Applied Investment Theory

Les Coleman

Applied Investment Theory

How Markets and Investors Behave, and Why

Les Coleman
University of Melbourne
Parkville, Victoria, Australia

ISBN 978-3-319-43975-4   ISBN 978-3-319-43976-1   (eBook)
DOI 10.1007/978-3-319-43976-1

Library of Congress Control Number: 2016957298

© The Editor(s) (if applicable) and The Author(s) 2016
This work is subject to copyright. All rights are solely and exclusively licensed by the Publisher, whether the whole or part of the material is concerned, specifically the rights of translation, reprinting, reuse of illustrations, recitation, broadcasting, reproduction on microfilms or in any other physical way, and transmission or information storage and retrieval, electronic adaptation, computer software, or by similar or dissimilar methodology now known or hereafter developed.
The use of general descriptive names, registered names, trademarks, service marks, etc. in this publication does not imply, even in the absence of a specific statement, that such names are exempt from the relevant protective laws and regulations and therefore free for general use.
The publisher, the authors and the editors are safe to assume that the advice and information in this book are believed to be true and accurate at the date of publication. Neither the publisher nor the authors or the editors give a warranty, express or implied, with respect to the material contained herein or for any errors or omissions that may have been made.

Cover Design by Liron Gilenberg

Printed on acid-free paper

This Palgrave Macmillan imprint is published by Springer Nature
The registered company is Springer International Publishing AG
The registered company address is: Gewerbestrasse 11, 6330 Cham, Switzerland

For Millie, and her siblings and cousins.
Yours will be the best generation yet.

Preface

Summary of *Applied Investment Theory*

Applied Investment Theory (AIT) explains how mutual fund managers invest in equities. This is one of modern finance's most important questions because mutual funds are the largest investor group in most developed economies, where their management of individuals' retirement savings is a critical agency relationship.

AIT builds on core principles of standard investment, namely efficient markets and rational investors, and overlays real-world conditions so that: markets are subject to frictions; rationality is conditional on restricted foresight; and risk becomes aversion to loss and uncertainty. AIT also relies on well-recognised finance concepts: equity value is contingent on state of the world; and equities have attributes of real options, multiple components to their value, and are ranked according to opportunity costs. In addition, mutual funds form a global oligopoly and their revenue is linked to funds under management. These structural influences from markets and the investment management industry combine with moral hazard and agency theory to explain fund managers' behaviour. Understanding the last addresses the economically important puzzle of funds' poor financial performance.

AIT incorporates six innovations:

- Financial performance of mutual funds is described through the structure-conduct-performance paradigm where fixed features of the industry interact with transient data flows to shape fund manager decisions and determine fund performance. Agency theory and moral hazard further explain fund manager behaviour
- Humans have significant influence over equity prices because they control the release, and often timing, of market information. Other human control arises from growth of institutions to dominate ownership of equities which makes their market oligopolistic, and leads to a classic sawtooth price pattern of gradual rises and sharp falls, with negative skew. Funds also window dress results according to the reporting calendar

viii   Preface

- Markets display significant inefficiency, and flows of public information have small, transient impact on valuations. Because transactions provide continuous new information of importance to valuation, investors incorporate prices in their utility functions.
- Investor risk relates to uncertainty in wealth. Possibility of loss is caused by anticipated return because a higher target return leads to greater difficulty in achieving the expected increase in equity value. There is no link between equity return and its volatility.
- Investors' lack of predictive capability and large, systematic swings in markets make it impractical to project returns of individual equities. Thus they think in terms of equity price, and rank values of candidate investments in light of their opportunity cost.
- Investors implicitly value equities as if they have three components, which comprise: the value of current operations; a long real call option whose price depends on value improvements; and a sold real put option whose value loss depends on unexpected adverse developments.

Key precepts of Applied Investment Theory are:

1. The managed funds industry is a global oligopoly whose fees are typically unrelated to performance, and which has a business model built around lifting funds under management (FUM). Mutual funds are free to self-regulate because few clients react to performance, most observers are captives, and fund operations are opaque and characterised by information asymmetry.
2. Equity prices are contingent on an unpredictable future state of the world, and are usually not related to public information nor predictable from lagged firm and security traits. Equity prices are subject to deliberate human action because people control most information flows and have discretion over timing. Dominance of open-ended portfolios leads to a sawtooth price pattern in equity markets.
3. Modern markets are informationally efficient; but they are subject to frictions, and cannot eliminate information asymmetry, nor costlessly enforce equity contracts. Prices trend and cluster, and technical analysis is of use over the short term. Procyclical demand for equities makes them Veblen goods which have an upward sloping demand curve.
4. Mutual funds are marked by extensive socialisation and complex game-theoretic interplays with competitors, clients, investee firms and industry observers where the common mixing variable is a search for proprietary information.
5. Moments of equity returns are not related, and risk for investors relates to the possibility of loss. Equities' target return indicates the difficulty of achieving any value improvement and causes price uncertainty.
6. Fund managers price securities rationally on the basis of information available at the time, within a theme that describes their investment assumptions. They are loss averse, use higher discount rates for nearer term revenues, and a higher discount rate for losses than gains. Thus ideal investments avoid short term loss while providing reasonable medium term return.
7. Investors are unable to form economically meaningful forecasts of equity returns. They look at the cross-section of equities in terms of opportunity cost and relative rank:

Subjective Preference $= U\{$Relative value, Relative uncertainty $\mid I \subset \Omega\}$
$\mid \{$Market price, State of the world$\}$

where I is information available, and Ω is total information set.

8. Investor estimates of value and uncertainty are developed from historical data and proxies for firm performance, including valuation ratios, management ability, hedonic features of the security such as size and governance, and market conditions.
9. The process followed by investors in ranking equities is equivalent to separately considering three economic components: value of current assets; a long real call option whose value reflects expected return; and a short real put option whose value reflects uncertainty and possible loss.
10. Fund managers do not add value for clients because it is fundamentally hard to outperform their benchmarks, their employers seek FUM growth even at the expense of performance, and they are loss averse and herd to protect their human capital. Business issues and transaction costs effectively cancel out any fund manager skill.
11. Mutual fund performance is best explained through the structure-conduct-performance (SCP) paradigm where stable structures of markets and the investment industry interact with more transient macroeconomic conditions to drive fund manager conduct and so determine performance. In addition, moral hazard and agency costs can be destructive of investor wealth.

This perspective aligns investment with other decisions that incorporate non-economic considerations, and resolves many investment puzzles, including those of behavioural finance. Shifting the way we perceive and model fund manager valuations should better explain fund performance and improve investor decision making.

This book has a specific focus, which is to understand how mutual fund managers invest in equities. This addresses one of the most pressing questions in modern finance, and findings are set out in a comprehensive *Applied Investment Theory* (AIT).

Mutual fund investment is an important topic because funds are one of the largest investor groups, and in most developed countries hold a third or more of equities (Aggarwal et al. 2011). Funds under professional management surged after the 1980s when governments began to fiscally encourage, and then mandate, retirement savings. Most investment was contracted out to mutual funds, which have huge resources and highly skilled managers. Funds became economically significant, and – as managers of workers' retirement savings – central to one of the most important principal-agent relationships in modern economies. Despite the importance of mutual funds, there is not a good, theoretically based description of their investment process.

The second reason to examine mutual funds is that they are one of the few professional groups that cannot best amateurs (Cochrane 1999): for decades it has been clear that funds' performance is indistinguishable from that of the market benchmark (Jensen 1968), and this is a globally robust phenomenon because the average equity mutual fund in major countries underperforms its benchmark (Ferreira et al. 2012). It is a puzzle why skilled, well-resourced institutional investors can nowhere add value for clients. Intuitively, the answer lies in better understanding what influences performance.

To date, the most successful explanation of equity investment is the neoclassical investment paradigm, which is often termed Modern Portfolio Theory (MPT). Whilst MPT has proven resilient since it was finalised around 1980, there have been sweeping changes since then in financial markets and investors. The most important has been transformation of investors from largely risk-averse individuals to financial institutions operating in an oligopolistic global industry. The significance of this is that revenue of financial institutions comes as a commission on funds under management (FUM), and so – unlike individual investors for whom MPT was designed – their principal goal is not to maximise risk-adjusted returns but to maximise FUM. This significant shift in objectives of the dominant investor group means that MPT may no longer be relevant. Assumptions underpinning market mechanics have also shifted because of the dominance of institutions, rapid expansion of traditional bourses and emergence of huge derivatives markets.

Another motive to revisit standard investment is the steady accumulation of evidence from empirical studies in accounting and finance literatures which cast doubt over MPT's real-world applicability (e.g. Fama and French 2004). Emphasising this point, surveys of fund managers confirm they are aware of MPT, but the majority do not use it (see, amongst many: Amenc et al. 2011; Coleman 2014c; Holland 2006).

A further need to re-assess the current investment paradigm follows from crises that rolled across northern hemisphere credit, banking and sovereign debt markets through 2008–2011, and yet again highlighted gaps in the tenets of modern finance and in the skills of leading finance researchers and practitioners (Coleman 2014b). Foundations of the investment industry have been further roiled by numerous ten and even eleven figure fines imposed on leading banks in recent years for defrauding customers and tolerating corruption among their investment advisers and money managers.[1]

---

[1] Large settlements that global banks agreed with the US Justice Department include $US13 billion by J P Morgan Chase in 2013 and $17 billion by Bank of America in 2014.

These and other issues are well recognised. For instance, Bob Merton (2003), whose Nobel Prize came from contributions to MPT, wrote of the need to make investment practices more effective, but included the important qualification that it is "a tough engineering problem, not one of new science."

This book agrees by holding true to core investment tenets of MPT, but re-engineers them using the large body of disparate material compiled by researchers in the last half century, especially field research into the process followed by fund managers.[2] The result links real-world data to recognized theoretical drivers and explains influences on fund manager decisions from markets and their industry. The objective is to develop a parsimonious, but comprehensive, explanation of what we know with certainty about markets and investors, incorporate theoretical underpinnings, and extend MPT to better interpret and explain empirical observations of fund managers' investment techniques. The applied focus is consistent with my conviction that the best way to explain financial outcomes is to detail links along the way from decision stimuli through investor decisions to market response. Thus field research augments empirical studies by amplifying their environment.

Let me summarise the key aspects of *Applied Investment Theory* (AIT).

AIT starts with the two core premises of standard investment in MPT, namely that markets are efficient (Fama 1970) and investors are economically rational in valuing securities (Mill 1874). Under AIT, however, idealised assumptions are relaxed and real-world conditions introduced.

AIT's first step in re-engineering MPT addresses efficiency of markets, which so speedily process newly available information that most is reflected in prices well before it appears in any media (Coleman 2011). However, the flow of new information about any security is dwarfed by the existing stock, and so most news has limited, short-lived market impact. Markets are also subject to frictions, which mean they cannot eliminate information asymmetry, nor ensure that the contractual obligations inherent in equities are costlessly enforced. The second core principle of MPT is investor rationality, which AIT incorporates with two provisos. One is that return to an equity is contingent on state of the world at the time of its liquidation (Arrow 1964). The other proviso is that investors have limited forecasting ability: according to Yan and Zhang (2009: 894), for instance, institutions' long-term trading does not evidence any ability to forecast returns, nor is it related to future earnings news; so investors must rely on currently available information.

---

[2] See Hellman (2000) for a survey of research into institutional investors, Coleman (2015) for a review of interview-based studies of institutional investors, and Stracca (2006) for survey-based research.

AIT incorporates other concepts that should be familiar to finance researchers: equities have real option features because of shareholders' flexibility to modify their return (Myers 1977); equity value has multiple components (or equals the sum of its parts) comprising assets in place plus future changes (Miller and Modigliani 1961); and – as is done with multiples valuation – equity values are ranked according to relative opportunity costs.

Another familiar concept incorporated in AIT is the structure-conduct-performance (SCP) paradigm (Bain 1959), under which the relative performance of firms is determined by their conduct, which in turn depends on their industry's structure. Applying SCP to investment sees the stable structure of markets and the investment industry interact with more transient conduct of investors and macroeconomic conditions to determine fund managers' valuation processes which in turn drive fund performance. SCP proves a neat prism to synthesise the huge amount of data available on fund manager investment, and combines with moral hazard and agency theory (Ross 1973; Jensen and Meckling 1976) to explain fund manager conduct. SCP explains other striking features of the managed investment industry such as returns that only match benchmark (Ferreira et al. 2012), and frequent deception of clients (e.g. Partnoy and Eisinger 2013).

The most prominent structural features of the mutual fund industry are that it is a global oligopoly, and has a business model that derives revenues from commissions as a proportion of funds under management (FUM) rather than performance (Alpert et al. 2015: 21). This industry model best manages funds' business risks and is enabled by clients who tend to be disengaged from management of their savings (Agnew et al. 2003), which – in combination with funds' opaque operations and weak regulatory overnight – leaves them free to self-regulate.

An important influence on fund manager conduct is information, which is intuitively important to equity valuation. However, modern regulation and corporate governance ensure that most price-sensitive data quickly becomes publicly available, and information advantage is only feasible by superior interpretation of public data or obtaining superior insights such as through private communications with firm executives (Drachter et al. 2007). This search for better data combines with funds' co-location in financial enclaves and common scrutiny by ratings agencies and regulators to promote extensive socialisation of fund managers with competitors, executives of investee firms and industry observers (e.g. Fligstein 2001).

Fund managers share similar processes and performance criteria; and meet expectations of colleagues, clients and industry observers by adopting processes and communications that promote favourable impressions of their skill

(Schlenker 1980). Other influences on fund manager conduct come from the oligopolistic nature of the industry such as market concentration, non-price competition, co-location and high profitability. In addition, investment professionals are able to exploit their agency role with clients because of the opacity of fund operations and information asymmetry between financial institutions and clients.

Turning to valuation of equities under AIT, an important structural limitation is that fund managers cannot accurately predict future equity prices (Yan and Zhang 2009). One reason is that investors do not understand determinants of returns. As examples: even ex post it proves impractical to explain the most significant moves in prices of individual stocks (Bouchaud et al. 2009) and major equity indexes (Fair 2002); few announcements of intuitively price-sensitive information bring significant price reaction (Cutler et al. 1989); and event studies show that news of events which intuitively should permanently affect stock prices usually brings only a small, short-lived cumulative abnormal return (Brown 2011). A second reason is that – even though many systematic and firm-specific factors have been identified ex post as explaining returns – these relationships between returns and lagged firm traits are unstable over investors' time horizon and so are of little value in ex ante prediction (Ferreira and Santa-Clara 2011). Finally, investors cannot develop useful forecasts of factors that are thought to be important to future returns. For instance, individual shares' price changes are explained roughly equally by systematic shifts and cash flows (Chen et al. 2013). However, expert forecasts of macroeconomic factors are no better than random numbers (Chan et al. 1998), and analysts' year-ahead forecasts have crippling errors (e.g. Espahbodi et al. 2015). Not surprisingly, models proposed to predict returns do not outperform naïve estimates (e.g. Simin 2008). A practitioner valuation primer gave a précis of the difficulties by saying that the process is so challenging that a fund manager "who is right 60 to 70 percent of the time is considered exceptional" (Hooke 2010: 9).

These experiences reflect the fact that equity value is contingent on state of the world (Arrow 1964), and thus is situation dependent, time varying and unpredictable. Because fund managers cannot make reliable forecasts of future value, they face uncertainty (Knight 1921).

All this leads to two steps that explain many seemingly anomalous behaviours. The first is that fund managers subjectively consider the cross section of candidate equities, and focus on relative valuations. The ranking process begins with reliable current financial data, and augments it with proxies for future return and uncertainty. These cover a wide range of observable features relating to future return (such as price-to-book ratio), management's operational and strategic capability (firm performance measures), and uncertainty in cash flows (such as governance and sustainability indicators). Fund managers are also loss averse because investors withdraw from badly performing funds (Del Guercio and Tkac 2002).

This first process can be described as follows:

$$\text{Subjective Preference} = U\{\text{Relative value, Relative uncertainty} \mid I \subset \Omega\}$$
$$\mid \{\text{Market price, State of the world}\}$$

where: I is available information, and Ω is the total information set.

In words, fund managers decide rationally, but recognise that equity return is contingent on an uncertain future state of the world for which it is impractical to develop economically meaningful predictions. They are limited to use of information available at the time, and look at the cross-section of equity prices to determine relative value and uncertainty of each potential investment.

The second process step is equivalent to treating equities as if their value is the sum of multiple economic components (Miller and Modigliani 1961). Components incorporate real option features because shareholders have flexibility to modify return through timing of purchase and sale, and leverage (Myers 1977), and equities' contingent value makes them an option over changing state of the world. The first component of a share is the value of its current operations, which is proxied by a multiple of assets, revenues or normalised earnings. The second component is a real call option whose value reflects expected improvement in future cash flows, and is captured by investor stock selection ability. The third economic component of a share is a short real put option, which responds to deterioration in the state of the world and brings value loss that is beyond the investor's control. The strike price of the real call and put options is value of current assets, and their respective premia reflect expectations of future value growth and its monetised uncertainty.

It is not proposed that fund managers explicitly value equities as the sum of three components or rank them. However, empirical analysis supports the intuition that they at least implicitly follow these steps.

This depiction of fund manager investment can resolve several puzzling behaviours. For example, including historical prices in utility function explains investors' use of technical analysis (Menkhoff 2010), and contributes to trending, momentum and mean reversion in prices. Also, purchase price establishes a benchmark that creates hindsight bias and mental accounting which can readily see attribution of wealth gain and loss to, respectively, the investor's stock selection skill and unexpected exogenous events that affected state of the world (Kahneman 2011).

The conduct or behaviour of FMs is shaped by structural features of markets and the managed funds industry which mean that fund managers' strategic alternatives boil down to either using proprietary skills to advantage, or eschewing any pretence of skill and herding or following less ethical means. As already noted, fund managers on average do not outperform benchmarks, and – suggesting this is largely due to lack of skill – there is little evidence that any investment professionals can generate good forecasts of inputs to standard valuation models such as macroeconomic state variables, cash flows and firm performance (e.g. Guedj and Bouchaud 2005): consistent, superior performance appears impractical, except possibly for an exceptional few. Fund managers' second alternative is herding, which is a pronounced feature of the managed funds industry (Sias 2004). Less ethical approaches are common, too, because finance has distinguished itself as the only industry whose major players have paid ten and eleven figure fines in recent years for defrauding their customers (e.g. Partnoy and Eisinger 2013).

Fund managers know that their employers' objective is to maximize growth in funds under management (FUM), clients take limited interest in fund performance as long as it is reasonable (Del Guercio and Tkac 2002), their compensation is only weakly influenced by funds' performance (Ma et al. 2013), and it is doubtful whether they can achieve consistent outperformance. A rational fund manager who wants to protect their own human capital will probably target a small margin above peers' median return, with strong aversion to significant loss. This is confirmed by evidence that fund managers assess their relative performance through the year, and will bank good results or increase risk following poor results (Clare et al. 2004).

AIT's description of fund manager equity valuation is theoretically-based and consistent with real-world evidence. It can also explain a number of puzzles in investment, especially why highly skilled, well-resourced fund managers cannot beat the market average: poor results can be traced to fund managers' inability to make reliable forecasts and the weak incentive structure of their industry where nobody is motivated to deliver superior performance. Similarly, the role of price and current information explain many anomalies identified through behavioural finance. In short, the model provides a comprehensive theory of applied investment.

The chief implication of the model for mutual funds is that structural features of markets make their current business model logical. Investors should accept that funds cannot beat the market average, and put their money in either low cost index funds or extra market vehicles such as private equity funds. Regulators should recognise that the mutual funds industry should be made more competitive and performance focussed. Researchers should be excited with the opportunities opened up by a new approach to investment.

Thus we need no longer look at markets or investors as something beyond understanding, but as the products of logical forces that guide them inexorably to repeatable outcomes. We can use this knowledge to inform industry regulatory policy and investor choices.

* * *

An impetus for this book is growing dissatisfaction with existing models of finance theory and practice, which is reinforced by recurring market collapses and financial scandals. A few of many critical comments include: the LSE's *Future of Finance* report (Turner et al. 2010) which concluded that "the evidence of the past decade has served to discredit the basic tenets of finance theory"; "The Financial Crisis and the Systemic Failure of Academic Economics" which criticises financial and macroeconomic models that rely on steady-state markets, assume that economies operate efficiently and rationally, and ignore recurring crises (Colander et al. 2009); Nobel economics laureate Paul Krugman who held nothing back in his regular *New York Times* column (2 September 2009): "The central cause of the [economics] profession's failure [to foresee the GFC] was the desire for an all-encompassing, intellectually elegant approach that also gave economists a chance to show off their mathematical prowess"; and Professor Barry Eichengreen of the University of California, Berkeley who wrote in *The National Interest* (May 2009): "The great credit crisis has cast into doubt much of what we thought we knew about economics."

In 2014 I published *The Lunacy of Modern Finance Theory & Investment* (Routledge, London) which rang a loud bell in its sub-title: how weak theory, poor governance and ineffective regulation failed investors with a decade of low returns.[3] It was classic Heathrow literature. Although academic reviewers sniffed that much of its material was known to most practitioners and researchers, readers appreciated the voice I gave to a lot of otherwise quiet elephants in the rooms of academia and financial institutions. To me, though, this Monday morning quarterbacking or using an academic's sinecure to deride those who do real jobs is cowardly. I have vowed throughout my career never to criticise anyone whose job I would not do. Thus this companion book responds to acid enquiries: "well, Les, what *does* work?" I preferred a book format because it permits broad explanations and richer messages than are possible in piecemeal

---

[3] John Quiggin (2012) cast an equally critical eye over economic policy in his best-selling *Zombie economics: how dead ideas still walk among us.*

academic papers. Hopefully this contributes to what should become industrial scale development of new theoretical perspectives that close chronic and damaging gaps in the knowledge of financial economists.

To make this material both relevant to researchers and accessible to practitioners, several compromises have been made. The first relates to referencing: despite its tedium for non-academics, no innovation in thinking can gain traction unless its foundations are clear, and so I have substantiated all evidence and theoretical explanations. A second compromise arises because decision process is the meat and potatoes of institutional investing and – to develop an applied theory – must be closely examined. Thus granularity strays into several discussions that unpack a central theme.

Like previous publications, this one combines learnings from my industry and academic careers along with many people's insights. Numerous academic colleagues have provided support and encouragement, and further rigour has come from feedback on my analyses by editors and referees of journals, and participants at conferences and seminars who proved unstinting in their commentary. Over decades, I have been fortunate in gaining the right industry experience and insights to form and shape my ideas, and acknowledge the input of colleagues at Mobil, ExxonMobil and Anglo American Corporations, IOOF Holdings Ltd, Australian Ethical Investment Ltd and other companies; and also from hundreds of interviewees and survey participants literally around the world who have generously provided their time and thoughts.

Finally, much of this book was written whilst I was on sabbatical at London Metropolitan University, and I gratefully acknowledge the hospitality of Professors Stephen Perkins and Roger Bennett, Dr Ke You and their colleagues.

Whilst warmly thanking my many advisers and informants, I affirm they bear no responsibility for this work and that any errors and omissions are mine.

The University of Melbourne   Les Coleman
Parkville, VIC, Australia   January 2016
e-mail: les.coleman@unimelb.edu.au

Contents

1	Introduction	1
Part I	Investment Theory and Practice	13
2	Current Paradigm: Neoclassical Investment Theory	15
3	Behavioural Biases in Investor Decisions	29
4	Uncertainty in Investor Wealth	53
Part II	Structure, Conduct and Performance of Fund Manager Investment	73
5	Building Investment Theory Using the Structure-Conduct-Performance (SCP) Paradigm	75
6	Structure of Equity Prices	83
7	The Mutual Fund Industry: Structure and Conduct	121
8	Fund Managers' Conduct: The Story of How They Invest	131

9	Performance of Mutual Funds	151

Part III Towards an Enhanced Theory of Investment 163

10	Piecing Together the Jigsaw: *Applied Investment Theory*	165
11	Real World Application of Applied Investment Theory	203

Bibliography 215

Index 243

About the Author

Les Coleman is a finance academic at the University of Melbourne and is a member (part time) of the Investment Policy Committee of IOOF Holdings Limited. At the University of Melbourne he completed a bachelor's degree in Mining Engineering (1974), and a PhD by thesis which was published as *Why Managers and Companies Take Risks* (Springer, 2006); he also holds a Master of Economics from Sydney University and a BSc (Economics) from London University.

Prior to returning to study in 2002 and then moving into academia, Les worked for almost 30 years in senior management positions with resources, manufacturing and finance companies in Australia and overseas. He started as a mining engineer with Anglo American Corporation in Zambia, and then joined Mobil Oil in Melbourne where highlights of his career include four years in Mobil Corporation's international planning group at its global headquarters near Washington DC, and six years as regional treasurer for ExxonMobil Australia. He has been a trustee of two employee superannuation funds and a public offer superannuation fund, and a director of ten companies involved in finance, retail and distribution, including Australian Ethical Investment Limited and Strasburger Enterprises Pty Ltd. Les has written and spoken widely on finance and investment strategies, and for four years was a weekly columnist with *The Australian* newspaper.

Les has published five books, four book chapters and close to 30 journal articles. His main research interest is applied finance, especially financial decision making by investment funds and firms. His most recent book *The Lunacy of Modern Finance Theory & Regulation* (Routledge, 2014) analysed shortcomings in finance theory using insights from extensive field research, including interviews with over 40 fund managers in Istanbul, London, Melbourne and New York. He also has an interest in sustainability and risk as decision stimuli, and his book entitled *Risk Strategies: Dialling up optimum firm risk* (Gower, 2009) foreshadowed a body of theory to manage risk strategically (in much the same way as human physiology and physical sciences support modern medical and engineering techniques, respectively). He delivers

About the Author

executive education programs in Australia and overseas, and has received research and teaching awards. Les is a member of the editorial board of two academic journals, and is a joint recipient of an Australian Research Council linkage grant.

Les has three adult children and lives in the coastal hinterland near Melbourne.

List of Figures

Fig. 1.1	Equity holdings of US financial institutions	4
Fig. 1.2	Turnover of NYSE shares 1950–2015	5
Fig. 1.3	S&P 500 value ratios	6
Fig. 1.4	Slumps in price of global equities and US corporate bonds	9
Fig. 4.1	S&P 500 Index level and volatility	59
Fig. 4.2	US Equity Risk Premium	62
Fig. 4.3	Contributors to loss in shareholders' wealth	63
Fig. 4.4	US Misery Index	64
Fig. 5.1	Model of fund manager investment	80
Fig. 6.1	Log of S&P 500 Index and skew in returns	91
Fig. 6.2	Today's return vs. range of yesterday's return	93
Fig. 6.3	Regime shifting in S&P 500 Index returns	95
Fig. 6.4	US bond yields and 15–34 year old population	100
Fig. 6.5	Five-year ahead return vs. price/dividend ratio	111
Fig. 6.6	Fama-French size and value factors	112
Fig. 8.1	Model of a firm's share price	135
Fig. 9.1	Finance industry's share of US GDP and corporate profits	159
Fig. 10.1	Waterfall diagram of a share's three components of value	175
Fig. 10.2	Multi-period framework of three-component equity model	191
Fig. 10.3	Schematic of Applied Investment Theory	194

List of Tables

Table 1.1	Growth in face value of US security types	6
Table 3.1	Biases that affect decisions	33
Table 3.2	Drivers of behavioural decision biases	50
Table 4.1	Components of UK and US equity risk premia	61
Table 4.2	Indicators of future firm uncertainty	71
Table 6.1	Regression of S&P change on prior day's return	94
Table 6.2	Common firm-specific variables whose lagged values explain returns	108
Table 6.3	Regression of excess S&P 500 returns on price/dividend ratio	110
Table 9.1	Recent analyses of mutual fund performance	153
Table 10.1	Regression of value ratios against three equity components	177
Table 11.1	Prediction of S&P 500 Index using error correction model	211

1

Introduction

The Key Takeaways of This Chapter Are

- Modern portfolio theory (MPT) is the dominant investment paradigm, and has proven resilient since its structure began to emerge in the early 1960s
- In recent decades, important changes have occurred in investment that were not comprehended during MPT's development. These include growth in scale of traditional markets and emergence of huge derivatives markets; and transformation of investors from largely risk-averse individuals to financial institutions operating in an oligopolistic, global industry
- MPT has proven unable to explain stylised market and investor facts, most obviously biases in decisions of skilled investors, the regular cycle of significant equity price collapses, and waves of systemic corruption and weak governance in financial institutions
- Although institutions are amongst the most sophisticated investors, they make limited use of MPT
- Management of workers' retirement savings by mutual funds is one of the most important principal-agent relationships in modern economies. Despite the importance of mutual funds, there is no comprehensive theory that explains their behaviour
- In short, there is a need to significantly extend the existing investment paradigm.

© The Author(s) 2016
L. Coleman, *Applied Investment Theory*,
DOI 10.1007/978-3-319-43976-1_1

2   Applied Investment Theory

This chapter sets out the case for reading the book, which boils down to answering the crucial question: why bother to extend the existing investment paradigm (which is generally termed modern portfolio theory, MPT; or neoclassical finance theory)? After all, it explicitly incorporates four Nobel Prize winning ideas – mean-variance portfolio optimisation, the capital asset pricing model, valuation of derivatives, and efficient markets – plus a number of well-established economic concepts (many of them bringing Nobel Prizes, too), including arbitrage, agency theory, flat or downwards sloping demand curves, and rational pricing. Further, MPT is elegant; longstanding, with most of it developed before 1980; widely taught in business schools around the globe; and has elements such as alpha and portfolio optimisation which are common parlance way beyond financial markets. MPT's robustness should give pause to any suggestions of change, much less endorse the search for a new finance paradigm.

The argument in favour of greater openness to extending investment theory rests on significant developments in recent decades that have overtaken MPT's foundations. Perhaps the most important has been the change in investors from predominantly risk-averse individuals with accurate future knowledge to highly trained institutional investors competing in a global oligopoly. At the same time, markets were transformed by expansion in the trading volume of traditional bourses and emergence of huge derivatives markets.

A further development is that MPT's analytical tools prove hard to apply because each requires data about future firm or market performance that is impractical to forecast with precision. Thus standard investment theory has been unable to explain many stylised facts – or what we know with confidence based upon empirical evidence – about markets and investors; the catalogue of these biases or irrationalities is so extensive as to support the discipline of behavioural finance. Nor can MPT explain puzzles such as emergence since about 1980 of a short cycle (roughly four years, rarely longer than five to seven years) of globally co-ordinated falls in prices of equities and other assets. These are associated with bouts of systemic weaknesses and endemic corruption, or runaway asset price inflation, but prove resistant to explanation, much less prediction and control.

Let us amplify these justifications for expanding investment theory, and indicate the book's approach.

1.1   Developments in Financial Markets over Recent Decades

This section discusses changes in financial markets and investors that were not comprehended by MPT.

1.1.1 Transformation of the Equity Investor Base

The most significant development in equity markets in recent decades is that the dominant investor group has transformed from risk-averse individuals to institutional investors (mutual funds, pension plans, insurance companies and other pooled investment vehicles) which compete in a global oligopoly. This can be traced to introduction in the United States of tax-advantaged retirement savings in 1978. Because individuals tend to contract out specialist services ranging from car maintenance to health care, wage and salary earners invested their retirement savings through professional money managers, and the managed investments industry expanded rapidly.

As an example, the following figure shows that the United States has seen consistent growth in investments of financial institutions so they now hold around half of all listed shares (of which, mutual funds own 46%; about 16% each for private pension plans and State and local Government pension plans; and about 12% each for insurance companies and exchange traded funds).[1] Similar developments have occurred in other developed economies, and institutional investors have risen to dominate financial markets across modern economies (Aggarwal et al. 2011)[2] (Fig. 1.1).

The rise of institutional investors has had sweeping effects. For instance, institutions are much larger than individual investors in terms of funds under management and trading volume, and have superior research capabilities. Also important is that replacement of atomised investors by powerful, well-resourced institutions brought strong performance pressures on firms, which – as shown in the figure – saw the profits of corporations rise in lockstep with their institutional ownership.

Emergence of institutional investors has been accompanied by two surprises: the managed investments industry developed as a global oligopoly; and, almost alone of all pursuits, investment professionals are unable to best amateurs and outperform the market (Cochrane 1999).

Funds management first expanded in the United States where legislation restricted entrants, and the industry formed as an oligopoly. When other countries began promoting retirement savings, US funds took advantage of their infrastructure and expertise to move in, so that members of a small group of large fund families have typically secured between a third and half

---

[1] Sources: equity holdings and US market capitalisation from *Flow of Funds Z.1 files* (Table L213) at www.federalreserve.gov; corporate profits from BEA *National Data* (table 6.16D) at www.bea.gov.

[2] Not surprisingly, there has been considerable research on impacts of these large investors, with surveys by Edwards and Hubbard (2000) and Sundaramurthyet al. (2005).

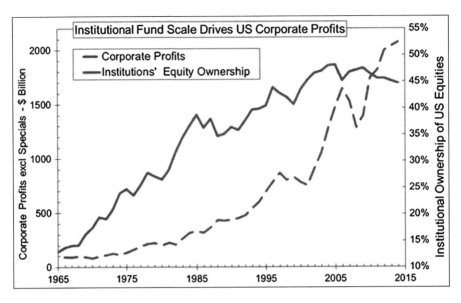

Fig. 1.1 Equity holdings of US financial institutions

the market for funds management in most countries (Ferreira and Ramos 2009). Other features of the managed funds industry are that its rate of innovation is glacial; funds offer similar products, and share common processes, data, and even locations; and the industry has high barriers to entry and is highly profitable. These features mark the managed funds industry as a classic oligopoly, especially as participants compete on non-price measures such as reputation and investment strategy.

The final important feature of mutual funds is that they collectively cannot beat the average market return. This has been recognised for half a century, and is true wherever mutual funds operate because the average equity mutual fund in most countries underperforms its benchmark (Ferreira et al. 2012). Given the important role of mutual funds as the custodians of retirement savings, the inability of their highly skilled and well-resourced money managers to add value is one of the most troubling puzzles in finance.

1.1.2 Inflation in Scale and Scope of Markets

A second significant change in financial markets since the 1980s has been sharp growth in trading volume on traditional bourses, and expansion in the size and offerings of derivatives markets (Greenwood and Scharfstein 2013). As an example, consider equities listed on the New York Stock Exchange: in 1980 the market's capitalisation was $508 billion and annual turnover was $382 billion or 73%; by 2010 the numbers were $14.5 trillion capitalisation and turnover of $12.0 trillion or 83% (US Census Bureau, 1990 and 2012). In 30 years, the NYSE increased 28-fold in size and turnover, which is an average rate of growth of 12% PA and several times the rate of increase in GDP, profits, savings and population. The growth in scale is displayed in the following chart which shows the turnover of NYSE shares as the ratio of annual volume to the number of shares listed (source: www.nyxdata.com) (Fig. 1.2).

Derivatives markets have also seen significant growth, both in absolute terms and relative to physical markets. The following table shows that face value of derivatives traded in US markets rose from about $20 trillion in 1995 to $270 trillion in 2014 (equivalent to 13% per year), largely because debt derivative markets grew from about 0.6 times the value of total credit outstanding to four times the value. Similar – although less economically significant – growth occurred in the foreign exchange market with a doubling in derivatives' face value as a multiple of the value of exports of goods and services (from about 5 to 11 times) (Table 1.1).

Although equity derivatives markets are only a fraction of the physical, the possibility of speculative spillover from debt and currency markets is indicated by significant inflation of equity valuations. For example, the next figure shows dimensionless measures of value on the US S&P 500 as ratios of market price to earnings and book value, which have both increased since the 1980s (Fig. 1.3).

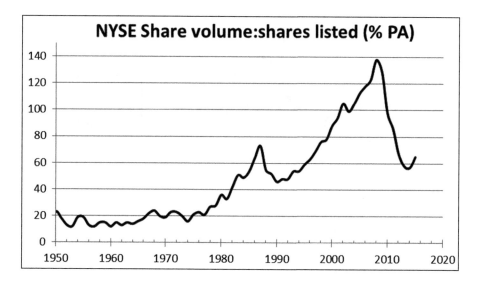

Fig. 1.2 Turnover of NYSE shares 1950–2015

6   Applied Investment Theory

Table 1.1 Growth in face value of US security types

Face value of US security types: $US trillion				
	Underlying Security			
Asset class	Description	Physical market	Futures markets[a]	OTC derivatives
1995				
Debt	Debt outstanding	18.7	3.1	11.1
Currency	Trade in goods and services	1.0	0.1	5.4
Equities	Market capitalisation	5.8	0.2	0.4
Commodities	Ex gate production	0.9	0.5 (est)	
2014				
Debt	Debt outstanding	58.7	40.2	183.4
Currency	Trade in goods and services	2.9	0.2	33.2
Equities	Market capitalisation	26.3	4.2	2.6
Commodities	Ex gate production	1.7 (est)	0.8 (est)	1.2

Sources: Credit market debt outstanding: US Federal Reserve *Flow of Funds Accounts of the United States* (table L1); US equity market capitalisation: World Federation of Exchanges *WFE Market Highlights* (www.world-exchanges.org); commodity production is agriculture, minerals and fuels from *Statistical Abstract of the United States*; futures markets data are from Bank for International Settlements *Exchange traded derivatives statistics* (www.bis.org/statistics/extderiv.htm) and Datastream for commodities; and OTC derivatives data are from *Report on Bank Trading and Derivatives Activities* (www.occ.gov)
[a]Covers North America

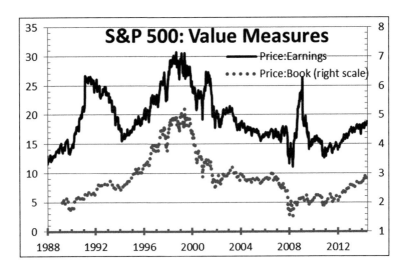

Fig. 1.3   S&P 500 value ratios

It is not obvious whether higher equity valuation comes from exogenously-driven asset price inflation, inherently greater value in firms, lower uncertainty in endogenous accounting measures of earnings and assets, or some other cause. One possibility is that the wide variety of all but free social media and other internet-based enhancements has increased the value of firms' traditional assets. According to a study by consultant McKinsey entitled "The Great Transformer" (www.mckinsey.com), the internet makes up 3.4% of GDP in developed economies, which seems a gross under-statement of its contribution to people's quality of life, and hence to the market value of corporate assets. Whatever the cause, the important implication of the chart is that recent decades have seen prices incorporate additional factors of significance to valuation.

1.1.3 Importance of Non-economic Factors in Investment Decisions

An important development in investment since MPT emerged is evidence that investors who are well-trained, well-resourced and highly motivated do not base their decisions solely on rational economic criteria, but also incorporate non-economic considerations.

One example is that professional investors take account of historical security prices, which is most obvious in their widespread use of technical analysis (Menkhoff 2010), and in skilled investors' common use of recent price highs as estimates of value (e.g. Baker and Wurgler 2006). Trends occur regularly, too, so that a rising price increases investor's preference and leads to crowded trades and herding. These and other behaviours contradict central propositions of standard finance such as the efficient markets hypothesis where prices do not contain value-relevant information; and the longstanding premise in economics of a downward sloping demand curve where price moves in the opposite direction to volume. Another example of irrationality is that investors incorporate publicly available data that should have no relevance to return such as lagged financial ratios, management ability, hedonic features of the security, size and governance, which explain up to a quarter of returns (Ferreira et al. 2012).

A specific pressure on fund managers to incorporate non-economic considerations in their investment decisions arises because their employers' income is typically a proportion of funds under management (e.g. Alpert et al. 2015), and they are subject to complex forces from socialisation of their industry (e.g. Arnswald 2001). Although a variable component of fund managers'

8   Applied Investment Theory

compensation is related to outperformance of their funds (Ma et al. 2013), this is generally limited to a relatively small portion to discourage speculation or worse (Dass et al. 2008). Moreover, they need pay only limited heed to clients' return because existing investors are not sensitive to anything other than serious underperformance (Agnew et al. 2003), and new investors are attracted by factors unrelated to return such as reputation and process (Foster and Warren 2015).

Thus fund managers have limited pecuniary interest in maximising return, reducing price uncertainty, or managing systematic risk: their perspective is very different to that of individual risk-averse investors for whom each is important.

1.1.4 Systemic Weaknesses in Financial Systems Reliability

The fourth set of developments in the investment industry in recent decades is the emergence of systemic weaknesses in the financial system, with a regular cycle of widespread collapse of markets and endemic corporate corruption.

The next chart shows the maximum peak to trough decline in prices of global equities and US corporate bonds during each 12 month period since the mid 1980s. The MSCI World Index saw rapid collapses during 1990, 2002, 2009, and 2016; and Moody's US Baa corporate bonds had additional pronounced, if smaller scale, collapses in 1994, 1999, 2006 2013, and 2015. It is clear that – in the real world – there are collapses in the prices of equities and/or bonds every four years, or so. Not shown here, is a longer, but sometimes even more serious, cycle of global housing market collapses that is evident to most investors (Fig. 1.4).

Like clockwork, each quadrennium the global bond and/or equity market melts down. The exact reasons for each are not clear (Goldstein and Razin 2015), but contributing factors include globalisation of markets, reduced restrictions on trade and investment flows, and global co-ordination of monetary policy, which have led to increased co-movement of asset prices and a greater frequency of the bubbles that precede financial collapse (Agénor 2003).

Whatever the cause, markets have proven far more volatile than can be explained by the current paradigm's assumptions of rational investors and efficient markets. Consider the visit by Queen Elizabeth to the London School of Economics in the wake of the 2007–8 global financial crisis when she asked: "why did no one see the crisis coming?" (Besley and Hennessy 2009).

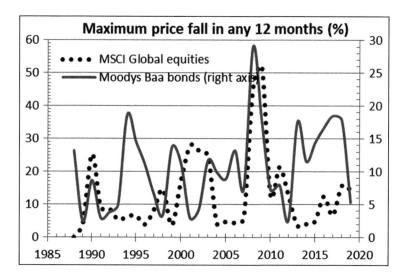

Fig. 1.4 Slumps in price of global equities and US corporate bonds

The prestigious British Academy responded by holding a seminar which concluded that it was "principally a failure of the collective imagination of many bright people, both in this country and internationally, to understand the risks to the system as a whole." Hardly a ringing endorsement of modern investment theory and practice.

A second systemic weakness in the modern investment industry is poor governance of its major institutions and of non-financial corporations, which brings regular waves that shatter seemingly reputable and robust companies every five years or so. Examples include: BCCI and Robert Maxwell in 1991; Barings and LTCM in 1995–8; Enron, Parmalat, Tyco and others in 2001–2; ABN-Amro, Madoff Investment Securities, Société Générale in 2008; and Olympus and Tesco in the early 2010s.

Mutual funds have frequently been part of these governance failures such as Lehman Brothers and Merrill Lynch in 2008. It seems that lack of investor scrutiny, weak regulatory oversight, and the absence of a link between investment return and mutual fund income leaves the industry open to deep agency conflicts, which emerge as bouts of fraud against individual investors. These recurring, serious shocks highlight a paradox in contemporary finance which is that the investment industry is highly profitable (BCG 2015), and yet it has a business model that is often inimical to the interests of its stakeholders.

Regular shocks, abuses and crises in investment cannot be explained within the existing investment paradigm.

1.1.5 Difficulty of Transitioning MPT to Investment Practice

The final shortcoming of the neoclassical investment paradigm that has become apparent since its development is that it has not transitioned well to practice. Specifically, MPT has seen only limited practical application: surveys over different periods and countries show that as few as one in three institutional investors uses MPT (see, amongst many: Amenc et al. 2011; Holland 2006). The main reason given by fund managers is that MPT is built around mathematical expressions that require data about future financial conditions, none of which is observable, nor predictable from past values (Coleman 2014c). Future financial conditions are not forecastable to a sufficient level of accuracy to apply MPT.

Pointing to broad practical shortcomings of standard investment theory is that – in addition to professional investors who underperform their benchmarks (Ferreira et al. 2012) – it gives poor results when applied by financial experts to large investment decisions. These include M&As that add little value (Henry 2002), and IPOs that are significantly underpriced (Ritter and Welch 2002).

MPT faces yet another practical challenge in its inability to explain anomalies in market prices and investor behaviours that have become so numerous as to support the discipline of behavioural finance (e.g. Barberis and Thaler 2003; Subrahmanyam 2007). These anomalies are attributed to investors' cognitive deficiencies (especially miscalibration of probabilities) and decision biases (especially over-confidence and situational risk propensity). Whilst this might explain the puzzling catalogue of statistically detectable anomalies, it opens up another puzzle with the intuitively improbable explanation that sophisticated, strongly motivated, professional investors suffer cognitive shortcomings that are so strong as to establish an environment of persistent, meaningful mispricings.

As Lord Keynes (1937: 213) observed: "the fact that our knowledge of the future is fluctuating, vague and uncertain renders Wealth a peculiarly unsuitable subject for the methods of the classical economic theory."

1.2 Motivation and Plan of This Book

The gaps noted above are so widespread as to suggest that modern investment theory does not describe the world that we see. It does not seem sensible to maintain a paradigm that can only be reconciled to empirical evidence by implausible assumptions (Thaler 1988). This provides strong justification to re-engineer the standard investment paradigm.

On the other hand, the resilience of the half century old MPT and its intuitive and logical framework should be capable of being made more complete and thus better describe fund manager equity investment. So this book's intent is to build from existing theory, and incorporate literature that details important features of markets and investors. My approach is bolstered by advocates of greater use of field data which dates at least to the AFA Presidential Address by Irwin Friend (1973), and was reaffirmed by Allais (1988: 274) who asked rhetorically: "how can the validity of axioms and their implications be tested without referring to observed facts?"

The way forward will likely be similar to paths that have proven successful in providing explanations of social (rather than scientific) phenomena in fields such as politics, sociology and psychology. A particularly relevant approach is given by research in medicine – which like finance is an archetypal hands on, intuitive discipline – that is termed knowledge translation, and refers to explicit efforts to impound field practice in theory so that each informs the other (Straus et al. 2009). The research approach in these disciplines suggests that a theory of investment should incorporate time-varying relationships that explain market behaviour and hominological precepts to describe human actions. The result would combine existing theory, published research and field studies to enhance the existing investment paradigm and narrow the gap between finance theory and practice.

Looking ahead, we will follow a robust process in assembling pieces of the investment jigsaw, detail existing theory and what needs to be done to improve it (Steiner 1988), and then – as foundations for new theoretical precepts – compile stylised facts and structural features of the equity market, managed funds environment and industry, and fund managers. The intuition is that industry and market structural features shape fund manager behaviours, and thus mutual fund performance.

The structure of the remainder of this book is pretty straightforward. Chapters 2 and 3 lay the foundations for a re-engineered investment theory by describing the current paradigm of equity investment along with its principal alternative in behavioural finance, and some alternative approaches. Chapters 4, 5, 6, 7, 8 and 9 discuss uncertainty in finance, and detail what we know empirically about markets and investors. Whilst much of this material is familiar to finance researchers and practitioners, it sets out the evidence that needs to be reflected in a more descriptive investment paradigm. The final part of the book combines the data into a unifying theory; introduces the structure and precepts of Applied Investment Theory; and discusses how it should be taught, researched, and applied.

Part I

Investment Theory and Practice

2

Current Paradigm: Neoclassical Investment Theory

The Key Takeaways of This Chapter Are

- The framework of the current investment paradigm – neoclassical finance or modern portfolio theory, MPT – was largely developed by 1980, and remains the staple of business courses and research around the world
- MPT is designed for individuals who own shares (i.e. investors are principals)
- Core assumptions of the current investment paradigm are that investors:

  – Are fully informed and risk averse, and unconditionally maximise return
  – Perceive risk as the dispersion of possible outcomes around expected value, and proxy it with the historical standard deviation of returns
  – Measure investments' utility in terms of expected return and standard deviation

- The capital asset pricing model (CAPM) is the centrepiece of modern investment, and assumes that market return causes the return of individual equities so that a share's return covaries with the market return in proportion to its beta, or systematic risk related to market-wide risk factors.
- Other techniques value firms in isolation, and include multiples and discounted cash flow analysis.

© The Author(s) 2016
L. Coleman, *Applied Investment Theory*,
DOI 10.1007/978-3-319-43976-1_2

16   Applied Investment Theory

Scientific progress comes by compiling ideas into a theory, and then continually testing it to winnow out duds and ensnare promising new concepts. A vibrant discipline experiences continuous innovation in its paradigm, which Thomas Kuhn (1970, 2nd edition) defined as a constellation of universally recognised facts, theories and methods that provide model solutions to practitioners, and are set out in current textbooks.

In order to extend the existing investment paradigm, we need to start by describing it, which is the objective of this chapter and the next. The discipline of finance involves efficiently matching the funds of investors and savers on one hand to the financing needs of entrepreneurs and governments on the other hand. Its success increases the utility of investors and borrowers by allowing them to spread consumption across time. That is, savers can defer spending until contingent expenses arise (whether planned such as college education or retirement, or unplanned such as loss of employment) and borrowers can stream investments ahead of earnings. Thus investment returns are a function of the benefits to borrowers of bringing forward consumption and the disutility to investors of postponing consumption and exposing their funds to risks of loss or underperformance.

The principal approach to making such decisions is standard finance, which has impressive foundations and a rich history that are intuitively appealing and pedagogically tractable. Research since the 1950s has built an elegant paradigm which is usually termed modern portfolio theory (MPT) or neoclassical investment theory. MPT links the CAPM of Sharpe (1964) and others, along with arbitrage pricing theory (Ross 1976) to mean-variance portfolio optimisation of Markowitz (1952, and later). It also incorporates a number of traits of investors (such as risk aversion and an unconditional objective of maximum risk-adjusted return), securities (such as price based on present value of future earnings, and uncorrelated returns), and markets (such as efficiency and the importance of information to pricing). Modern investment is often described as being based around Miller and Modigliani's arbitrage principals, Markowitz' efficient portfolio construction, the capital asset pricing model of Lintner and Sharpe, and the option pricing theory of Black, Merton and Scholes (e.g. Statman 1999). In any event, MPT is a staple of business school finance courses around the world.

To describe the contemporary investment paradigm, this chapter draws on texts which are used in finance MBAs and final-year undergraduate courses, including: *The Economics of Financial Markets* by Roy Bailey (2005), *Investments* by Bodie et al. (2011), *Fundamentals of Corporate Finance* by Brealey et al. (2012), *Investment Valuation* by Aswath

Damodaran (2002), *Modern Portfolio Theory and Investment Analysis* by Elton et al. (2010), *Modern Portfolio Theory* by Francis and Kim (2013), and *The Theory of Corporate Finance* by Jean Tirole (2006). Whilst the texts overlap in content, they provide a variety of perspectives through differences in discipline and geography.

The linear approach followed here introduces concepts as needed and expands each step to describe its implementation. Readers should also recall earlier discussion that the objective of this book is to understand the processes followed by fund managers in selecting equities for investment, so this chapter omits discussion of portfolio theory.

2.1 The Building Blocks of Investment

Investment involves giving up wealth in expectation of receiving a future profit, and typically involves a contractual arrangement through purchase of securities such as stocks or bonds. Investors' objective is to obtain the highest return, but they must forego liquidity and take on counterparty risk (non-performance by the securities' issuer) and investment risk (because future returns cannot be determined). Thus investors evaluate equities as the probability-weighted return across possible investment scenarios and choose those commensurate with their own risk appetite. They trade off between expected return and expected risk, even though neither can be directly observed.

Investment theory is founded on the concept of 'economic man' (*homo economicus*) who is rational, self-interested and sufficiently informed to be able to maximise utility. This can be traced back to John Stuart Mill (1874) who wrote that political economy "is concerned with [man] solely as a being who desires to possess wealth, and who is capable of judging the comparative efficacy of means for obtaining that end." Economic man has since been augmented by numerous concepts that underpin value-based decision making, and these constitute the paradigm of modern investment.

In brief, concepts that support equity valuation comprise:

- Theoretical

    - Markets provide the best indicator of true value. This dates to at least 13th century philosopher Thomas Aquinas who wrote in *Summa Theologica* that "the quality of a thing that comes into human use is measured by the price given for it"

18　　Applied Investment Theory

- – "Movements in security prices are associated with market-wide information that differentially affects the value of securities" (Scholes 1972: 188)
- – Markets are efficient (Fama 1970), and do "not allow investors to earn above-average returns without accepting above-average risks" (Malkiel 2003).
- – Investors perceive risk as the dispersion of possible outcomes around the expected value, and proxy it with the standard deviation of returns.
- – There is a positive link between security risk and return (Sharpe 1964), so the price of an asset is set by a state-dependent risk-adjusted discount factor. Thus investors optimise their portfolio through efficient diversification by trading between the mean and variance of returns (Markowitz 1952).
- – All investors are exposed to the market as a whole, so differential returns come only through acceptance of higher non-diversifiable risk (e.g. Malkiel 2003). "The market will price assets such that the expected rates of return on assets of similar risk are equal" (Scholes 1972: 182)
- – At the firm level, corporate structure (mix of debt and equity) and distribution policy distinguish the timing of cash flows, not their quantum, and thus do not affect value (Miller and Modigliani 1961). This concept of irrelevance began with economist David Ricardo who argued in his 1820 "Essay on the Funding System" that the source of government funding – taxes or debt – was irrelevant because spending would be the same and paid from taxes, with debt merely deferring the timing of tax receipts.

- Mix of theory and observation

  - – Factor models provide projections of asset returns (e.g. Sharpe 1964; Fama and French 1993)
  - – A nexus exists between the prices of derivatives and their underlying securities (Black and Scholes 1973)
  - – Finance has many cases where principals (typically investors or shareholders) must employ agents (such as money managers and corporate executives) whose actions cannot be monitored, and so the principals establish incentive contracts to minimise agency costs while avoiding moral hazard (Jensen and Meckling 1976)

- Theory imported from economics

  - – Investors are: perfectly informed about prices, securities, and the state of the world (Walras 1877); homogenous and risk averse (Bernoulli 1738); and economically rational by seeking to unconditionally

2 Current Paradigm: Neoclassical Investment Theory 19

maximise expected utility (Mill 1874). Investors can form reliable estimates of future return and risk, and choose between securities on the basis of their expected values

- Securities have a fundamental value determined by identifiable characteristics which is equal to the discounted present value of future cash flows (Boulding 1935; sometimes attributed to Williams (1938)). That is the price paid by rational investors
- Markets are complete so that contracts are available for all securities in all states of the world
- Markets clear at a price that matches supply and demand, and demand curves are flat or downward sloping (Smith 1759)
- Securities have a single price in all markets (law of one price)
- Security transactions do not have frictions (or cost) (Arrow and Debreu 1954), and have no impact on fundamental value

- Important (often unstated) assumptions

- Investors are small, with no individual ability to affect prices
- Markets achieve equilibrium.
- Security returns are independent and identically distributed
- The distributions of security returns are sufficiently stable that historical observations can be used to predict expected return, risk and covariance.
- Data flows are exogenously determined (if not random), and reach all investors simultaneously
- Financial contracts can be costlessly enforced
- Price inflation is zero.

It is actually surprising to see the distant origin of many investment principles. One of my favourite examples involves managing investment risk through diversification which was succinctly described five centuries ago by Antonio in Shakespeare's *The Merchant of Venice*[1]:

My ventures are not in one bottom trusted,
Nor to one place; nor is my whole estate
Upon the fortune of this present year.
Therefore my merchandise makes me not sad.

Antonio knew it is hard to pick winners and just as hard to avoid losers. He trusted to the power of diversification to provide a steady return from a portfolio of assets spread across a variety of good prospects.

---

[1] Act 1, scene 1. 'Bottom' refers to a ship.

2.2   Utility Theory and Investor Risk Propensity

Financial economists assume that investors assign a value to the utility of holding each alternative security, and then choose the highest. The inherently uncertain nature of investment means that expected utility, $E(U)$, will be a combination of expected return, $E(r)$, and risk, σ:

$$E(U) = \Phi\left[E(r), \sigma\right]$$

Investors' state and psyche set their attitude towards risk, so that each investor has an individualised utility function, such as:

$$U(p) = E(r_p) - \text{½}.A.E(\sigma_p^2)$$

where: p is a prospect, and A is a measure of the investor's risk aversion.

A risk averse investor will require a premium for taking on uncertainty, and prefer a security that is priced below its fundamental value so that it provides an abnormal return. Thus positive values of A in the equation above imply risk aversion, with higher A implying greater risk aversion. The value of A is negative for risk loving investors; and zero for risk neutral investors. When utility is considered in mean-variance (or return-risk) space, a risk averse investor requires increasing expected return per unit of risk and her indifference curve slopes up and is convex. That is, as the risk increases, a risk averse investor will require a greater proportionate rise in expected return.

The risk aversion co-efficient, A, is not directly observable and so is not straight-forward to evaluate. Typically it is assessed on an individual basis using risk-tolerance questionnaires, or by direct observation of preferences such as portfolio holdings (and estimates of their riskiness). The risk aversion of groups can be calculated from revealed behaviour such as their level of insurance cover and the labour rates for occupations of different riskiness.

2.3   Capital Asset Pricing Model

During the mid-1960s a series of papers by Sharpe (1964), Lintner (1965) and others emerged that gave more structure and theory to earlier investment techniques. This material became known as the Capital Asset Pricing Model (CAPM), and describes return from a security in terms of the risk-free rate, r_f, and the security's risk:

2 Current Paradigm: Neoclassical Investment Theory   21

$$\text{Expected return} = \Phi\left[r_f,\text{risk}\right]$$

CAPM assumes equity markets behave as follows:

- The market is composed of numerous investors, who are each so small that their trades do not affect prices, and who share common traits such as: planning for a single holding period, paying no taxes or transaction costs, and being price takers.
- These investors share the same view of the world and analyse securities in the same way, giving rise to homogeneous expectations, and act in an economically rational manner to optimise the return-risk trade-off
- Return on individual securities is given by the security market line (SML) and shows expected return-risk for each security, i, through the following expression:

$$E\left(r_i\right) = r_f + \beta_i.\left[E\left(r_M\right) - r_f\right]$$

where: $\beta_i = \dfrac{\text{Covariance}\left(r_i,r_M\right)}{\sigma_M^2}$ and r_M is return *on* the market.

The slope of the security market line is equal to $r_M - r_f$, and the unexpected return of the security is equal to $r_i - E(r_i)$.

CAPM is a technique to evaluate the return of individual securities, rather than portfolios. It assumes that investors hold a diversified portfolio of securities, and partitions security risk into two components. One is systematic, and linked to market factors that must be borne by all investors. A second component is idiosyncratic, or specific to individual equities, and – because its random fluctuations are cancelled out within a balanced portfolio – it is not rewarded. Only systematic risk, or contribution of the security to variance in portfolio return, is rewarded; and beta, or the co-movement of the stock's return with the market, "is a complete measure of the risk of a security" (Fama and MacBeth 1973: 610). The return of any security relative to the market is a linear function of the risk it contributes to the market portfolio.

Empirical tests of the CAPM using real-world data raise a number of issues. Two are practical: the model incorporates the whole market, which means it is impractical to test (e.g. Fama and French 2004); and it uses expected values of risk and return which cannot be observed. A third issue is that analyses show CAPM explains little of the cross-section of equity returns.

Axiomatically, equity return must incorporate other parameters (e.g. Black et al. 1972), which has led to a number of extensions of the model.

22   Applied Investment Theory

The intertemporal CAPM (ICAPM), for instance, relaxes the single period assumption, so investors trade continuously to optimise their investments in light of changing income and consumption. Investors will take account of these additional risks, and generalise the SML to incorporate additional risk factors, k:

$$E\left(r_i\right) = \beta_{i,M}.E\left(r_M\right) + \sum_{k=1}^{K}\beta_{i,k}.E\left(r_k\right)$$

Another version replaces r_M in the traditional CAPM with r_C which is growth in investor consumption. This recognises investors will focus on risks to the buying power of their wealth, rather than the return it generates.

Over the years, CAPM's authority has waned as studies found that equity returns respond not just to beta but also to a number of firm characteristics such as capitalisation (Malkiel and Xu 1997) and book-to-market ratio (e.g. Fama and French 1995). The conclusion that idiosyncratic risk is rewarded (Goyal and Santa-Clara 2003) accelerated analysis of firm traits that explain firm-specific risk. This reflects interest in reduction of firm-specific risk amongst investors (Olsen and Troughton 2000) who have particular concern over downside components of systematic and diversifiable risks (e.g. Estrada 2006).

2.4   Factor Models and Arbitrage Pricing Theory

A broad set of extensions to the market model of CAPM are termed multifactor models that – rather than assessing return solely on the basis of market risk – add additional factors to capture other systematic risks. The general expression for the return of a security becomes:

$$r_i = E\left(r_i\right) + \sum_{j=1}^{n}\beta_j.F_j + \varepsilon_i$$

$$\sigma_i^2 = \beta_i^2.\sigma_M^2 + \sum_{j=1}^{n}\beta_j^2\sigma_F^2 + \sigma_{\epsilon i}^2$$

where β_j is termed factor beta, and relates to additional price-sensitive information contained in a systematic factor that drives return away from its expected value (everything from labour rates and household consumption to firm traits such as size). The factor betas can be thought of as compensation for bearing systematic risks, F. There is no theory of which factors should affect returns, and their betas are usually derived empirically by data mining.

A well-known alternative specification of a security's price comes from the relationship between expected return and expected risk as given by the market, or single-index, model which is the most familiar depiction of CAPM to practitioners:

$$E(r_i) = \alpha_i + \beta_i.E(r_M)$$

This is combined with the factor model concept to give an arbitrage pricing approach:

$$E(r_i) = \alpha_i + \beta_{i,M}.R_M + \sum_{x=1}^{n} \beta_{i,j}.F_j + \varepsilon_i$$

where alpha (α_i) is the outperformance of security i, and the betas relate to its co-movement with the market ($\beta_{i,M}$) and other common factors ($\beta_{i,j}$).

This general approach has come to be called arbitrage pricing theory (APT). It starts with the assumption that markets are competitive with no arbitrage opportunities and identifies non-diversifiable, market-wide influences that require compensation in the form of higher return. APT is less restrictive than CAPM because it can be applied across multiple periods. Conversely it offers no guidance on how many factors should be used, or how they should be identified.

An example is the popular Fama-French-Carhart four-factor model that incorporates firm characteristics to quantify systematic risk (Carhart 1997). This is shown below:

$$r_i = \alpha_i + \beta_{iM}R_M + \beta_{iSMB}SMB_i + \beta_{iHML}HML_i + \beta_{iMOM}MOM_i + \varepsilon_i$$

where: *SMB* is small-minus-big and shows the excess return of a portfolio of small stocks above that of a portfolio of large stocks; *HML* is high-minus-low and shows the excess return of a portfolio of high book-to-market stocks above that of a portfolio of low book-to-market stocks; and *MOM* is momentum, or recent price change.[2]

Again this model is largely theory free, merely quantifying longstanding observations that factors such as firm size, book-to-market ratio and price momentum systematically affect returns. They are generally assumed to proxy for some extramarket (i.e. non diversifiable) sources of risk (Fama and French 1993).

---

[2] Factors are available from Ken French's website at http://mba.tuck.dartmouth.edu/pages/faculty/ken.french/data_library/f-f_factors.html.

2.5 Other Valuation Models

Where CAPM and similar models derive expected return based on equities' links to systematic factors, an alternative perspective derives their standalone value.

The most common explanation of security prices is that they represent the present value of future cash flows expected by the security holder (for shares, that is dividends and perhaps a terminal price), which are discounted at a rate set by the security's risk relative to alternative investments. The concept was first set out by Ken Boulding (1935) and is probably the most common assumption of all in finance. For example, the standard corporate finance textbook by Brealey et al. (2014) begins its list of "the seven most important ideas in finance" with the fact that shares are priced at their net present value which is obtained by discounting future cash flows at the opportunity cost of capital.

The intuition is that purchase of a security buys future earnings, and its fundamental value equals the present value of expected future cash flows. Cash flows are projected using publicly available data such as company financial statements, and additional information is obtained from study of the company, overlain by the analyst's expectations. The discount rate is typically calculated using CAPM or a factor model. Decisions to purchase a security assume that any mispricing will be corrected by the end of the single period used in the analysis. While security analysts acknowledge the need to also use intuition and qualitative factors, they affect an analytical approach which protects against bias and emotion.

Equating share prices to their present value seems so obvious that it is not often discussed. But its use or applicability is quite unprovable. To calculate a share's value in this way requires a decade or more of cash flow forecasts, a projection of the risk-free rate of return over that time, and an evaluation of the risk specific to the cash flows. None of this data is observable, so nobody can confidently say it underpins the market's valuation of any stock; nor can the assumption's validity be tested as investors cannot forecast future cash flows and opportunity costs. For instance, studies of analysts' forecasts of even one-year ahead earnings generally have an absolute error of around 35% (e.g. Espahbodi et al. 2015) and management forecasts are similarly inaccurate (Hutton et al. 2012). In practice, little weight can be placed on cash flow projections, and discount rates are equally hard to determine (Hooke 2010), which makes developing NPVs a Herculean task.

As a simple example, consider valuation of an offshore oil field that is intended for production. The capital required for a new platform and associated infrastructure and their standard operating costs are well known in the oil industry. Thus DCF analysis should be straightforward.

It can, however, take decades to bring a field into production, including five or more years for design and construction; all this while the outlook is clouded by shifting political, economic and technical risks.[3] And, of course, the major determinant of cash flows is oil's price, which is notoriously unpredictable (Coleman 2012a). Even with technologies and operations that are well understood, it is complicated to calculate the quantum and timing of cash flows; and difficulty is compounded when determinants are less familiar.

Limits to CAPM and DCF analyses encourage analysts to use other techniques such as relative valuation that calculates the price of (say) an equity by reference to prices of comparable asset. The usual approach is to identify variables that the equity has in common with other securities such as growth, assets, sales or profit. The variables, or comparables, are scaled by market capitalisation to obtain a market value per unit of the common variable. This prices firm traits such as earnings (whose after tax value when divided by the stock's market capitalisation gives the price to earnings ratio), book value of assets (price to book ratio), sales and so on with the intuition that values should be roughly comparable for similar stocks (particularly those in the same industry and of similar size). Ratios serve as a benchmark indicate over or under-valuation, and can be used to estimate the market value of any asset including those that are not listed.

While these ratios may appear simple, many actually have complex drivers and linkages. A good example is given by the price-to-earnings ratio (PER), which is negatively related to future return (see: Basu 1977; Penman 1996). The link is easily seen by using the dividend discount model to unpack PER into its dividend, D, expected rate of dividend growth, g, cost of equity, k_e, and the payout ratio:

$$P_t = \frac{D_{t+1}}{\left(k_e - g\right)} = \frac{E_{t-1} \ast \left(1 + g\right)^2 \ast \text{Payout ratio}}{\left(k_e - g\right)}$$

$$\text{Price : Earnings} = \frac{P_t}{E_{t-1}} = \frac{\left(1 + g\right)^2 \ast \text{Payout ratio}}{\left(k_e - g\right)}$$

---

[3] A typical example is the ExxonMobil Corporation Hebron project which is in about 100 metres of water off north-east Canada. The field was discovered in 1980, and required about six years to design and construct after 2009. It is expected to have a total capital cost of around USD 6 billion and produce up to 180 thousand barrels of oil per day for 30-plus years (Development Application Summary, 2011 available at www.hebronproject.com).

This shows that PER reflects a complex mix of firm financial performance and strategy. This gives a credible basis for the negative link between return and lagged PER: growth is uncertain and higher growth requires a higher expected return, which reduces price, so that lower PER stocks earn higher returns.

Another ratio indicating firm value is market-to-book which proxies for the importance of uncertain, high risk opportunities relative to the value of lower risk assets in place. If a firm contracts due (say) to declining revenues, its future opportunities become more uncertain, which lowers the value of future returns from existing assets and so reduces market-to-book. The ratio can also be associated with the possibility of financial distress and indicate default risk.

The comparables approach to valuation is qualitatively different to that of DCF analyses because relative valuation relies on observable data and makes no allowances for its quality or expected change. It also relies on historical data, and has practical limitations as few companies have identical twins. Where DCF analysis seeks a fundamental standalone value for a security, relative analyses rely on current market prices. Moreover, DCF analyses produce a single valuation (albeit with associated uncertainty or error bars), whereas relative valuations typically produce a range of estimates depending on choice of the variables and comparable firms. These can be hard to reconcile.

Another approach to investment is technical analysis (TA), which studies market action rather than what the market trades. It interprets financial and economic data in light of investor behaviour and supply-demand pressures, and uses maths and images to project the trajectory of securities and markets (Ciana 2011). TA uses a variety of data sources: most obviously market transactions (everything from prices to IPOs), but also economic data, surveys of investor and analyst outlook, and a variety of sentiment-type indicators such as closed-end fund discounts and margin lending. I tell my students that TA "uses numbers to beat the market."

Despite general scepticism amongst finance researchers about the merits of TA, even simple technical trading rules can add value over the short term (see, for example: Brock et al. 1992; Shynkevich 2012). This explains wide use of TA by investment practitioners for whom it is the most important decision tool for horizons up to a month (Menkhoff 2010).

There are also less quantitative approaches to the theory and practice of investment, and – without presuming to cover a burgeoning field – it is useful to briefly describe a few of the many eclectic perspectives.

An early depiction of investment followed from interviews with managers at US banks and observation of their investment decision processes, which were then captured in a computer program (Clarkson 1963). Another atheoretical model was developed during the 1950s by Philip A. Fisher (2003) who chose stocks using information from the business grapevine to determine the strengths and weaknesses of potential investee firms (he termed it the 'scuttlebutt' method). To this end he listed 15 indicators of core company attributes, which – although hard to quantify such as products with untapped sales potential – were critical for price appreciation.

Other approaches proposed new lenses through which to interpret investment. Thus the adaptive markets hypothesis explains how investors continually refine simple heuristics in order to cope with changing environments (Lo 2004); the theory of fair markets intuits that "society is better off when markets are fair rather than efficient" (Frankfurter 2006); and the integrative investment theory extends neoclassical investment to include topics such as agency issues, governance and risk (Ambachsheer 2005). More broadly, a wide variety of research findings have been linked to hypotheses from the natural sciences to serve "as building blocks for a more robust theory of financial decision making" (Olsen 2010), which has been extended into a theory that explains the organisational process and individual decision making by fund managers (e.g. Holland 2014).

A middle ground between quantitative and qualitative investment approaches is occupied by the Austrian School of Economics which reflects elements of behavioural finance and technical analysis. Adherents of the Austrian School think of financial decisions as conditional on their institutional context, but made within an organic system involving human actions. Thus human actions are at the centre of investment decision making, and serve as determinants of security value, which is different to neoclassical finance that sees markets as some human designed mechanism that functions mechanically (for a review, see Kirzner 1987).

For Austrians, no investor can know how other investors' decisions will shape prices of securities, which makes risk more complex than generally assumed. Investors may be value maximisers, but they face a real world dogged by fundamental uncertainty and ignorance so they are never fully informed. Markets' inextricable linkages to wide-ranging social and political issues makes them so dynamic that they may be unable to reach equilibrium (Boettke 1994), which is further reinforced when alert investors trade every market move (Benink and Bossaerts 2001). This limits the applicability of utility analysis, and successful investors need to constructively use intuition and incomplete knowledge (Dempster 2011). George Soros (a Hungarian born investor) captured this uncertainty in his Theory of Reflexivity where thinking participants help shape the future by responding to other investors' decisions and market transactions and inducing feedback and non-linearity in prices (Soros 1994). To some observers, the Austrian school is philosophical rather than mathematical, and Austrian economists acknowledge their discipline can appear vague to financial economists schooled in more mathematically rigorous approaches.

2.6 Conclusion: Useable Hypotheses of Neoclassical Investment Theory

The neoclassical investment paradigm is founded on a series of hypotheses and findings that have been intuited or statistically identified. It has been extended by adding real-world factors that – to the extent they are uniquely relevant to return – better explain investment decisions.

The contemporary investment paradigm has been described by Statman (2010) as having four foundation blocks that were laid by the mid-1960s: rational investors and efficient markets, where investors employ mean-variance optimised portfolios, and expected security returns respond only to systematic risk. Together these underpin most models advanced in research and teaching. Ross (2002: 129) is typical of those who admire its success and robustness:

> The basic outline of neoclassical finance is now complete … [T]he success of the theory is the envy of the social sciences. There is probably no construct in the social sciences that has had a greater impact on the practical world than that of modern finance.

3

Behavioural Biases in Investor Decisions

> **The Key Takeaways of This Chapter Are**
>
> - Ex post examination of investor behaviour and tests of market prices against theoretical predictions reveal numerous anomalies and puzzles.
> - Despite the large catalogue, most biases can be attributed to a few factors:
>   - Simplification of the decision process
>   - Reliance on past values
>   - Status quo bias that avoids excessive reaction
>   - Personal identification with the decision
>   - Social factors
> - Most biases disappear after relaxation of the assumptions that investors are fully informed and are unconditional ex post value maximisers
> - There is limited evidence that behavioural biases cause substantial mispricings.

Behavioural finance (BF) is the most important depiction of investment after the standard finance paradigm set out in previous chapter. It examines why investors deviate from the normative, rational approach to investment (i.e. unconditionally maximise return), and – in sufficient numbers to be economically apparent – apply alternative criteria. These irrationalities arise in psychological biases or cognitive errors that are typically traced to incorrect

© The Author(s) 2016
L. Coleman, *Applied Investment Theory*,
DOI 10.1007/978-3-319-43976-1_3

29

information processing or to embedded misbeliefs, and contribute to erroneous expectations and suboptimal outcomes (Barberis and Thaler 2003; Subrahmanyam 2007). The discipline began to take shape with an analysis of rationality in decision making by Simon (1955), and now comprises a lengthy catalogue of departures from rational decision making and efficient pricing.

The yardstick for identifying biases is that of a rational, fully informed investor. Most seem to reflect a few core investor attributes, including attitudes towards risk, bounding, incorporation of personal preferences, situational features, and the way information is received. The intuition is that the information which investors face is too voluminous and uncertain to thoroughly process, and so they use mental shortcuts to reach a decision, including heuristics developed through trial and error (which suggests evolutionary causes).

BF studies violations of the standard investment paradigm's conviction that "behaviour can be explained by assuming that rational agents with stable, well-defined preferences interact in markets that clear" (Rabin and Thaler 2001: 219). It sits at the interface between quantitative analyses of investment with the assumptions of perfect foresight and perfect markets, and humans' generally subjective processes when facing decisions whose outcomes are unclear. Where MPT optimises asset selection, behavioural finance studies how to operationalise investment decisions, and seeks to improve market efficiency.

One limb of BF research identifies anomalies in market prices and traces the causes to non-rational decisions. The most obvious examples are herding, momentum, and bubbles that can be so serious as to attract the Greenspan depiction of "irrational exuberance" (Olsen 2000). Other examples are sustained departures from fundamental values that would be expected to be closed by arbitrage, such as IPO under-pricing and violations of the law of one price.

A second limb of BF – and the focus of this chapter – examines the process of financial decision making from a psychological perspective. It explains biases in investors' decisions. as arising from social, cognitive, and emotional impacts on decisions.

The volume of finance decision biases is now so large as to be perplexing to anyone with even a cursory knowledge of the field (see, amongst many: Hirshleifer 2001; Rabin 1998). However, they are often combined into about ten principal groups, with herding and overconfidence typically amongst the leaders. As an example, a survey of CFA members asked 'Which of the following behavioral biases affects investment decision making the most?', and replies were split: herding – 34%;

confirmation – 20%; overconfidence – 17%; availability – 15%; loss aversion – 13%; and others – 1% (Kunte 2015).

Proliferation of biases has prompted efforts to rationalise them, especially through construction of empirically verifiable theories. One perspective is that of psychology which describes the behaviour of individuals and identifies anomalies that reflect personal cognitive biases. A second is economic sociology which describes how individuals make financial decisions in group settings that result in non-rational biases. A third perspective is neurofinance which – following the availability of cheap MRIs – traces decisions to mechanics of the brain. Technology is also promoting individualised approaches to help optimise investment performance, such as giving investors biometric bracelets that measure their respiration, heart rate and perspiration, and linking this to market data and a diary to record trades and other events (Solon 2015).[1]

The balance of this chapter discusses behavioural decision biases that are evident in the real world, with particular emphasis on the handful that are specific to investment.

3.1 The Catalogue of Cognitive Investment Biases

Decisions of individuals are central to investment. No matter how large or small the investor, nor the extent of their information and computational efforts, each must choose what data to incorporate in their decision, the analytical methodology to be employed, and how conclusions will be actioned. With all investment decisions subject to human influences, none is without bias using its meaning of distortion or prejudice.

Central to decision bias is the concept of bounding. This was well captured by behavioural finance pioneer Daniel Kahneman (2003) who accepted the Nobel Prize in economics with an address entitled "Maps of Bounded Rationality" that placed information processing at the heart of decision biases. A prime reason why investors diverge from the rational agent model is that the volume of decision data they face is so voluminous or uncertain that they are overwhelmed and need to adopt heuristics or mental shortcuts to reach a decision.

A second reason for investor irrationality is that people's attitudes towards risk and other aspects of a decision are situational: for example, they will take

---

[1] This work is being conducted by a number of firms. See: www.essentia-analytics.com and www.sybenetix.com, amongst others.

32   Applied Investment Theory

greater risk when in a poor position. The third departure from rationality occurs because decisions can be affected by the way information is framed or transferred to investors. There is a fourth important driver of decisions and that is hedonics, or an object's non-economic value, which is sourced in sensation or state of mind. Adding in the traditional economist's goal of utility maximisation, this gives five cognitive influences on decisions.

Researchers also identify individuals' attributes that impact investment. These come from inherited traits (Cesarini et al. 2010) and experience, and show up in personality (more or less risk prone or conservative), emotion (loss aversion, self-control), motivation and world views. Age and gender also contribute to differences in behaviour. As examples, younger fund managers are less risk prone and have greater career concerns, which encourages them to herd; and, female fund managers – by comparison to their male counterparts – are less risk prone and have a more measured investment style as evidenced by less frequent trading (Niessen and Ruenzi 2007).

Investment decisions incorporate techniques used in non-finance decisions, such as reducing the range of prospects by considering only those with specific non-economic attributes, or hedonics. Using car purchase as an example, these include identifiable factors such as brand (Ford vs. Porsche), colour, and size; along with more qualitative features such as the vehicle's environmental attributes and country of assembly, and success of its manufacturer's team in motor sports events. A good example of an investment hedonic is preference for firms with a superior ethical or sustainability record. Thus many decision makers "base their decisions on qualitative information" (Omenn et al. 1997: 90).

Behavioural influences bias estimates of probability and value, which systematically affects expected utility and leads to economically irrational valuations and sub-optimal risk taking. Consensus of the academic and practitioner literature is that these biases should be eliminated (for a survey, see Hirshleifer 2001).

There are numerous catalogues of decision biases, and I use Bachmann and Hens (2010), Montier (2007), and Ricciardi (2004), amongst others to develop the following table. Many of these biases prove to be common across different types of decisions and so can be thought of as heuristics, which are rules of thumb that simplify and speed up decision making.

The table identifies impacts of biases on financial decisions, and separates the few decision biases that are unique to investment decisions in panel B (Table 3.1).

Let us now consider principal biases that shift people's decisions away from objective assessment.

Table 3.1 Biases that affect decisions

Bias	Description	Impacts on financial decisions
Panel A: Biases that are common across decision environments		
Affect heuristic	Reflects the emotional response (affect) of a decision maker and instinctively brings positive or negative feelings	• Shades valuations based on psychological judgements • Promotes glamour stocks • Determines ever-changing 'sentiment' in markets
Ambiguity aversion	Reflects dislike of situations where the distribution of outcomes is unknown	• Preference for more familiar investments (home country bias or brand names)
Anchoring and adjustment	Identifies a reference point in decision choices (e.g. an expert's prediction, or an initial value) and adjusts it in light of assumptions	• Investors under-estimate the possibility that current prices or economic conditions could change dramatically.
Availability heuristic	Draws on a mental sample of intuitively obvious or easy to recall events which are typically vivid, well-publicised or recent. Leads to over-estimation of recognised or believable events	• Choose securities that match experience or are familiar (home country bias) • Rely on easily available information (e.g. recent events, popular media) • See significance in big figures (e.g. 10,000 level on the Dow). • Market focus on particular events or statistics
Base rate neglect	Failure to consider the objective probability of an event, generally in light of historical data. Contributes to representativeness bias and law of small numbers	• Under-estimate the frequency of extreme market events
Bounded rationality	Reflects inadequacy of data, resources and/or time to make rational decisions	• Incomplete decision making
Confirmation bias	Overweights information that supports the decision maker's opinion	• Herding by analysts and investors
Conservatism	Preference for past decisions even as they turn out to be incorrect	• Infrequent portfolio updating

(continued)

Table 3.1 (continued)

Bias	Description	Impacts on financial decisions
Dread risk	Fear of catastrophic events over which the decision maker has no control and are highly unwelcome (involuntary exposures).	• Opportunity cost from excluding risky choices • Overpay for put options and insurance
Endowment effect	Overvalues what is owned	• Bias towards status quo and current portfolio
Familiarity bias	Relates a decision to recognisable or similar past event(s)	• Preference for known or recognisable securities
Framing	Relates to the way a choice is presented (e.g. loss or gain, high or low risk) and brings different responses to identical data	• Investors are more willing to accept positively framed choices.
Gambler's fallacy	Belief that independent events such as roulette spins are related	• Leads to expectations of mean reversion and trending
Hedonics	Takes non-economic factors into account in a decision or in calculating the utility of a prospect	• Prices security attributes such as ESG and reputation
Herding	Reflects correlated decision making arising in some coordinating mechanism such as receipt of shared information, observation of others' decisions, or a common decision stimulus such as price	• Leads to momentum trading where markets trend for extended periods. • Causes bubbles and slumps
Hindsight bias	After observing an outcome, places higher weight on it than before the outcome occurred. Can promote complex interpretations of major events	• Distorts judgement of how readily forecasts can be made
Homogenizing probabilities	Tendency to assign equal probabilities to distinct events, which over-weights improbable events and under-weights frequent occurrences	• Leads to too many very low risks (under-investment) and very high risks
Hyperbolic discounting	Higher discount rates for risks or costs than benefits, and for near term benefits. Leads to homogenisation of future outcomes, and promotes instant gratification.	• Inadequate savings for retirement • Neglect of possible downside outcomes

Illusion of control	Belief in the ability to control outcomes of preferred choices, even in the case of random events (such as choosing specific lottery ticket numbers).	• Investors see lower risk in their own choices • Can over-concentrate portfolios to a few preferred stocks
Loss aversion	Greater weight is placed on a given loss than an equivalent gain	• Unwillingness to dispose of poorly performing stocks and thus crystallising a loss (disposition effect) • Over valuation of loss protection products (insurance and put options) • Use of technical analysis
Mean reversion	Reflects an assumption that most natural processes are stationary, so that – when a system departs from its long term average – it will tend to return to it	• Expectation that previously underperforming stocks will do better than outperforming stocks (disposition effect) • Greater willingness to spend windfalls
Mental accounting	Partitions wealth into separate accounts according to timeframe or use, and considers each in isolation.	
Mood	Emotional reactions to non-financial factors influence decisions	• Explains abnormal market returns related to local weather and national sporting events
Optimism	Over-estimates the probability of favourable outcomes; and vice versa. Linked to overconfidence	• Investors overestimate the precision of their information and predictions
Overconfidence	Heightened expectation of own skill that leads to over-estimation of the accuracy of predictions (i.e. error bars are too narrow)	• Investors over-concentrate portfolios • Leads to higher risk portfolios and excessive trading
Over or under-reaction	Comes from errors in evaluating new information, with under-reaction due to a conservative response	• Post announcement drift (i.e. incomplete response)
Prospect Theory	People are normally loss averse, but – in the domain of losses, defined as below target wealth – can be risk prone. Gives an S-shaped utility function	• Risk propensity is situation dependent, and can rise following a loss
Regret aversion	Fear that a decision will prove wrong and be regretted	• Unwillingness to rebalance portfolio

(continued)

Table 3.1 (continued)

Bias	Description	Impacts on financial decisions
Representativeness bias	The assumption that most examples of an event resemble each other, so results of a small sample are over-generalised and stereotypes emerge	• Investors choose securities with a good brand or reputation
Panel B: Biases that are limited to financial decisions		
Asset-liability management	Investors match the characteristics of their investments or assets (maturity, currency, and volatility) with those of anticipated liabilities	• Home country bias
Disposition effect	Arises from loss aversion (unwillingness to crystallise a loss); or the assumption of mean reversion (losers will outperform winners).	• Tendency of investors to sell winners rather than otherwise equivalent losers. • Investors hold losing securities longer than winning securities
Home country bias	Arises from familiarity bias (see higher risk in unfamiliar offshore investments); or prudent asset-liability management given that most expected expenditures are domestic.	• Investors commit a disproportionate portion of their portfolio to domestic assets.
Hot hands	Expectation that historical performance will continue (equivalent to trend following)	• Investors prefer recently successful advisors or fund managers
Longshot bias	This could be a preference for skew (affect), or improbable events with high payout; or due to some combination of the availability heuristic (recall of longshot winners), illusion of control, or overconfidence.	• Over-pricing of securities with volatile/skewed performance such as mineral exploration stocks • Tendency amongst bettors (but common across financial markets) to overpay for low probability bets (i.e. high odds runners, or longshots in the jargon) • Makes expected return positively related to win probability.

3.1.1 Affect Heuristic

The affect heuristic reflects the tendency for decision makers to react to a decision in proportion to the emotion it generates, which is the psychological meaning of affect. They refer to a mental database of images and feelings that tags objects and events with favourable or unfavourable affects, and incorporate the resulting emotional cues (Finucane et al. 2000).

Affect arises in investors' personal circumstances, instinctive reaction to the decision's content, expectation of its impacts on them, and the extent of their control over it (Slovic and Gregory 1999). Affect can also link the expected risk and benefit of an event through the intensity of decision makers' reaction to its consequences, which explains why many people will – in direct contradiction to the assumptions of finance theory – inversely relate expected risk and return: as the perceived personal benefit of an event rises, it is increasingly preferred and the associated risk is perceived as falling. This can favour decisions with particularly attractive potential results such as highly skewed or lottery-type outcomes, which has a variety of names, with the most graphic coming from studies of wagering markets: long shot bias.

Affect can lead to massive blunders, such as the proclamation by celebrity economist Irving Fisher just days before the 1929 stock market crash that "stock prices have reached what looks like a permanently high plateau." The subsequent loss of much of his wealth suggested that Fisher was talking affectively about what he hoped would happen, not necessarily what he thought was probable. Blind optimism has been in plentiful supply ahead of many subsequent crashes: Bloomberg, for instance, reported (27 June 2007) statements by Merrill Lynch's CEO, Freddie Mac's Treasurer and Lehman's CFO that rising problems in the mortgage market did not pose risks to other markets.

Affect also contributes to the availability heuristic where investors give disproportionately high weighting to a graphic or memorable outcome. Thus an event that is easily recalled – such as recent media reports of increased company profits – is considered more probable than other less memorable events. This leads to over-estimates of the probability of vivid, well-publicised or easy-to-believe events.

3.1.2 Anchoring and Adjustment

Anchoring and adjustment refers to the tendency of decision makers to seize on a number that is offered to them in the early stage of decision evaluation – perhaps an offer price or the probability of a market rise – and then adjust it according to the perceived bias of the number's source (e.g. Baker and Nofsinger 2002).

38   Applied Investment Theory

A property investor, for instance, might heavily discount the valuation that a real estate agent gives of the investor's own house (assuming she is seeking to lock in a contract and secure a sales commission), but inflate a valuation that the same agent gives of a house that she is about to auction (assuming it is low in an attempt to attract buyers).

3.1.3 Asset-Liability Management

Investors often match the duration and convexity of assets such as savings with characteristics of anticipated liabilities as a form of crude risk management. For example, many investments are intended to meet local currency liabilities such as retirement expenditures or children's education, and so domestic assets can be preferred as a natural currency and inflation hedge, which appears as a home country bias (e.g. Covall and Moskowitz 1999).

In addition, non-financial components of investor wealth – that is human capital and residential property – are too lumpy to be diversifiable and can only be protected through insurance. This leads to over-valuation of put options (the option smirk) and non-economic purchase of insurance (which is a real put option).

3.1.4 Bounding

Investors operate in complex, fast changing environments that constrain their ability to gather and process information in a timely fashion. When decisions must be made quickly or information is lacking or ambiguous, complex analysis is not practical or justified and decision makers are forced to limit their options and adopt heuristics. These streamline complex decision making and help achieve quick judgments, but – unless limited to routine settings where variability is low – can lead to systematic biases (McFadden 1999).

An aspect of bounding that is important for investment relates to the spread of information between investors. To the extent that security valuations are information based, investors benefit from more information,[2] which is why regulation requires firms to continuously disclose information relevant to security performance and risk. As new information flows, it is tested against investors' paradigm, which triggers an effective response and either confirms or refutes pre-existing assumptions (often called prejudices).

---

[2] The slogan of eSignal which markets trading workstations is 'You'll make more, because you'll know more' (www.exacteditions.com, February 2013).

3 Behavioural Biases in Investor Decisions 39

When new information contradicts decision makers' paradigm, they must reject one or the other, and will experience cognitive dissonance. To avoid this, decision makers are prone to accept information that confirms their views and reject contradictions, often with little consideration about the source and quality of the new data. They can interpret ambiguous data to confirm their position and ignore information that challenges it; and seek out evidence that is confirmatory rather than contradictory.

Decision makers can also require less information to support a desirable event than they do to conclude that an undesirable event may occur (Zackay 1984). This is the confirmation bias which over-weights information that supports a preferred position, and limits investors' openness to conflicting evidence. It is strongest with entrenched beliefs, personal wealth or status, and emotional issues.

A related bias is ambiguity aversion where people are uncomfortable with uncertain or conflicting data, and hence have a preference for familiar settings and investments. Thus media and other information channels select and frame news reports to suit their clienteles.

Bounding explains one of the puzzles of financial scams such as Ponzi schemes which is that many investors are known to each other and are attracted by word of mouth (Rantala 2015). Individual investors can rarely do much of their own research, and – to cut out the demands and complexity of identifying good investments – will almost blindly follow those they trust, even when the latter lack relevant investment skill.

An interesting corollary to biases from information limits is the conjunction fallacy where receipt of additional information, irrespective of its merit and plausibility, increases confidence in decisions. As an example, consider the following evidence:

Matthew is 35, outgoing and intelligent. When a child, he was introduced to investing by his stockbroker father, and later completed a finance MBA at a prestigious school. He has an investment property and diversified stock portfolio.

Is it more likely that Michael is: a) a fund manager; or b) a fund manager with a Chartered Financial Analyst (CFA) accreditation?

Most people typically answer b, which is illogical because fund managers with CFAs are a subset of all fund managers, and so – without any other information – b is less likely than a.

Other studies have shown that risk propensity and confidence can rise with receipt of additional data, even when it is not central to the decision (Yates 1990). Thus the stock analyst who is able to ask many questions of a CEO and

3.1.5 Disposition Effect

One of the best-studied decision biases in finance is the disposition effect, in which investors are slower to crystallise losses than gains. This has been best demonstrated in several natural experiments using data from stockbrokers to show that investors sold stocks which had performed well ('winners') in preference to losers (e.g. Grinblatt and Keloharju 2001;Odean 1998). This is also consistent with evidence that losing investments are held for longer periods than winners (see Frino et al. 2015). The behaviour is variously attributed to some combination of loss aversion and regret avoidance, so investors do not wish to sell an under-performing asset because this crystallises a loss (Fogel and Berry 2010).

The disposition effect, though, is also consistent with mean reversion, whose existence has been well documented in the field (e.g. Camerer et al. 1997). Consider an investor who (say) buys two stocks, after which one rises in price while the other falls. In the absence of new information, it is rational to expect mean reversion and assume that the loser will outperform the winner (e.g. Da Costa Jr. et al. 2008).

3.1.6 Framing

Framing describes presentation of identical data with a different emphasis that shifts a decision maker's expectation of the outcome (Highhouse and Yüce 1996). An example of framing in finance comes from a study which found that the performance of a group of investors declined after they switched from telephone trading to internet-based trading. The explanation is that the investors gained access to more information, but lost personal feedback (Barber and Odean 2001).

Framing complements the affect heuristic so that the way a proposal's personal and social impact are described will elicit different emotional responses in different decision makers, and thus shade their assessment of its probability and benefits. For example, describing a situation as a threat or opportunity, possible loss or probable gain will elicit different responses from the same individual: risk averse decision makers overweight worst-case outcomes and are concerned at ambiguity and threats; risk neutral decision makers evenly weight losses and gains and focus on expected outcomes, and are particularly swayed by experts' judgments; whilst risk-prone decision makers look for opportunities and best-case outcomes (Pablo et al. 1996).

Framing itself can be framed. In keeping with the confirmation bias, decision makers self-frame a decision by editing materials to be analysed through instinctive perception of the costs and benefits of each outcome (Wang 2004). Similarly, framing can be introduced through manipulation of data. As one example, many decision makers have a natural aversion to choosing extremes, which is why survey responses tend to cluster around the middle of the range, irrespective of whether it makes objective sense or not. Thus unscrupulous analysts can shift respondents' apparent preferences by simply adding an outlier value to a questionnaire (Tourangeau et al. 2007).

3.1.7 Herding

Perhaps the most common – and certainly the most obvious – behavioural bias in investment is herding. Herding over-rides individuals' judgement so that investors react en masse to some coordinating mechanism such as receipt of shared information, observation of others' decisions, or a common decision stimulus such as news (Devenow and Welch 1996). Fund managers herd because of shared data and paradigms, pressures from competition and through scrutiny by ratings agencies (for a survey, see: Bikhchandani and Sharma 2001).

Thus institutions follow prior trades made by themselves and competitors (Sias 2004), and individuals react to recent price action. This leads to price momentum, crowded trades and build-up of sentiment. Traders quip that investor herding follows the 'cockroach theory', whereby the sight of one means that more are on the way.

A common correlating measure for herding by equity investors is price: significant moves are attributed to decisions of powerful investors, and observers who suspect this is based on superior information react in concert. Herding can entrap investors who seek to avoid a risk – everything from wealth loss to reputation damage – because they cede decisions to the majority.

Are members of a herd in denial? Not those who trade price momentum while being aware of overbought and oversold conditions. Nor those who know that information is central to valuations, but the probable price impact of any data innovation is uncertain. Thus investors who recognise that their private information is relatively weak can see herding as a prudent risk transfer mechanism because it at least achieves the average outcome (Ackert et al. 2008).

42   Applied Investment Theory

Although going against the consensus can be fatal until momentum slackens, a number of investors deliberately keep their distance from the herd. A good example is fund managers who avoid crowded trades and search for points of distinction, which is consistent with evidence that portfolios of the smallest and best performing funds diverge furthest from the index (Cremers and Petajisto 2009).

Thus herding in markets is a social phenomenon because investors form opinions from interaction with others and act in light of other decision makers' behaviour. It is not only a common bias, but economically significant because – at the extreme – it leads to pricing inefficiencies which cannot be closed by arbitrage and so cause market bubbles and crashes.

3.1.8 Hindsight Bias

When people look back at the outcome of a previous decision they have different data, and the knowledge that they were correct or not (see: Roese 2004). This leads to a bias in which favourable outcomes are seen to reflect skill, whereas unfavourable outcomes are ascribed to intervention by unpredictable events. The hindsight bias is part of a mechanism to gain closure on past decisions – no matter how bad – and allow decision makers to move ahead (Biais and Weber 2009). However, it can so badly interpret decision outcomes that – even in the face of evidence to the contrary – people will persist in belief in their own ability or preferred paradigm through an illusion of skill (Kahneman 2011).

Another aspect of the hindsight bias is the attitude towards post-audits or retrospectives. They are not common even in the wake of major decisions, which suggests little value can be gained by examining history. When post-audits are conducted, particularly of serious incidents using root cause analysis, the hindsight bias can encourage identification of a chain of linked events that allows sense to be made of the incident, even though the mechanisms involved cannot be observed or validated. This leads to suggestions that surprising events such as the 9–11 terrorist attacks on the US and collapse of Enron Corporation were predictable (Bazerman and Watkins 2004).

The hindsight bias complements a generally optimistic outlook amongst decision makers, which is consistent with over-confidence.

3.1.9 Homogenizing of Probabilities

A consistent decision bias amongst investors is poor calibration of event probabilities. Thus low probability events are seen as more likely to occur than is projected by objective measures such as historical occurrences or market valuations; and high probability events are seen as less likely (Camerer 2000).

There are several contributors to poor probability estimates. Affect, for instance, can see people swayed by memorable or extreme outcomes and so ignore more statistically rigorous estimates of probability. Decision makers can be averse to ambiguity, in which case they categorise data as either factual and relevant, or not; dismiss the ambiguous data; and roughly equally weight remaining possible outcomes. Another contributor is that even expert judgments have such wide error bars that once an outcome is accepted as possible there is little to distinguish its probability of occurrence from that of most other possible outcomes. Each of these approaches homogenizes probabilities, so all outcomes are given similar weight, irrespective of their objective probability of occurrence.

Poor estimation of probabilities reflects neglect of the base rate, which refers to the objective probability of any event occurring. This becomes important in settings where the prevailing paradigm is uncertain, and the base rate gives an outside view (Lovallo and Kahneman 2003). Obvious examples are bubbles following emergence of new and poorly understood financial products that lead to a rapid run up in prices, and investors should be alert to an almost inevitable reversion to the mean.

3.1.10 Hyperbolic Discounting

Although finance assumes that elapsed time is the only factor separating the same decision made now and in the future, comparison of decision alternatives across time reveals a preference for immediate gratification (Leiser et al. 2008). This reflects high opportunity costs from delay, so that a higher discount rate is used for short-medium term decisions than for more distant decisions.

A finance implication of hyperbolic discounting is that investors place disproportionate importance on near-term events (Knetsch 1995). As an example, they attach less importance to a fixed time gap as it moves into the future, which minimises distinctions between quite varied cash flows (Sagristano et al. 2002). This emerges as a preference for receipt of a lump sum this year rather than next year, with less concern about receipt of the same lump sum in 20 rather than 30 years.

A second feature of comparisons within actual decision making is that people use a higher discount rate for costs or negative outcomes than for benefits (Shelley 1994). Thus losses are felt more strongly than comparable gains.

These two behaviours combine so that early losses are particularly unpleasant, and so fund managers have a natural aversion to an early bad outcome because it is disastrous for stakeholder perception and – by reducing the portfolio base – harder to recover from. Preferred investments for fund managers have limited near-term risks and attractive long-term returns, which can be viewed as a focus on short-termism.

3.1.11 Mental Accounting

Mental accounting arises when decision makers do not consolidate or equate all components of their wealth, but partition it into separate accounts according to the expected time and purpose of expenditure, assign different priorities to accounts, and administer each in isolation. In the case of households, for instance, retirement savings and home equity are not fungible with current income: the last tends to be totally consumed, whereas assets are rarely touched. Decision makers will also treat wealth differently according to its source: unexpected windfalls – such as an inheritance or lottery winnings – can be spent freely; whereas anticipated extra revenues – such as a salary bonus or tax refund – will be saved (Thaler 1999).

More broadly, mental accounting can give investors a portfolio perspective. Consider a successful academic with tenure: her human capital is secure, and tax-effective retirement savings are scheduled to build adequately. Thus she may rationally take on sharply higher risk when allocating other elements of her assets, and put (say) all of a modest allocation to direct shares in high risk, potentially high payout mineral explorers or R&D firms. By extension, a nation or epoch that is characterized by rapid growth and societal stability which foreshadows low risk to human capital (through unemployment or other calamity) may see an increase in risk-prone behaviour, including with investment.

3.1.12 Overconfidence

De Bondt and Thaler (1994) propose "the most robust finding in the psychology of judgment is that people are overconfident." Overconfident decision makers have unjustified certainty about their own skill and so underweight alternative opinions and under-react to new information. According to Matthew Rabin (1996: 50):

We are over-optimistic regarding our health and other aspects of our life; we feel we are less vulnerable to risk than others; and we are more responsible for our successes than we are for our failures. We think that we are superior to others in all sorts of ways: we are better at controlling risk, better drivers, and more ethical.

Overconfidence is higher amongst experts and in more complex tasks requiring skill. This is part of a pattern which psychologists term self-enhancing biases, and complements the affect heuristic and confirmation bias.

Overconfidence also leads to miscalibration of probabilities, where decision makers over-estimate the precision of their knowledge. Thus they under-estimate randomness (or at least unpredictability) in events and are regularly surprised by unexpected outcomes. A good example is the hypothesis that hubris is a common catalyst for corporate takeovers (Roll 1986), which leads to lack of objectivity by managers of the acquiring firm in assessing the value of the target and the complexity of integrating the two firms.

Not surprisingly, overconfidence is a bias commonly attributed to investors. This was seen, for instance, in a study where money managers revealed excessive confidence in their meta-knowledge by reporting 90% confidence ranges that contained only half the correct answers (Russo and Schoemaker 1992). Overconfidence is also seen in under-estimation of the possibility of error or loss which leads to higher risk portfolios and excessive trading (see: Scheinkman and Xiong 2003).

Overconfidence does not always produce a negative outcome. For instance, it can encourage risk-prone investing which leads to higher returns (see: Kyle and Wang 1997); and being an aggressive early trader captures benefit when slower moving noise traders enter or exit a stock. These situations are a sort of reverse arbitrage where irrational investors thrive at the expense of rational investors.

3.1.13 Prospect Theory and Situational Attitudes Toward Uncertainty and Loss

A prominent bias is that decision makers shift their preference for uncertainty or risk according to the decision and situation.[3] A useful framework for explaining this is the Prospect Theory of Kahneman and Tversky (1979), which argues that the utility of actual or expected outcomes is determined relative to a benchmark: outcomes above a reference point such as an income

---

[3] For reviews from different perspectives of the influence of risk on decision making, see: Camerer et al. (2011), Fox and Tversky (1998), Kőszegi and Rabin (2007), Lopes (1994), Oliver (2013), Reyna (2004), Ricciardi (2008), Shefrin (2006), Sitkin and Pablo (1992) amongst many others.

46   Applied Investment Theory

target are seen as 'gains'; but results below that level are considered as 'losses', and losses are weighted more heavily than gains because they push decision makers further towards non-preferred wealth levels. This gives an S-shaped curve when utility of an outcome is plotted against expected outcome.

The fact that any loss is felt harder than the equivalent gain is termed loss aversion (Barberis and Huang 2001), and can skew investor preferences so they prefer to avoid uncertain prospects even if this results in lower expected return. As an example, consider investments that are intended to meet inflation-influenced expenses (e.g. retirement savings), or contingent calls due to adverse events (e.g. job loss). Because the expected value of liabilities is stable, many investors avoid securities that are subject to price uncertainty which makes them appear to be loss averse (Hwang and Satchell 2010). This can intensify as the anticipated expenditure approaches because the possibility of recovery from any loss steadily declines.

A second consequence of risk sensitivity is that prior outcomes influence future decisions. Thus decision makers who are above their reference level can become risk averse to remain in the domain of gains and seek more certain outcomes, including a bias towards the status quo. Conversely, those below their reference point become risk prone with an increased preference for risky alternatives in the hope of achieving a positive outcome and moving into the realm of gains.

Prospect Theory complements the wealth effect, where the willingness to spend varies directly with wealth. A finance example is termed the house money effect where successful gamblers (investors?) will take higher risks with their winnings than their original stake (Thaler and Johnson 1990). The net is that investors' wealth influences their decisions: changes in equity prices that affect wealth lead to shifts in absolute and relative ranking of investment preferences. This has the interesting implication that – as investors' wealth wanes or waxes – they become more or less willing to take on uncertainty, and so do not have a constant rational price for any security.

The implication for investment is that – along with other personalising biases such as affect and framing – risk is not an unambiguous, objective measure but is a personal and social construct.

3.1.14   Regret Aversion

Regret aversion describes the fear that a decision will prove wrong and thus be regretted (Humphrey 2004). This is part of a set of biases that favour the status quo, in which decision makers cope with surprises and rapid change through lethargic response that reflects their preference for avoiding change. They can be averse to making a decision that could bring loss; resist knee jerk reactions to new data by waiting for confirmation; insist on proper process before agreeing to change; and rely blindly on yardsticks such as heuristics and affect. As an example in finance, regret aversion leads investors to neglect regular evaluation of their portfolios.

3.1.15 Sentiment

Anecdotally, many investors display sentiment. One analysis covered more than 20 measures using investor surveys, technical indicators calculated from market data, and various measures of trading activity (Brown and Cliff 2004). It found strong correlation between measures; that sentiment is strongest amongst institutional investors in large stocks; and that equity returns cause future changes in sentiment. A similar analysis developed a sentiment index incorporating closed-end fund discount, NYSE turnover, IPO first day returns and dividend premium, and found that it explained half the variance in returns for US stocks during 1962–2001 (Baker and Wurgler 2006).

In a related area, a good deal of analysis has been conducted into the influence on returns of non-market factors that are assumed to proxy for investors' sentiment. Event studies have found mood-based biases related to weather, holidays and disruption to sleep patterns (Shu 2010). To comprehensively study weather's effects, one study compiled trades of individuals with a large national brokerage and found no evidence that cloud, rain or blizzards in investors' city of residence affected returns (Loughran and Schultz 2004). Another example of investor sentiment is the effect from outcomes of sporting events with national importance: loss in a World Cup soccer match leads to a 49 bp drop in stock prices, with smaller, but still significant, drops following losses in international cricket, rugby, and basketball games (Edmans et al. 2007).

An important aspect of sentiment is that it can potentiate asset pricing anomalies. That is, during or after periods of strong sentiment, there is a strengthening of anomalies that relate to investor over-reaction, particularly excessive optimism (Jacobs 2015).

3.2 Could There Be a Common Behavioural Denominator?

No doubt the most unsatisfactory aspect of behavioural finance is its fragmentation, so that there is not yet an accepted framework or theoretical paradigm that explains the many biases in investment decisions. There are, though, several approaches with promise.

48   Applied Investment Theory

The first is to expand decision makers' utility functions by explicitly incorporating behavioural measures. For example, one study of inconsistencies in investor behaviour across different periods assumes that returns follow a random walk, whereas investors expect they will either trend or mean revert (Barberis et al. 1998). Investors identify the regime by sequential moves: two in the same direction are a trend, while two in opposite directions signal mean reversion. The result is to explain equity price behaviour through biases in individual investors and their interaction with the market.

A second way to cohede biases is to incorporate them within a central intuition. One finance example relies on the premise that information drives security prices, and assumes that heterogeneous agents trade as a consequence of conflicting expectations formed by arrival of price-sensitive information which they variously interpret or receive at different times. Under this mixture of distributions hypothesis, information affects both price and market volume (Clark 1973).

Models such as these show how investor and market activity influence price. They are coherent, with sound theoretical bases in sociology, psychology and economics, and can explain a wide variety of observed investor and market behaviours.

There is promise, too, in identifying common factors amongst decision biases. Many, for instance, can be traced to incorrect data collection that leads to erroneous forecasts and suboptimal outcomes, and to difficulty in determining an appropriate distribution for decision outcomes. Investor rationality is constrained, too, by information asymmetry, lack of data about the future, and insufficient computational resources. Examples of resulting decision biases include over-weighting of recent experience, overconfidence, conservatism and sample size neglect. Other biases arise during information processing, including framing, mental accounting, regret avoidance and situation-based risk propensity. Also, investors weight alternatives according to circumstances, such as higher discount rates for costs or negative outcomes than for benefits, and alter risk propensity according to their situation. Finally, financial decisions incorporate a wide range of non-economic stimuli typical of those used in other choices.

In fact, just a handful of decision stimuli can explain virtually all investors biases (De Bondt et al. 2008). My own rough ordering of core biases from most to least important is:

- Bounding that encourages simplification of the decision process through heuristics. There are simply too many decisions to make, and few people have the time, skill or inclination to fully analyse each. Thus a large number of apparent biases simply describe shortcuts that are typical of natural decision processes including framing, mental accounting, regret avoidance and situation-based risk propensity.

- Constraints on the size of the sample used (which reflects bounded capability) that leads to erroneous forecasts through over-weighting of recent experience, overconfidence, conservatism and sample size neglect. As examples, investors rely on past values and incorporate price in utility functions, and assume predictability in markets so that short term momentum promotes technical trading and medium term mean reversion encourages them to hold losers in the disposition effect
- Status quo bias which recognises that the continuous flow of information with its surprises and rapid change can whipsaw investors. They avoid excessive reaction through a lethargic response that is averse to making a change that could bring loss.
- Personal identification with the decision, which explains affect and non-economic stimuli or hedonics typical of other choices (whether a new car, household appliance or holiday destination), including reputation of dealers, social pressures and psychic rewards
- Attitude towards risk, especially loss aversion and situational risk propensity. Thus investor decisions incorporate recent experience, weight alternatives according to circumstances, and apply higher discount rates for costs or negative outcomes than for benefits.
- Social factors in which decision makers identify better informed people and copy their decisions, which can lead to herding and momentum effects.
- Self-deception where decision makers over-estimate their own skill, underweight alternative opinions and under-react to new, conflicting information.

The following table shows how cognitive and emotional behavioural biases can be consolidated around these few basic drivers to produce a parsimonious system of classification (Table 3.2).

3.3 Conclusion

Although many financial economists consider that behavioural finance is distinctly different to standard finance, they both achieve similar ends. Standard finance, for instance, values securities using discounting, a factor model or similar and maximises return per unit of risk. Behavioural approaches allow for risk aversion amongst investors, and incorporate security traits such as name recognition and favourable management attributes. The effect of

Table 3.2 Drivers of behavioural decision biases

	Drivers of behavioural decision biases							
	Bounding/ Decision simplification	Incorrect data collection	Status quo bias	Personal identification	Reliance on historical data	Social factors	Self-deception	Situational risk propensity
Affect	X			X	X			
Ambiguity aversion	X	X	X					
Anchoring	X				X			
Availability	X		X	X	X			
Base rate neglect		X	X				X	X
Bounded rationality	X							
Confirmation bias		X	X	X			X	
Conservatism			X				X	
Disposition effect					X			
Dread risk				X				X
Endowment effect			X	X				
Familiarity bias	X	X	X	X		X	X	
Framing				X		X		
Gamblers' fallacy					X			
Hedonics	X			X		X		
Herding					X	X	X	
Heuristics	X			X				
Hindsight bias		X	X		X			
Home country bias	X			X		X		
Homogenising probabilities	X	X						
Hot hands		X			X			
Hyperbolic discounting	X							
Illusion of control		X		X				

Involuntary exposures							X
Longshot bias		X					X
Loss aversion	X						
Mean reversion						X	X
Mental accounting			X	X	X		
Mood				X			
Optimism							X
Overconfidence							X
Over or under-reaction		X		X		X	
Regret aversion		X	X	X			
Representativeness	X			X			X

following both standard finance and behavioural finance is to lead investors towards diversified portfolios of good stocks with low risk.

The distinctive feature of behavioural finance is that it seeks to explain investor biases or departures from rational, unconditionally economically optimised decisions. It catalogues mistakes to avoid, and perhaps techniques to profit. Given that there is hardly a finance decision where testing has not revealed an anomaly, it is easy to understand the concern expressed by proponents of behavioural finance that "poorly informed and unsophisticated investors might lead financial markets to be inefficient" (De Bondt et al. 2008).

Despite the richness of behavioural finance, it has a number of shortcomings. In particular it plays down the conclusion of Herb Simon (1978) that "almost all human behavior has a large rational component, but only in terms of the broader everyday sense of rationality, not the economists' more specialized sense of maximization." Put simply, it can be hard to distinguish a behavioural bias from a well-founded belief or judgement.

Behavioural finance also has some interesting gaps. There is not much research, for instance, into culture-specific pricing anomalies, even though it is clear that people's upbringing and cultural environment shape much of their decision making (Hofstede 1997). Similarly there is limited research on how corporate culture impacts decisions, nor the effect of investor socialisation with colleagues, competitors, clients and other observers (but see Sect. 8.3, below). Little is known about how individuals' decisions respond to factors such as self-selection and hiring into a particular finance role or firm, nor about fund manager attributes and motives (many people in finance, for instance, display criminal attitudes, seek thrills and are contrarian). This opens up the whole question of investment industry culture: does one exist? If so, how is formed, shaped and maintained? What is its impact on markets? (Beckmann et al. 2008).

Another topic that is lightly covered by behavioural finance is agency issues. They loom large in corporate finance research, and seem equally significant to investment decisions given that so many are made through, or under the influence of, agents. The last could be expected to maximise their own utility and that of associated third parties, and fail to maximise value for investors. A good example involves financial advisors who construct portfolios according to their own preferences rather than clients' circumstances (Canner et al. 1997).

Finally, there is no doubt that every investor can see BF's echoes in their own decisions and in the actions of colleagues. Even so, an intuitively troubling aspect of BF's catalogue of statistically detectable biases is their attribution to cognitive shortcomings of sophisticated, strongly motivated investors. This seems improbable. It is equally difficult to accept that biases continue to cause significant loss, because any that produce meaningful mispricings would surely be arbitraged away and their adherents forced to leave the market.

4

Uncertainty in Investor Wealth

> **The Key Takeaways of This Chapter Are**
> - There is no empirical evidence to support a stable relationship between equity return and its statistical uncertainty.
> - Investments with high expected return are usually accompanied by high possibility of loss, so that target return causes risk or uncertainty.
> - Investors are loss averse, and risk for them is uncertainty in future value of their wealth.
> - The possibility of wealth loss reflects Knightian uncertainty, which investors estimate through a variety of proxies, most of which are correlated because they represent different measures of a common underlying parameter
> - The possibility of investor loss is analogous to writing a put option whose value derives from failure to achieve expected cash flows and adverse developments in the state of the world.

Investment involves foregoing consumption of current wealth in exchange for claims on a larger amount that is uncertain because it depends on future cash flows, counterparty performance and state of the world. For equity investors, risk represents how poorly their choice performs under a wrong scenario (Porter 1985).

The first source of possible wealth loss is investor over-estimation of value because of information asymmetry, use of an incorrect analytical paradigm, or misjudging counterparty performance. A second source of loss is endogenous

© The Author(s) 2016
L. Coleman, *Applied Investment Theory*,
DOI 10.1007/978-3-319-43976-1_4

to the investee firm and reflects failure by its management to achieve expected improvements in cash flows from projects and strategies in prospect. This stems from underestimation of difficulties in executing new strategies and initiatives, high transaction costs and negative synergies within the firm, or poor management of operations. A third source of investor wealth loss is exogenous to the firm and involves adverse developments that could not be reasonably expected (everything from natural disasters to competitor breakthroughs), and weaker than expected conditions in the economy and financial markets. Finally, terminal value of the investment depends on a set of ill-defined, state-dependent contingent claims on the firm, which arise from decisions by the firms' managers and through moral hazard from institutions and other forces impacting on the firm.

Let us consider uncertainty associated with equity investment.

4.1   Background

Uncertainty is central to investment. This is because investment realigns intertemporal wealth by trading a liquid, known sum against a future amount that is uncertain because of time varying state determinants such as economic regime or financial outlook that can cause wealth to vary unexpectedly. Investment outcomes reflect events that have not yet occurred and the only data available to assess them relates to the past, which may be of poor quality or – because of information asymmetry – unavailable along the chain of security supply and demand. It is also yet to recognise data that will not become available until the future, and is largely unknowable. There is also uncertainty in the intentions of agents with influence over investor wealth such as directors and managers, regulators and legislators.

Thus it is not possible to form more than a general impression of the future and scientific objectivity is impracticable. Moreover, uncertainty and knowledge become fungible, so that more of one means less of the other (Coleman and Casselman 2016). Examples of improved knowledge that has lifted equity valuations in recent decades are legislation and enhanced governance that improved corporate reporting to be more reliable and detailed; and higher liquidity which provides additional data on other investors' value estimates (Friederich et al. 2002).

The obvious importance of uncertainty to investors encourages firms to develop strategies that signal less risk to counterparties. These include building a reputation for reliability, adopting financially prudent policies, and enhancing governance. The best signals are negatively correlated to expected risk and difficult to manipulate or misreport (Riley 1975), which has seen emergence of a variety of independent industry benchmarks promoted by low risk firms. As examples: a group of international banks developed the Equator Principles to ensure that projects they finance meet acceptable social and environmental criteria (Scholtens and Dam 2007); another group developed the Global Reporting Initiative which provides Annual Report type data for non-financial measures (Brown et al. 2009); and numerous professional and regulatory bodies have developed best practice guidelines. Because it is easier for low risk firms to signal their relative risk, they have an incentive to self-select into risk measures, report against benchmarks, and upgrade the quality of their reporting. Investors who are seeking to reduce uncertainty from knowledge risk can free ride on these measures, and also others' monitoring such as independent ratings of creditworthiness and investment processes.

These steps to titrate the level of uncertainty or risk are only part of investors' task because they need to factor in their own risk propensity, which is their preference or aversion to loss or uncertainty. Decision makers have an inherent risk propensity related to their psychology, environment and actions of peers or competitors, which varies with endowment and recent risk history, and with sentiment and prevailing market conditions. This throws up a rich literature on risk, with disciplines of interest to investors comprising finance, decision science, organisational behaviour, psychology, and strategic management.[1]

Investors who are motivated to manage the possibility of failing to achieve expected return tend to avoid market based instruments because the required premium consumes most of the expected benefit.[2] Extra-market wealth protection alters the probability or consequences of contingent claims on the firm's cash flows. For investors, the only practical choices are avoidance and diversification. The firm, though, has more techniques available, including enterprise risk management (ERM), outsourcing of tasks that could damage wealth, and insurance against specific losses. These assess particular risks, but – even with a routine activity such as a factory process or corporate acquisition that has a large enough population to establish a base rate – each individual project has an uncertain outcome.

---

[1] Other disciplines with extensive risk literatures include engineering, medicine, politics and science.

[2] Consider a stock priced at $100 which is expected to provide an abnormal return of 20% over four years. Protection can be obtained through purchase of a put option with strike price equal to expected value. Using the Black-Scholes model (with 3% dividend yield, 3% interest rate and 20% volatility), a put option with a $120 strike price would cost $20.

56   Applied Investment Theory

Risk is one of the oldest topics in economics research, and dates at least to Bernoulli (1738),[3] but the risk literature has shortcomings that pose a "fundamental methodological challenge" for many researchers (Ruefli et al. 1999: 167–168). One is the absence of an agreed definition of risk. In finance and accounting, risk is measured as variability in market or accounting returns, and is a population-based measure with a reliable distribution that can be confidently modelled using historical data. In management and strategy, risk is a negative concept with connotations of downside loss that matches the dictionary definition as the chance of a non-preferred outcome, specifically the possibility of loss of value; it tends to be evaluated on a case by case basis.

A second fault line involves the nature and determinants of the link between risk and return. Finance intuits that investors require compensation to take on risk: thus expected return has a positive relationship with expected risk, and expected risk causes return. By contrast, other disciplines agree with fifth century BC Greek historian Herodotus that "great deeds are usually wrought at great risks" (Rawlinson 1964): the difficulty involved in executing a task is related to its expected benefit. Thus expected return causes risk, although the latter can be moderated by risk management and occurrence of unexpected developments: this results in no more than a weak ex ante link between return and risk.

A useful bridge over these fault lines is the framework proposed by Frank Knight (1921) that distinguishes between mechanical and biological risk. The former relates to probabilistic risk that is associated with events that have a known distribution such as flips of a coin. The latter is typical of markets and firms where outcomes are time varying and situation dependent, and risk for investors and managers reflects uncertainty.

No matter what specification of risk is used, no decision outcome is predictable. Certainly mechanical processes have known distributions, as do more organic processes such as corporate strategies. But each is independently distributed and/or has a time-varying distribution. For example, the abnormal first day return to IPOs has a large population, but is known to vary markedly (Ritter 1998). Similarly with the volatility of equity returns – which is the typical finance definition of risk – where even the most sophisticated models cannot predict more than 30–40% of variation in the next day's volatility, and this drops off quickly (Ghysels et al. 2005). Nor does implied equity price volatility – such

---

[3] For reviews of financial risk over more recent time, see: Knight (1921), Simon (1959), Slovic (1972), Trimpop (1994), and Ricciardi (2004). For more general reviews of firm risk, see: Cyert and March (1963), Mehr and Hedges (1963), Froot et al. (1993), Sitkin and Weingart (1995), and Coleman (2006).

as the VIX Index – improve forecasts beyond a month (Canina and Figlewski 1993); and fundamentals are of little use either (Engle and Rangel 2008).

Looking forward, we will recognise the richness of risk, but – unless otherwise made clear – use it with the *Oxford Dictionary* meaning of "the chance of bad consequence or loss", and treat it as uncertainty in Knightian terms. Risk, then, represents the cost of a non-preferred outcome of a decision, which lies in the left tail of the distribution of possible outcomes. Because this definition incorporates probability and consequence, it is multi-faceted and embraces most uses of risk across economics.

4.2 Risk in the Finance Literature

Within investment, there is no broad theory of risk. Sharpe (1964), for instance, identified "the absence of a body of positive microeconomic theory dealing with conditions of risk", which was still apparent half a century later to Bodie et al. (2011: 117) who noted that "there is no theory about the levels of risk we should find in the marketplace".[4] Although the broad topic of investment risk is a theory-free zone, aspects of it have stimulated some of the finance discipline's pre-eminent papers, including: Markowitz (1952), Sharpe (1964), Fama and MacBeth (1973), Jensen (1993), and Lakonishok et al. (1994).

In the equity investment literature, risk has four key aspects, and is: integral to asset valuations; a probability measure, and so objective; and driven by firm and industry business risk, and the firm's contracted liabilities, including debt. In parallel, investors' utility functions reflect their risk propensity.

4.2.1 Relationship Between Security Return and Uncertainty

It has been common for finance researchers to assume a positive relationship between risk and return, and thus: "an investor … may obtain a higher expected rate of return on his holdings only by incurring additional risk" (Sharpe 1964: 425). Put differently: "There is general agreement that investors, within a given time period, require a larger expected return from a security that is riskier" (Glosten et al. 1993: 1779). According to a classic discussion by Fama and MacBeth (1973: 608, 610): "the risk of a portfolio is measured

---

[4] In fact the lament echoes across disciplines along the lines that "very little is known about the relationship between corporate strategies and firm uncertainty, or risk" (Lubatkin and O'Neill 1987: 685)

58   Applied Investment Theory

by the standard deviation of its return ... [and] in a market of risk-averse investors, higher risk should be associated with higher expected return."

The intuition that return and risk have a positive link has two rationales: risk averse investors would require a higher expected return for taking on additional, non-diversifiable risk; and higher return investments are inherently more risky. Obviously, then: "As long as investors correctly perceive the riskiness of various assets, risky assets must on average yield higher returns than less risky assets" (Jensen 1968: 389). This positive link between expected risk and return conditional on data available at the time "is so fundamental in financial economics that it could be described as the 'first fundamental law of finance'" (Ghysels et al. 2005: 510).

The positive return-risk link is so central to standard finance and near universally relied upon in investment decisions that it is one of the most interesting research questions. Sadly, evidence does not support the assumed link. For instance, Glosten et al. (1993) report a variety of studies that show positive, negative and time varying relationships between return and risk; whilst more recently Bollerslev et al. (2013) conclude that: "counter to the implications from a traditional risk-return trade-off, or volatility feedback-type relation, returns are at best weakly positively related, and sometimes even negatively related, to past volatilities." Other empirical studies of the link between return and risk have variously concluded that the sign is positive, negative or insignificant (see: Anderson et al. (2009), Bali (2008), and Scruggs (1998)).

This finding is amplified in the next chart which shows the linkage since 1990 between the S&P 500 Index and the log of its volatility (calculated as the 30 day moving average of squared daily change). Consistent with uncertainty in the relationship found by most studies, volatility and price tended to move together during the first half of the period, and then inversely. This makes it obvious why ex post analyses show no consistent relationship between return and risk (Fig. 4.1).

Further evidence casting doubt on the positive return-risk nexus comes from studies of corporate performance which find a negative link between return and its volatility (e.g. Bromiley (1991) and Andersen et al. (2007)). Thus a study of nuclear power plants found that their operating safety is related to profitability (Osborn and Jackson 1988), which is a common conclusion.

The existence and direction of any causality in the return-risk relationship are highly uncertain. One possible contributor is that – for samples drawn randomly from a normally distributed population such as security returns – the standard deviation will not be related to the mean (Stuart and Ord 2009). Thus there should not necessarily be any nexus between equity risk and return given their definition, respectively, as the standard deviation and mean of samples of security returns (the occasional relationship detected between them would be due to sampling bias).

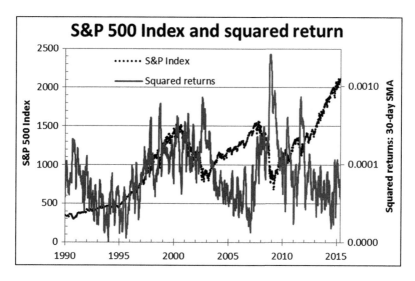

Fig. 4.1 S&P 500 Index level and volatility

Another contributor to conflicting signs for the return-risk relationship is that it could be concave as proposed in an early edition of *Dictionary of Political Economy* (Higgs 1926: volume III, page 224):

> [C]lasses of investments which on the average return most to the investor are neither the very safest of all nor the very riskiest, but the intermediate classes which do not appeal either to timidity or to the gambling instinct.

Such a concave, ∩-shaped relationship between return and risk has been identified in a real options model which shows "that the probability of investing is initially an increasing function of volatility, but after a certain point it becomes a decreasing function of volatility." (Sarkar 2000: 223), and confirmed by Walls and Dyer (1996) and other authors.

In terms of the return-risk relationship, the only certainties are that: higher observed risk is related to higher risk propensity; higher expected risk is related to higher observed risk; and there are insurmountable practical difficulties in developing economically valid expectations of return and risk.

Another ambiguous aspect of the relationship between security return and uncertainty relates to the appropriate return that should be obtained per unit of risk. The best example of incongruity here is the disparity in returns from equities relative to risk free Treasury bills, which – over long periods – has not been justified by standard asset pricing models. A typical depiction of what is termed the equity risk premium puzzle is that the annual yield on

60 Applied Investment Theory

Treasury bills in the United States averaged 3.7% during 1925–1995, whilst that on equities averaged 10.1% (Siegel and Thaler 1997). This unexpectedly high premium was confirmed as robust across time and countries (Campbell 1999).

To help unpack the equity risk premium puzzle, it is useful to reshape the test away from comparison of returns to equities and those from Treasuries which is unbalanced because equities have an infinite life, whilst Treasuries are short duration, discount securities. A more relevant comparison is between the risk premium for equities and a similarly long-lived risk-free asset such as Treasury bonds. This gives comparable time frames; and allows separate identification of the risk of equities relative to corporate bonds and the risk of corporate bonds relative to risk free Treasury bonds.

Thus a better way of thinking about the various premia for investing is:

> Risk premium on corporate investment = Return on corporate bonds – Return on Treasury bonds
> Risk premium on equity investment = Return on equities – Return on corporate bonds

Both premia are expected to be positive (reflecting higher risk from equity and corporate investment), and in low single figures in real percentage terms.

This breakdown is examined in the following table using 20 years of UK and US data.[5] Most obviously there is no recent evidence of an equity premium puzzle: the yield on equities in both Britain and the US has been only a few percent above cash since 1992. This is yet another anomaly that seems to have disappeared shortly after its publication! What the table does show, though, is two quite different puzzles: in both Britain and USA in recent decades the return from corporate bonds has been higher than, or equal to, the return from intuitively higher risk corporate equities; and the return from gilts and Treasury bonds has been higher than the return from intuitively higher risk corporate bonds.

In short, financial markets in Britain and the United States have been providing higher returns through the last two decades to intuitively lower risk assets. If nothing else, this equity risk deficit puzzle should conclusively reject any positive nexus between return and uncertainty or risk (Table 4.1).

The next chart amplifies this issue, with a plot of the annual equity risk premium as total return to the US S&P 500 minus return to Treasury bills and its

---

[5] Sources: *Barclays Equity Gilt Study, 2012*; US Federal Reserve (https://research.stlouisfed.org/fred2/); and Professor Damodaran (http://pages.stern.nyu.edu/~adamodar/New_Home_Page/datafile/histretSP. html).

4 Uncertainty in Investor Wealth

Table 4.1 Components of UK and US equity risk premia

	Britain			USA		
	2011	2002–2011	1992–2011	2011	2002–2011	1992–2011
Real Returns: % PA						
Equities	−7.8	1.2	4.8	−4.0	1.8	5.6
Corporate bonds	1.6	1.6		12.6	5.4	5.4
Cash	−4.1	0.2	2.1	−2.8	−0.7	0.6
Gilts/Treasury bonds	15.8	3.9	5.9	22.5	6.1	6.0
Spreads						
Equities – cash (proxy for equity risk premium)	−3.7	1.0	2.7	−1.2	2.5	5.0
Return premium on equity investment: Equities – Corporate bonds	−9.4	−0.4		−16.6	−3.6	0.2
Return premium on corporate investment: Corporate bonds – Gilts or T bonds	−14.0	−2.3		−9.9	−0.7	−0.6

five-year moving average (dotted line). The premium has varied significantly between periods: during the early period of the data, the ERP was several percent higher than the last few decades (an average of 9.8% during 1928–1957, and 7.5 during 1995–2015) (Fig. 4.2).

The most significant takeaway from this section is the striking lack of consistency in the relationship between return and statistical risk. Empirical studies show the relationship can be positive, negative or insignificant; and the equity risk premium has swung from puzzlingly high to inexplicably low and even negative.

Possible explanations come from a review piece by the equity premium puzzle's architects who noted that the puzzle: "… underscores the inability of the standard paradigm of Economics and Finance to explain the magnitude of the risk premium, that is, the return earned by a risky asset in excess of the return to a relatively riskless asset" (Mehra and Prescott 2003). They suggested three possible causes: the standard paradigm does not capture equity price dynamics; investors cannot implement the standard paradigm; or investors are irrational and do not follow the standard paradigm. The chart shows a somewhat different explanation which is that returns to equities are not systematically related to their medium-term risk.

To develop a more robust understanding of equity risk, we need to drill further into its determinants.

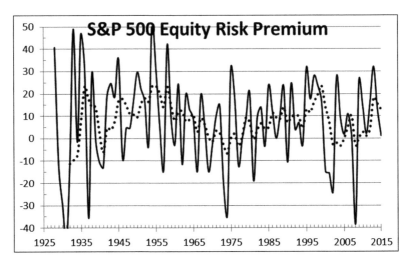

Fig. 4.2 US Equity Risk Premium

4.3 Unpacking the Notion of Uncertainty and Risk in Finance

Uncertainty for investors relates to the probability that the value of their equities falls below some yardstick, such as purchase price, estimated value, or market return. This section examines factors contributing to loss, as summarised in the following figure. The model distinguishes between *security risk*, which is the possibility of loss by shareholders in the firm, and *firm risk*, which is the possibility of a fall in the firm's enterprise value. As we will see, firm risk and security risk are distinct in terms of their drivers, measures and significance: it is inappropriate to conflate the two concepts (Fig. 4.3).

Enterprise value is at risk from factors under the firm's direct control such as operations, strategy and corporate structure. Other influences come from the firm's industry, especially competitor activities; along with technology and social, economic and political factors in the firm's environment. This in turn is overlain by market and financial factors and unexpected external events or news, which impact share price.

4.3.1 Exogenous Influences on Equity Uncertainty or Risk

The highest level exogenous influence on firm risk is the state of the world. This recognises that the performance of individual firms and securities depends on impacts from the macroeconomy on market parameters and

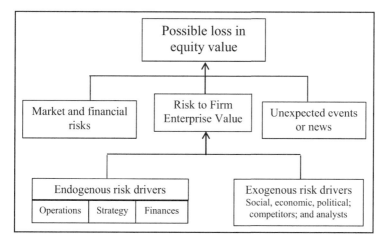

Fig. 4.3 Contributors to loss in shareholders' wealth

investor liquidity. An example of the last is widespread belief that US Federal Reserve was so fearful of fall-out from collapse of the irrationally exuberant stock market during the 1990s that it made pre-emptive reductions in interest rates. Investors saw this as a floor under the price of their shares, much as can be achieved by a put option, and termed it the 'Greenspan Put' (Miller et al. 2002), which was so powerful that: "only Alan Greenspan's reckless monetary expansion kept the bubble economy of the 1990s afloat" (Quiggin 2012: 26).

A number of proxies are available to monitor macro risks to investors, with one of the best given by the Misery Index, which is the sum of unemployment and inflation rates plus 10-year government bond yield less GDP change. This intuits that unemployment and inflation succinctly capture risks to human capital and wealth from loss of individuals' job or firms' bankruptcy; and the long-term interest rate less GDP growth is a proxy for restrictive monetary policy (Barro 1999).[6]

The following chart plots the US Misery Index with values inverted, and shows that it moves inversely with, and perhaps leads, the S&P 500 Index. This can be interpreted as equity values responding favourably to easy liquidity (low yields), along with strong employment and economic growth that are accompanied by low inflation (Fig. 4.4).

Interestingly, the Misery Index has also been shown to correlate well with a variety of adverse social indicators such as crime (Tang and Lean 2009). As

---

[6] Values of this Misery Index for most countries as at the end of 2013 are available at www.cato.org/publications/commentary/measuring-misery-around-world.

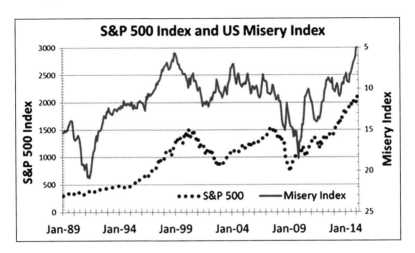

Fig. 4.4 US Misery Index

discussed earlier (Sect. 3.1), this could be consistent with mental accounting where people take a portfolio approach and relate their investment risk propensity to expectations about the value of their human capital. When social and political risks appear low, investors see relative certainty in their non-financial assets and will take higher financial risks.

By extension, risks in the macroeconomy are important to equity returns, and so most institutional investors adopt a tops down perspective. They expect that conditions in the political, economic, social and technological environment have synergetic effects on firms through conditions in the industry (such as regulation, profitability, competition) and markets (aggregate demand, interest rates, and commodity prices). This, for instance, guides credit default models that predict firm losses using exogenous variables such as economic conditions in the region or country, and historical recovery rates in the industry (Gupton and Stein 2005).

The economic cycle is also important because risks of adverse selection are pro-cyclical: for example, transaction volume is high at market peaks which reduces barriers to entry and throws up a higher than the normal number of investment choices (e.g. IPOs and acquisitions), many of which will not survive the inevitable downturn. Thus there is a lower probability of successful investment choice at cycle peaks than in other periods.

Another external influence on firms is industry regulation that shapes the quantum of monopoly rent available to industry participants, and thus deters competition and risk-taking. Regulation has long been important to risk within financial institutions and markets, such as the Glass-Steagall Act of 1933 that prohibited US bank holding companies from owning other financial companies.

Another exogenous influence on firm risk is moral hazard which is action by a third party that reduces the loss expected from a particular action, and hence increases risk propensity. Moral hazard can arise in factors as diverse as insurance, competitor strategic initiatives and the need to cater to various clienteles (Baker and Wurgler 2004). Far more common is reverse moral hazard which places a higher cost on risky actions and so deters them: criminal sanctions are the obvious example.

Shocks from endogenous risks can significantly impact investor wealth. For example: fatalities in major incidents such as airline crashes and hotel fires have been valued by stock markets at around $US50 million per death (Viscusi 1993); and crises typically trigger an immediate drop of up to 10% in share prices (Hooker and Salin 1999).

A pronounced driver of moral hazard amongst investors and financial institutions is the finance sector's core commodity, namely money, which provides investors with strong inducement to take risk. Reinforcing investor risk is the finance industry's practice of paying volume based commissions to investors' agents such as financial advisers, and this can encourage some to exploit less informed clients. Another contributor to moral hazard in investment is innovation by financial institutions that regularly introduces new products with option-like potential for huge, albeit uncertain, gains. Recent examples include telecommunications, media and technology (TMT) stocks in the 1990s and collateralised debt obligations (CDOs) in the 2000s: each held the promise of such spectacular possible return that it led to suspension of doubt by investors and sufficient investment to induce bubbles in asset prices whose implosion brought global recession.

Across the finance industry, regulations promote moral hazard because of the virtual absence of sanctions against corporate executives for poorly judged decisions. The concept of limited liability caps shareholder exposure, and – by materially reducing their risks – has promoted equity investment. There is similar protection for management because legislation does not impose criminal and financial penalties on executives in the event of their firm's financial distress. In fact, it is unusual for a firm's management to be convicted even for the most egregious actions: thus a study of US bankruptcies between 1980 and 2006 found that not a single outside director was prosecuted for breach of their duties (Black et al. 2006). That is, even though more than 270 companies with assets in excess of $1 billion went bankrupt during the period (plus far more smaller firms) and outside directors were expected to protect shareholders' interests, not one *legally* failed to do so! This confirms that there are rarely consequences for individuals who abuse their insider advantages.

4.3.2 Endogenous (Non-human) Influences on Uncertainty in Firm Value

Taking a resource based view of the firm (Hart 1995), its structure establishes optimum pathways for development and the resulting call on resources. These structural firm features – such as size, leverage, diversification – are relatively stable and follow from gradual evolution through trade-offs in the firm's products, processes, capital structure and counterparties. This constitutes a firm's culture, part of which determines its medium term risk.

The most important risk-related structural feature of a firm is size. Larger firms tend to have a diversified portfolio of assets that – through the co-insurance effect (Hyland and Diltz 2002) – makes them more resilient to any given loss. This is enhanced by their generally higher level of slack or surplus resources such as greater capacity to raise capital to replace any loss (which is self-insurance); and by economies of scale that make it easier to execute activities with high transaction costs such as raising debt, and to establish specialist functions such as risk management.

Recent performance can also impact firms' risk propensity because – in line with Prospect Theory – firms with results below a reference level tend to take more risk. Thus an analysis of American firms concluded: "poor performance triggers risk taking … Most firms, when faced with poor performance, would undertake decisions that would only further their decline" (Singh 1986: 582).

Finally, risk is driven by latent parameters, which is consistent with a risk-based attractor and leads to a long memory for high or low risk that persists until the firm is restructured (La Porte 1996). The existence of an attractor explains anecdotal evidence that firms can suffer a series of seemingly independent losses, and whole industries can be swept by crises, with banking contagions providing a good example.

4.3.3 Human Influences on Uncertainty in Firm Value

Intuitively the strongest contributor to uncertainty in firm value is the actions of executives who control its cash flows: thus firm chief executives are the "most important factor in stock prices" (Jackofsky et al. 1988: 48). Executives alter cash flows through operational decisions, and through strategies such as acquisition, investment, and re-organisation. The importance of these decisions is clear from studies of large corporate collapses which invariably find that few are due to acts-of-god or crippling competition, but occur because of inadequate strategies and weak processes that were the responsibility of management and should have been brought under control by diligent directors (e.g. International Federation of Accountants 2003). Study after study shows that bankruptcy can be traced to a few key generic causes: dysfunctional culture and unmanaged organisational knowledge; poor internal processes, especially the inability to produce accurate financial accounts; failure to understand the implications of financial activities such as hedging and use of derivatives; poorly executed strategies, particularly acquisitions; unskilled directors and disengaged chief executives; and excessive debt (Marshall et al. 1996).

Experience has taught investors to be cautious about the extent of uncertainty inherent in executives' actions because research shows they have a poor track record: as many as half of all managers' decisions are wrong (Nutt 1999), which rises to three quarters for one-off strategic initiatives (Coleman 2009), and close to 100% for high profile corporate decisions (Henry 2002). M&As provide a simple example of the uncertainty associated with managers' decisions, because as few as two thirds of announced mergers are actually completed (e.g. Ang and Cheng 2006), and most of these do not achieve their planned benefits (e.g. Moeller et al. 2005). Compounding the poor record of executives' strategic decisions is that investors cannot monitor them, but only infer their quality from observation of noisy, aggregated outcomes including investor briefings.

Thus the market generally places little value on the strategic capability of executives, and its typical response to even the highest profile corporate decisions is typically a short-lived, trivial price move. As an example, announcement of an acquisition between listed bidding and target companies is followed by a slight fall in their combined market value (Roll 1986), which indicates negative expected synergies. This common result suggests that investors lack access to relevant data because of information asymmetry and bounded rationality, and so lean towards population-based measures of uncertainty such as industry mean (Lovallo and Kahneman 2003). At the very least, this outsider view provides an anchor around which to adjust estimates in light of managers' skill.

An indicator that can be used to adjust population-based estimates of a firm's human-related uncertainty is composition of its board and senior management. Make up of the board influences risk propensity because reaching consensus is promoted by relevant expertise and common thinking and less diversity of directors' personal traits (Gummer 1998). Board size is important, too, with the optimum number typically seen as around eight (Jensen 1993). Another impact on risk propensity is the proportion of outside directors because they bring diversity and can be expected to act in the interests of all shareholders (not just managers).

Below the Board level, senior executives make the important day-to-day decisions, and the aggregate of their risk propensity determines firm risk taking. Studies of executive psychology show that less than half of all managers are risk-prone (see, for example: Levy and Levy 2002; MacCrimmon and Wehrung 1984; Williams and Narendran 1999), which matches the typical observation that decision makers' risk propensity is too low (e.g. Wu et al. 2003). Other indicators of managers' risk propensity are that risk-prone managers tend to be male, younger, and better educated; and they adopt multiple risky behaviours such as smoking and adventure sports (Grable 2000). These observable traits can be useful guides to managers' likely impact on firm behaviour and performance (Bertrand and Schoar 2003).

There are also links between firm risk propensity and managerial compensation. First, the nature of executive compensation responds to exogenous risks faced by a firm because an incentive component is more likely when agency problems are greatest because it is when shareholders are more exposed to managers' independent judgement and skill (Prendergast 2002). Compensation drives risk because managers who are risk averse – that is, the majority – require higher compensation to offset their lower risk-adjusted income; otherwise they will protect their human capital by reducing variation in firm value through low risk strategies and extending risk management. Compensation of risk-averse managers through stock and options links with their human capital to compound the proportion of their wealth that is concentrated in the firm. It can exacerbate shifts in risk propensity with options encouraging risk and stock promoting risk aversion.

Thus employee compensation interacts with managers' risk propensity to influence their decisions and firm risk propensity (Coles et al. 2006). As Tufano (1996: 1129) dryly observes: "managers' private preferences seem to affect corporate risk management choices".

4.3.4 Governance, Ethics and Sustainability

Corporate governance has many definitions, most of them built around the idea of balancing competing stakeholder interests. Thus it can be about "who controls corporations and why" (Kaen 2003), or – as proposed by Jim Wolfensohn, President of World Bank (*Financial Times*, 21 June 1999) – is directed at "promoting corporate fairness, transparency and accountability." My favourite description is that "governance deals with the ways in which suppliers of finance to corporations assure themselves of getting a return on their investment" (Shleifer and Vishny 1997: 737).

4 Uncertainty in Investor Wealth 69

The last definition opens up a range of corporate responsibilities given that financial performance depends on reliable suppliers, productive employees and satisfied customers; and all firms rely on a social license to operate successfully. Thus return rises when firms limit costs imposed on others through physical damage such as emissions, moral hazard such as predatory lending, or through defaulting on obligations to counterparties (Coase 1960).[7]

Governance can also be impacted by the firm's environment because rapid change or tough competition is a partial substitute for governance (Börsch-Supan and Köke 2002). An example in finance of how exogenous factors enhance governance arises because the rights of creditors are better defined and protected than those of shareholders (Shleifer and Vishny 1997). Thus the processes around securing and retaining debt (such as communicating to lenders and obtaining a rating) promote reduction in information asymmetry between the firm and stakeholders.

The mechanism whereby governance and related concepts such as good ethics and environmental and social responsibility lift shareholder return is identified in a pioneering scrutiny of investor protection which reviewed firms' constitutions or similar documents, identified provisions or rules that were inimical to shareholder interests, and summed their number into a governance index (G Index) (Gompers et al. 2003). The authors then compiled portfolios of firms according to G Index, and identified an abnormal return of 8.5% per year for firms in the decile with strongest shareholder rights (which have a low G Index, or count of anti-shareholder provisions) versus those in the decile with weakest rights (termed dictatorship firms due to their dominance by managers).

The most obvious – and thus most appealing – explanation for this result is that governance causes performance. This is expected given that the G Index quantifies the strength of management rights relative to those of shareholders through provisions that complicate or prevent takeovers, limit shareholders' voting power, and protect management. Anti-stakeholder provisions empower entrenched management to act against shareholder interests through fewer strategic and operational initiatives which reduces its value as a real option, and by limiting information flow which lifts uncertainty around management of the firm (Ferreira and Laux 2007). As a result, the G Index contributes an important set of indicators of certainty in firm cash flows.

---

[7] Adam Smith (1776: 112) put this succinctly in *The Wealth of Nations* by reference to employment: "The wages of labour vary with the ease or hardship, the cleanliness or dirtiness, the honourableness or dishonourableness of the employment".

70   Applied Investment Theory

Other indicators of firms that avoid wealth destruction by favourable treatment of stakeholders over the longer term come from measures of ethics and environmental, social and governance standards (ESG). Not surprisingly, the financial impact of ethical and sustainable strategies has garnered much empirical interest in the fields of finance (e.g. Ferreira and Laux 2007) and strategy (e.g. Luo et al. 2015). Within both literatures, beyond-compliance strategies are typically seen as acting like incentives to alter management behaviour, which leads investors to observe or anticipate a change in performance and adjust security prices accordingly.

The intuition that good ethics and ESG lift returns has wide (if sometimes only lukewarm) support in the literature, with a typical conclusion from meta-studies that there is "a positive, but also highly variable, relationship between corporate citizenship and corporate financial performance" (Orlitzky 2008: 127).[8] This is sustainable investment, which supports mutual funds that seek "to achieve long-term competitive financial returns together with positive societal impact", and this sector comprises 15% of US assets under management (US SIF 2015).

4.3.5 Proxies for Uncertainty in Firm Performance

Loss averse investors will seek firms with characteristics that proxy for reliability or certainty in performance, and thus avoid the unobservable possibility of loss in value (Berk et al. 1999). This has motivated research across finance, management and other disciplines to identify firm traits that indicate uncertainty. A number of authors have developed catalogues of empirical findings, which – in addition to those already cited – include Bartram (2000), Coles et al. (2006), and Mayers and Smith (1990).

A few of the more relevant proxies or indicators of firm uncertainty are summarised in the next table (Table 4.2).

As an aside, it is typically assumed that measures of uncertainty are titrating different firm traits. In practice, though, most are correlated as if each is measuring some aspect of a common set of latent risk parameters. Thus an evaluation of 13 measures of downside risk found that half the correlations between them were highly significant (Miller and Reuer 1996); and another study grouped different measures of firm risk into income stream risk, stock return risk and strategic risk, and found statistically significant correlations between the principal component variables (Miller and Bromiley 1990).

---

[8] A survey of the literature by Van Beurden and Gössling (2008) suggest that more recent analyses provide stronger support for a positive return-CSR relationship.

Table 4.2 Indicators of future firm uncertainty

Firm variable	Relationship with future uncertainty
Size (assets, market capitalisation)	–
Leverage	+
Recent financial performance (ROE, equity return)	–
Narrow shareholder base	–
Credit rating	+/–
Compensation of managers with options	+
Compensation of managers with stock	–

Quite different measures of firm operational risk are typically linked, so – for example – airlines with higher bond ratings and hence lower expected financial risk have better operational safety records (Noronha and Singal 2004).

4.4 Conclusion: The Return-Uncertainty Link for Equities

Investor uncertainty relates to possibility of wealth loss at the time equities are sold, which has complex determinants including environmental influences, structural factors, management actions and shocks.

Uncertainty is a consequence of both strategic decisions and firm performance in line with the truism in finance and management that "large gains tend to require large risks be taken" (Sanders and Hambrick 2007: 1055). This makes uncertainty in achieving any value change proportional to its magnitude, although potential losses can be moderated through risk management. Thus the return-uncertainty link for equities looks something like:

$$\text{Equity uncertainty} = \Phi\left(\frac{\text{Expected return}}{\text{Risk management}}\right).Z,$$

where Z is a vector of equity-specific variables.

That is: the return from any prospect establishes the challenges in achieving it and hence determines uncertainty, which can be moderated by managing the risk (using some combination of market instruments, insurance, or techniques such as enterprise risk management), and is affected by variables specific to the firm that affect implementation of value-generating strategies (such as size and leverage, which proxy for capability).

72 **Applied Investment Theory**

The monetised value of equity uncertainty becomes a function of firm-specific features, risk management, and the difficulty of achieving expected improvements in return. This embraces concepts such as exposure, consequence, range of outcomes and potential for catastrophe (Sanders and Hambrick 2007). It also depicts equity uncertainty as contingent on specific attributes of the firm and its risk management strategy: each can be moderated at the discretion of the firm and alter the range of possible outcomes. These give equity uncertainty the characteristics of a real put option, which complements the familiar depiction of an equity as a real call option because of the holder's discretion to vary the length of holding and other factors (e.g. Myers 1977).

Let me briefly summarise key findings of this chapter.

First, investors' greatest concern is over loss of wealth at the time it is required. This wraps in loss aversion and downside risk. It also opens up uncertainty: what can investors know about risks associated with their investment in the market, operations and agents?

Second is the relationship between return and uncertainty, or risk. Return and possibility of loss are jointly determined by the nature of the decision and successful investments are achieved with minimal loss. Thus looking forward, an objective with high return implies stretch goals, difficult execution of the investment, and high possibility of loss, especially with projects that are not well understood. Looking backwards, return is positively related to factors that proxy for sound execution such as safety, reliability and productivity. Thus ex ante, expected return causes higher possibility of loss and uncertainty in outcome of the investment; while ex post, return reflects low loss of wealth through successful implementation.

The fact that the relationship between return and the possibility of loss in wealth or uncertainty is positive ex ante and negative ex post highlights the critical role of execution of any investment strategy, including management of its risks. This incorporation of real optionality is why simple measures of risk or uncertainty such as historical share price volatility prove of little relevance.

Part II

Structure, Conduct and Performance of Fund Manager Investment

5

Building Investment Theory Using the Structure-Conduct-Performance (SCP) Paradigm

> **The Key Takeaways of This Chapter Are**
>
> - Good theory sets out how and why phenomena occur, explains real-world behaviour, and is parsimonious. Its hypotheses are verifiable in natural experiments
> - While many finance theories are intuitive and mathematical, others are descriptive and based on observation
> - A comprehensive investment theory will incorporate natural and hominological components
> - The lack of investor foresight points to a qualitative, descriptive theory, albeit with some mathematically specified elements
> - The structure-conduct-performance paradigm is suitable for describing mutual fund investment

Markets are dynamic, and even cursory study reveals many examples of time varying exogenous pressures, internally generated vitality, and natural selection that continuously optimises their structures (Lo 2004). The challenge for this book is to reconcile the many structural and transient features of markets and investors with central tenets of the current investment paradigm, and establish empirically validated linkages. The objective, of course, is to build a parsimonious theory of applied investment by mutual fund managers that has logical theoretical underpinnings and is consistent with field evidence. Let us develop a pathway to good theory.

© The Author(s) 2016
L. Coleman, *Applied Investment Theory*,
DOI 10.1007/978-3-319-43976-1_5

5.1 What Is a 'Good' Investment Theory?

Every discipline is built around its paradigm, or state of knowledge, which is a linked mixture of theory and practice. Theory is knowledge gained from speculation or contemplation, and has the meaning of "a statement of concepts and their interrelationships that shows how and/or why a phenomenon occurs" (Corley and Gioia 2011). It is encapsulated in a series of law-like statements that are related in a systematic way and universally applicable. Moreover, good theory will be robust to real-world application, and support practice with a set of principles or techniques that apply theory. Specific to the finance context: "a theory should be parsimonious, explain a range of anomalous patterns in different contexts, and generate new empirical implications" (Daniel et al. 1998).

Once theory and its principles and statements have been developed, they should – in the classical sense advanced by Popper (1959) – be falsifiable, with well-defined hypotheses that can be tested in natural experiments. Results should explain a significant proportion of the real-world empirical evidence or observed phenomena by identifying contributing influences. Evidence based models of this type rebut the observation that something is fine in theory but not in practice, and have particular advantages. The first is to incorporate the lessons of history, and – rather than glossing over inconvenient puzzles, biases and irrationalities – engage them as phenomena requiring explanation. A second is to eschew a normative framework and avoid being judgemental or politically biased.

In the last half century, financial economics has built an eclectic mix of theories. Certainly some of the best known are mathematically specified (including CAPM and arbitrage theory, and derivatives pricing models such as Black-Scholes); and they are tested using observed market data. But some theories with a numerical specification – such as capital structure and attitudes towards risk – are tested using qualitative data such as surveys and other field observations. Finally there are descriptive theories such as Jensen's agency theory and Lintner's dividend model which are tested using a combination of market and corporate data, as well as surveys and interviews.

Given the diversity of existing finance theories and tests, what form should we seek for a revised theory of investment and the tests of its hypotheses?

Although it would be nice to follow the hard sciences and base investment theory on quantitative expressions in the style of $E=mc^2$, this is only practical with closed systems that can be clearly defined and measured. In the case of investment, there are myriad influences from the economy, society, politics and environment that have state-dependent, non-linear impacts; and this unstable mix of drivers is overlain by unpredictable feedback as investors respond to market moves. Not only is it hard to identify and measure the many factors that determine equity valuations, their influence varies with state of the world. Thus markets never remain in equilibrium, and it seems impractical to develop a quantitative investment model.

For an investment theory to generate practical techniques that have explanatory power, it probably needs to be descriptive in order to capture central properties of the investment system that are generalizable over time and geography. It will likely be both physical given its natural application, and hominological in the sense that it incorporates elements unique to humans. Respective examples are that security returns are approximately normally distributed, and fund managers follow naturalistic decision processes.

Improved theory will also match a consistent thread running through this book which is that it should be evidence based and able to explain observed investor behaviour. This seems logical and is consistent with other sciences. Implications are that the theory will accept markets and investors for what they are and do, and refuse to accept normative simplifications and assumptions that cannot be empirically validated. This points to pursuit of positive science, which is a "body of systematised knowledge concerning what is" (Keynes 1891). Its logical corollaries are that assumptions match reality, and that the theory is applicable in the real world so its explanations of observed phenomena can be tested using empirical evidence. This meets the criterion of Aquinas that theory aligns beliefs and reality, and it should also generate instrumental wealth or utility by improving fund performance.

A promising approach for developing theory comes from medicine, which is an archetypal practitioner-driven discipline akin to investment. In a process termed knowledge translation, it captures evidence from field research and impounds real-world data in theory (Straus et al. 2009). This amplifies the field environment surrounding empirical research and disseminates practical knowledge back into research. Thus theory does not stagnate, and field research directs theory towards adding value for practitioners by improving decisions.

Following this lead, a re-engineered investment theory should explain why the largest investor group, namely mutual fund managers, act as they do, and what determines their performance. It should describe and explain real-world practice, which constitutes the first step in the grounded theory-making paradigm of observe-measure-hypothesize-test-theorise.[1] The most obvious

---

[1] This approach of constructing theoretically based hypotheses using field evidence in an inductive, or bottoms up, process follows multiple techniques, especially analytic induction of Lincoln and Guba (1985), grounded theory of Glaser and Strauss (1967), and the extended case method of Burawoy (1998).

78   **Applied Investment Theory**

evidence to be explained includes 'facts' about investment, actual behaviour of investors as identified in surveys, puzzles in investment such as poor performance of experts and the emergence and collapse of bubbles, and biases and anomalies that are unique to investment decisions.

5.2   Does Investment Theory Have to Be Quantitative?

For the last few decades, dominant theories in financial economics have been quantitative and based on hard data such as market prices and company financials. This is easily understood given the availability of extensive data and powerful econometric tools.

The quantitative approach, though, has had a number of unfortunate consequences. One is that researchers have come to expect that little value will come from softer data such as interviews and surveys. Thus they dismiss it as not necessarily reflecting actual behaviour because answers cost nothing and respondents can say anything.

A second is that robust analysis using hard data works well with variables that are directly measureable ex ante: the effect of firm size on payout ratio, for instance; or that of fund manager compensation on mutual fund performance. In these cases, quantitative analysis readily explains the nature of the relationship because ex post results can be regressed on ex ante drivers. In equity investment, however, ex ante decision stimuli cannot be observed much less measured. In addition, investment decisions are largely based on unobservable ex ante expectations about the future for which there are no reliable proxies. Moreover, investment is a qualitative process that requires choices about what data to look at, the time period covered, analytical protocols (e.g. will outliers be removed?), and evaluation of results (in absolute terms or against some kind of benchmark). This requires reliance on unverifiable hypotheses. Further, contributors to outcomes of investment decisions are interlinked and impose a joint test problem so that one unproven fact must be assumed in order to substantiate a second unproven fact. Testing fund performance, for instance, requires a model of valuation but the decision stimuli and process followed are unknown. Remote quantitative analysis and intuitive evaluation risk omitting or misunderstanding the most important drivers of outcomes, and thus lead to erroneous conclusions.

Although a qualitative descriptive model of investment has possible weaknesses (e.g. Aggarwal 1993), it has the important advantage of explaining investor behaviour, which enables development of new concepts that can help develop better theory. This book, then, will prefer a descriptive theory of investment over existing, largely normative, quantitative models because it can codify observed field practices and explain them using recognized theoretical precepts. That is, a descriptive model allows for investors to develop identifiable practices that satisfy their objectives under guidance from the invisible hand of Adam Smith (1759).

5.3 Structure-Conduct-Performance (SCP) Paradigm

A descriptive model must present material about fund manager investment in a way that provides a theoretical basis for their conduct and explains fund performance. This proved a challenge, but – after considerable research and experimentation – a satisfactory interpretative framework proved to be the structure-conduct-performance (SCP) paradigm that is commonly used across economics to explain industry behaviour.

SCP was developed by Bain (1959) and posits that the performance of an industry is determined by the conduct of firms within it, which in turn depends on the industry's structure. Structure describes relatively stable features such as concentration of supply and demand, product differentiation and barriers to market entry. Conduct relates to the way that buyers and sellers behave, which shapes firms' strategy, investment and marketing. Performance is relative between firms in the industry and is measured by profitability, market share, product quality and efficiency. SCP typically focusses on the determinants and effects of competition between actors in the industry (firms, suppliers and customers). A well-known application is the Porter (1980) model of industry profitability, and SCP has also been used as a framework to interpret performance of the banking sector (e.g. Hannan 1991).

SCP offers a useful basis on which to develop a theory of investment. Structure of the managed funds industry arises in legislation and the distribution of security returns. It is also seen in fixed features of financial institutions that consistently influence choices, including the industry's make-up (major players, profit levers, strategy) and organisation. There are also time varying exogenous influences such as state of the world, relationships between financial variables, and investor sentiment. Conduct – which responds to these influences and can be varied from one decision to the next – is reflected in investment decisions and allocation of fund managers' time, and leads to fund performance.

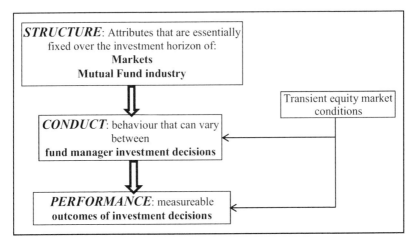

Fig. 5.1 Model of fund manager investment

Although I am not aware of any explicit application of SCP to financial markets, it has much in common with the 'building blocks' approach to investment proposed by Jensen and Smith (1984) that sets out the concepts, intuitions and relationships of decision making, and then uses them to show how investment theories form. In addition, finance research often uses structure and conduct in examining asset price performance. Structure is fundamental to the standard asset-pricing paradigm through fixed assumptions such as efficiency in markets, the absence of arbitrage, and stable return-generating operational functions (Campbell 2000). Conduct is central to behavioural finance when it examines biases in decisions of investors. Thus SCP is consistent with the intuition of research and practice that structural features of the managed funds industry influence the transient preferences of fund managers which interact with market action and characteristics of their institutions to shape investment decisions and fund performance.[2]

The model to be followed is set out above (Fig. 5.1).

---

[2] This obvious relevance of SCP to investment should address the caution that exporting models to another discipline may be an inappropriate generalisation (McWilliams and Smart 1993). Where SCP sees firm performance as set by industry factors, its main alternative of operational efficiency describes industry profitability in terms of the cost and quality of competing products, and sees profitability as stemming from firm-specific factors such as management skills, innovation, cost control, and scale.

5.4 Conclusion

This book's objective is to provide a parsimonious description of the process followed by mutual fund managers in making equity investments. The principal input data comprise empirically established facts, observations of field practice, and anomalies and puzzles in investment.

Although research in financial economics developed out of the strength of its data which promoted robust quantitative analyses whose results were intuitively interpreted (Ross 1987), this seems the wrong way to understand the relatively qualitative decision making process of investment. Moreover, there is nothing inherently superior about quantitative data. Its scope is limited to a slice of important valuation information. In fact, quite a number of important theories in financial economics are descriptive, and were developed from field studies of real-world behaviour. Myer's pecking order theory is based on observation of firms' capital structure, Lintner's dividend model arose out of his discussions with CFOs, and many elements of agency theory and risk-taking are descriptive.

Thus the re-engineered theory of investment will incorporate descriptive elements alongside mathematical specifications (see Rudner 1966; Wallace 1983). Within the theoretical framework, decision makers will be unequivocal utility maximisers using their own paradigm to analyse as much value-adding information as practical. Decisions will have identifiable drivers, which may arise naturally, be economically rational, meet investors' non-financial objectives such as maximization of human capital, or be imposed by third parties including employers, clients and regulators. Explanation for investors' decision process will be sited within traditional theories of financial economics and relevant disciplines, although each must be consistent with empirical evidence and intuition, and thus provide a causal model. The intent is to meet the test of Fama (1998) that any alternative to neoclassical finance theory must specify what causes investor behaviour.

The following three chapters summarise what is known as fact about the structure of equity markets and the mutual fund industry, the conduct of mutual fund managers, and performance of mutual funds. This progresses the observe-hypothesise-test-theorise process of scientific discovery, and sets out established facts as opposed to intuition, opinion or speculation so they can be explained and fitted into a structure-conduct-performance depiction of fund manager investment.

6

Structure of Equity Prices

> **The Key Takeaways of This Chapter Are**
>
> - Equity prices have roughly lognormal price distribution, with sufficient regularity for investors to capture abnormal returns
> - Equities' demand curve has a time-varying slope that can turn positive like a Veblen good so that prices move pro-cyclically (i.e. trend)
> - Links identified between equity return and lagged values of systematic and firm-specific factors are ex post explanations. They are unstable and noisy, and have little ex ante ability to predict returns over investors' time horizon
> - Investors do not have predictive skill, and ex post will not be judged as unconditionally making optimum decision choices.
> - Empirical evidence is that intuitively price-sensitive public information explains relatively little of the return to equities, whose prices usually move in the absence of new information.
> - Humans control virtually all market information and have discretion in timing some of the most important data
> - Price-insensitive investment managers who dominate ownership of equities are monopsonistic buyers, which leads to a classic sawtooth price pattern

© The Author(s) 2016
L. Coleman, *Applied Investment Theory*,
DOI 10.1007/978-3-319-43976-1_6

83

84   Applied Investment Theory

Financial markets arise to serve emergent liquidity and are integral to investment. Their very presence brings together willing buyers and sellers, which reduces search and transaction costs. Markets are also an allocative mechanism that facilitates trading use of present capital against future income. Finally, market interactions between buyers and sellers reveal prices of securities, which are the most frequent source of incremental information.

This chapter sets out empirically verified facts about equity markets and identifies contributing factors as inputs to a theoretical model.

6.1   Compilations of Facts in Finance

A fascinating compilation of stylised finance facts is provided by Richard Thaler and co-authors in a series of articles published in *The Journal of Economic Perspectives* during 1987–2006. Thaler (1987: 197) motivated the series using a quote from Thomas Kuhn: "Discovery commences with the awareness of anomaly, that is with the recognition that nature has somehow violated the paradigm-induced expectations that govern normal science." He later gave a pithy description of what constitutes normal science in his speciality (Thaler 1988: 121):

> Economics can be distinguished from other social sciences by the belief that most (all?) behavior can be explained by assuming that agents have stable, well-defined preferences and make rational choices consistent with those preferences in markets that (eventually) clear [bracketed asides in the original].

The intent was to examine observations that are inconsistent with standard theory or require implausible assumptions to explain, and so challenge the completeness of neoclassical financial economics. Thaler's equity price anomalies include: calendar-based patterns in supply and demand, price regularities such as mean reversion and over and under-reaction, violations of the law of one price, and mis-valuations such as the equity risk premium, closed end mutual fund discount, and the winner's curse. A similar catalogue by Jacobs (2015) lists 100 price anomalies that fall into 20 groups, and additions to Thaler's list include technical analysis, beta inconsistencies, earnings surprises, and the price role of public data such as accruals, industry effects and dividends.

Complementing the catalogues of anomalies, around the turn of the last millennium, a number of leading financial economists published articles setting out facts that conform to the current asset pricing paradigm. One by Professor Cochrane (1999) entitled 'New facts in finance' included:

6 Structure of Equity Prices   85

(i)   Asset returns are explained by multiple risk factors other than the market as a whole (which is the CAPM assumption)

(ii) Stock returns are unpredictable over horizons of less than a year, but have growing predictability over longer periods

(iii) Some mutual funds that follow mechanical styles can outperform market indexes.

A similar catalogue by Professor Christoffersen (2003) entitled 'Stylized facts of asset returns' included the following:

(i) Over long periods, daily returns exhibit little correlation. Thus the return on any average day has no ability to predict the following day's return.

My own calculation using daily data during 1950–2014 for the S&P 500 shows a significant positive correlation ($p<0.001$) between today's return and yesterday's return, but the co-efficient is small at 0.03 and the explanatory power is trivial at under 0.1%.

(ii) Also over long periods, a plot of the distribution of daily returns is roughly normal (or Gaussian), but has fatter tails than expected.

To amplify this, my own calculation shows that almost 2% of daily returns on the US S&P 500 from 1950 until just before the 2007 GFC lay more than two standard deviations above or below the mean, which is about twice the number expected if returns were normally distributed.

(iii) Looking at individual days of extreme returns, large drops are more common than similar sized rises. This skews the distribution to the left.

For the S&P 500 during 1950–2014, there are three times as many falls of greater than six standard deviations than equivalent rises, but roughly the same number of rises and falls for smaller moves.

(iv) The correlation between returns of different asset classes is time varying. In particular, correlations increase in volatile down markets; this can be quite marked, so that asset prices tend to move together in market crashes.

(v) Unlike returns, volatility (which is often measured by squared returns) is serially correlated.

86   Applied Investment Theory

My own calculation using daily data during 1950–2014 for the S&P 500 shows a significant positive correlation ($p<0.001$) between today's volatility and yesterday's volatility, with a co-efficient of 0.17 and the explanatory power of 2.8%.

(vi) From a statistical perspective, the standard deviation of returns dominates the mean.

Again, my own calculation shows that – for the S&P 500 during 1950–2014 – the mean daily return is 0.03%, while the standard deviation is 0.97%: it is therefore not possible to reject the possibility that mean daily return is zero (or even modestly negative).

(vii) For equities, variance and return are negatively correlated. When prices drop, variance generally increases by a larger amount than in the case of an equivalent price rise.

The balance of this chapter sets out further statistically certain facts, or what we know with confidence, about the structure and performance of equity markets.

6.2   Distribution of Equity Prices

Even though finance theory emphasises returns when making decisions to buy or sell a security, fund managers think of shares' value in terms of fundamental price (Hellman 2000), which makes equites' price distribution central to any theory of investment.

It has long been accepted that security prices are approximately lognormally distributed (e.g. Markowitz 1952), which is typical of variables that are driven by numerous multiplicative parameters (Leipnik 1991). Stock prices appear stationary in real terms over at least the medium term (Lim and Brooks 2011), and mean revert within a 5–7 year cycle (e.g. De Bondt and Thaler 1989) that can be punctuated by structural breaks.

Stationary equity prices are explained by the standard assumption that they represent claims on bundles of underlying assets such as raw materials, property and knowledge whose value is roughly constant in real terms. Stationary equity prices are consistent, too, with mean reversion in firms' financial performance (Fairfield and Yohn 2001).

6.2.1 Unexpectedly High Turnover and Volatility

A puzzling feature of equity markets is their unexpectedly high turnover. For instance, annual turnover of stocks exceeds the value of shares on issue, with an average holding period of about ten months for global equities.[1] This is far more than can be explained by incremental investment, which is only a trivial proportion of turnover.[2] Thus large investors who dominate most markets must engage in a lot of short term, tactical trading (which contradicts their claim to have a multi-year investment horizon![3]).

Apart from trading volume, equity price volatility is high. Consider my analysis of daily price moves during 1982–2014 for Apple, ExxonMobil and Wells Fargo, which are the three largest firms in the S&P 500 that come from different industries. Each year on average they respectively moved by 4% or more on 52, 7 and 23 days; and by more than 10% on 3, 0.4, and 1 days. Price volatility of this scale is far higher than can be explained by fundamentals given the low variability in price-sensitive factors such as dividends and discount rates and the relatively low frequency of innovations in price-sensitive information (see: Shiller 1981).

More broadly, the US S&P 500 Index suffers several daily falls each year of greater than 4%, and a daily fall above 10% each decade, often without any apparent justification. As an example, one of the worst falls was over 20% on Black Monday 19 October 1987. Four inquiries were set up in the US to study the crash, and staffed by people with intimate knowledge of the industry who analysed recent, well-documented events (not the future, or distant past). Despite this they could not link any factor to investors' decisions: the cause of the 1987 Crash remains in dispute (Headrick 1992). More generally, the economics literature cannot explain why stock prices shift abruptly (see: Cooper et al. 2008 and Goldstein and Razin 2015).

Of equal portent are flash crashes, or intraday declines in major market indexes of more than about 5% within not many more minutes. These occur even in deep and highly liquid markets such as a fall of 6% in the S&P 500 within 15 minutes on 6 May 2010; and another in the 10-year US Treasury bond market where yields fell on 15 October 2014 by 33 bp from 2.2%

---

[1] The World Federation of Exchanges *Market Highlights* (www.world-exchanges.org) reports that trading during 2014 on the world's equity exchanges totalled $US81 trillion, while their capitalisation averaged $67 trillion.

[2] Using US data, net acquisition of equities and non money market mutual funds averaged $400 billion per year during 2009–2014 (Board of Governors of Federal Reserve System, 2015: table F10), which is around 3% of equity markets' turnover.

[3] In a summary of US mutual fund traits, Chen, Desai and Krishnamurthy (2013) report their average annual turnover is 94% of assets.

88   Applied Investment Theory

(a 15% fall) and then recovered within 20 minutes. Neither crash could be tracked to innovative price-sensitive information,[4] and official SEC reports shed no light on their causes (see, for example: SEC 2010).

Despite the inability to explain these very large, short-lived moves, market manipulation is possible. It can be malicious as suggested by one review of the 2010 flash crash which concluded that it was not an accident given the range of tricks available through computers to manipulate the market, and some earlier smaller slumps that looked like dry runs (Rose 2011). Another credible suggestion of large scale manipulation is contained in a US Department of Defense document entitled *Economic Warfare: Risks and responses*[5] which argues that a three-phase economic attack on western economies began in 2007 through a tripling of oil prices with proceeds used to manipulate the stock market and bring on The Great Recession in the United States and Europe during 2007–9.

A second explanation for puzzling equity market volatility is speculation. Generally speaking, finance sees speculative activity as benign. Consensus of the literature seems to be that futures and physical/spot prices respond to the same fundamental factors and so move together, perhaps with futures prices leading (Garbade and Silber 1983). There is, however, strong evidence that activity in futures markets is not independent of the physical market, and there are crossovers in volumes that affect demand and hence security prices. Supporting evidence includes rapid price rises that seem inconsistent with fundamental valuations (e.g. Cheung and Wong 2000). The possibility of speculative forces is re-inforced because most flash crashes begin in derivatives markets.

6.2.2 Patterns in Markets

Equity returns are not randomly distributed, but display recurring behaviours, of which the most important are seasonalities, clumping and trends.

6.2.2.1 Seasonal Patterns in Markets

Many empirically validated calendar-based patterns in equity markets are built around seasonality in liquidity and risk (Jacobs 2015). Some are related to scheduled events such as regular savings contributions, releases of economic

---

[4] Of course, rapid price moves can sometimes have an obvious cause such as a false report attributed to Associated Press on 23 April 2013 that President Obama had been injured in an explosion in the White House, which saw US financial markets drop by 2% for a minute or two.

[5] www.archive.org/details/EconomicWarfare-RisksAndResponsesByKevinD.Freeman.

data and corporate accounts, and expiry of derivatives contracts. Thus tax year ends are popular times to rebalance portfolios and sell winners or losers to optimise capital gains taxes. Patterns can follow cycles built around seasons and holidays, such as the well-documented relationship between stock prices and phases of the moon (Yuan et al. 2006).[6] While summer vacations are often quiet on the markets, early autumn is busy after investors come back to work with new resolve. Other regular patterns are based on opportunism such as quarter-end window dressing by institutional investors, and intraday patterns related to markets' opening and close. There is also the practice of timing press releases according to the news cycle and market trading hours, with good news released in time for the morning network shows and bad news kept for after the close, often on Friday (Damodaran 1989).

These patterns have colourful names such as the January, weekend, or turn of the month effect. Even though a lot of pricing anomalies prove transitory or collapse under scrutiny, some have been established as economically significant across time and geography (e.g. Das and Rao 2011). The survivors typically have robust explanations relating to either liquidity (investment flows and security issuance) or extra return from holding assets during extended market closures (such as weekends and holidays).

Another set of patterns in markets have been attributed to what psychologists term seasonal affective disorder, which is characterised by seasonal mood fluctuation that expects depression in winter (Kramer and Weber 2012). This has been shown to be consistent with patterns in returns in both northern and southern hemisphere stock markets, and in asset allocation by mutual fund investors who reduce exposure to equities in winter (Kamstra, Kramer, Levi and Wermers, forthcoming).

More unusually, some analyses identify statistically significant influences on investors that seem to be quite unrelated to markets, such as the onset of daylight savings (Kamstra et al. 2000). I leave it to readers to decide if these reflect reality, data mining, or co-incidence.

6.2.2.2 Cyclical Features of Equity Prices

An often topical feature of equity markets is their recognisable cyclical features, with long periods of steady rises punctuated by short, sharp falls. For example, NYSE data for 1800–2000 show that bull markets are longer than bear markets at 21 and 15 months, respectively; and bull markets rise faster

---

[6] For an introduction to this extensive literature see Professor Kramer's website www.lisakramer.com.

90   Applied Investment Theory

than bear markets fall with respective median monthly absolute returns of 1.9 and 1.1%. (Gonzalez et al. 2005: Table 3). This negative skew is true across all major northern hemisphere markets (Wen and Yang 2009).[7]

The sawtooth pattern sees alternating periods of concave, serially correlated rising price and convex, sharper falls. A general depiction of price changes is given by (after Capozza et al. 2004):

$$\Delta \text{Price}_t = \alpha + \beta . \Delta P_{t-1} + \gamma . \left(P^*_{t-1} - P_{t-1} \right) + \delta . \Delta P^*_t$$

where: α, β, γ, and δ are constants; Δ refers to rate of change; P is price; and P^* is the fundamental, or long term mean, price.

Sawtooth patterns are common in nature, and across many markets which leads to frequent observation along the lines that 'prices go up via the escalator and down in the elevator'.

The sawtooth pattern of slow rises and sharp falls is characteristic of Edgeworth (1925) cycles that arise from competition between dominant buyers or sellers (Noel 2011). It is familiar to motorists in many countries where cycles in retail petrol prices are driven by competing sellers in oligopolistic markets (e.g. Lewis and Noel 2011).

The few interpretations of equity markets through the Edgeworth lens assume dominant players are dealers who compete to sell (e.g. Hasbrouck 2015). The evidence in equity markets, though, of prolonged price rises, sharp falls and negative skew points towards competition between buyers. This would be expected given that dominant equity holders are open-ended funds which have virtually continuous net inflows of compulsory or tax incentivised retirement savings that are relatively price-insensitive. As institutions' cash builds, they must offer a successively higher bid price, which is then matched by other buyers, and the price edges up in slight increments. Eventually the price reaches its highest feasible level, where large investors expect better risk-adjusted returns from holding cash and reduce their equity demand: price then falls quickly and is reset around a minimum fundamental value, after which the process repeats. The result is an equity price cycle marked by many small price rises during buyers' serial overbidding, and infrequent large falls as the price is reset. This sawtooth pattern is clear in the left of chart which plots the S&P 500 Index since the 1970s.[8]

---

[7] See Ekholm and Pasternack (2005) and Kee-Hong et al. (2006) for a discussion of equity skew. Harvey and Siddique (2000) discuss theoretical contribution of skew to asset prices.

[8] An alternative perspective on the sawtooth pattern is the price pressure hypothesis where the price of a security rises (falls) in response to a large buy (sell) order to induce sellers (buyers) to accommodate the

6 Structure of Equity Prices

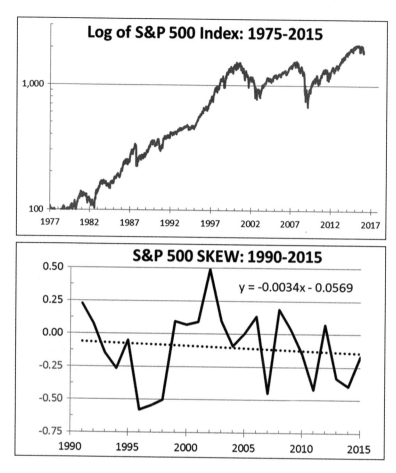

Fig. 6.1 Log of S&P 500 Index and skew in returns

The right hand chart plots annual skew in daily changes in the S&P 500 Index and shows (to a statistically weak extent) a steady decrease over time. This is a noisy aggregate of the skew in returns from individual stocks, but increased skew is consistent with greater competition between buyers as the funds management industry grew in size (Fig. 6.1).

Interpreting equity prices as subject to Edgeworth cycles explains a number of puzzles. First, creeping competition between investors gives prices a serially dependent dynamic, which explains why prices do not reach equilibrium. Also, as the underlying mechanism shifts into and out of competition between

---

order; the price then returns to its earlier value (assuming the trade has no information content) to provide the inducement (Scholes 1972). A succession of such trades will generate a sawtooth pattern. For a discussion of mutual fund price pressure see Ben-Rephael et al. (2011).

92   Applied Investment Theory

buyers (bull markets) and sellers (bear markets), it sets up both positive and negative skew in returns, which helps explain the thick tails in return distributions. The irregular cycles of slow climbs to a maximum realistic price followed by quick reset towards underlying value (and vice versa in established bear markets) within relatively stable limits explain the use of technical analysis, including channels, trend lines and resistance/support levels.

Another implication of Edgeworth cycles in financial markets is that the regular flow of essentially involuntary investments into mutual funds induces a positive bias in returns in physical and derivatives markets, which will push prices above fundamental value in a steady upward trajectory. Thus, where the traditional debate over equity returns is whether they are stochastic or mean reverting, dominance of predominantly long, price insensitive fund managers means equities are now deterministic with an upward drift.

Edgeworth cycles in equity prices can also explain their high volatility at market lows. Volatility reflects the rate of time variation in estimates of value or factors contributing to it, and – because fundamentals do not change significantly from one day to the next – high volatility must arise from increased fluctuations in sentiment or liquidity. The sawtooth cycles see institutions steadily build cash as prices peak and hold it until prices fall and reach support: the build up of cash lifts liquidity, and long-only fund managers are alert to price rebound.

Edgeworth cycles explain another puzzling phenomenon where equity market peaks are more concentrated in the later part of the year than is expected by chance. For instance, 8 out of 16 of the highest values of the S&P 500 Index during 2000–2015 occurred in December with 6 of them at the end of the month. This pattern is consistent with the common suggestion that fund managers window dress their returns (e.g. Brown et al. 2001). Calendar-based patterns in trading of dominant investors also explain use of Gann trading techniques.

Another point of support for Edgeworth cycles is evidence that big figures are important to markets. These are notable price levels – 10,000 on the Dow, or a gold price of $1,000 per ounce – that seem to attract investor focus. A typical study identified examples of clustering and price barriers around symbolic numbers tied to the decimal system, and concluded that round numbers become simple rules of thumb for investors to measure value, and so are used strategically in setting price targets (Mitchell 2001).

In the light of the structure-conduct performance depiction of institutional investment, Edgeworth cycles are an interesting example of how institutional investors' conduct drives market structure.

6.2.2.3 Clustering in Returns and Volatility

A central feature of neoclassical finance theory is random walk, where today's market level or security price equals yesterday's value plus a random move. Black and Scholes (1973: 640) provide a typical example of reliance on randomness by stating that their formula for the value of an option assumes that "the stock price follows a random walk in continuous time."

Although returns may appear random across a lengthy sample, tails of return distributions contain anomalies which suggest patterns that aggregate analyses miss. Consider the following chart that plots the value of the slope coefficient in a regression of today's return against yesterday's return. Results use daily data for the S&P 500 Index during 1950–2014 and two equal sub-periods. The difference from traditional analyses is to partition the data into eight sub-samples according to the number of standard deviations by which the prior day move was above and below mean return (i.e. mean ±0–0.99, 1–1.99, 2–2.99 and ≥3.0 standard deviations), and calculate the slope of regression between sequential moves (Fig. 6.2).

The figure has a number of takeaways. The first is that significant falls tend to reverse the next day: following a day where return is more than two standard deviations below the mean (which is less than about −1.9%), the direction of movement reverses and the next day's change is likely to be a rise that recovers half the previous day's drop. Partitioning the data by period confirms persistence in reversal of large price falls. Less obviously, large rises

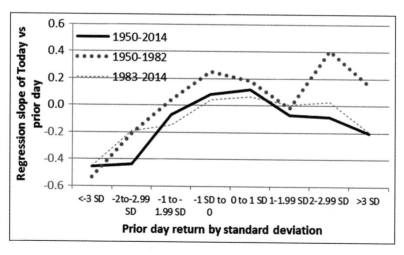

Fig. 6.2 Today's return vs. range of yesterday's return

94   Applied Investment Theory

may mean revert next day. Finally, there seems little serial correlation across the full sample.

Another take-away from the figure is that large falls are qualitatively different to large rises. To amplify this, consider only extreme moves of greater than six standard deviations. These can be described as follows:

$$R_t = \alpha + \left(\beta_1.\text{Dummy}_1 + \beta_2.\text{Dummy}_2 + \beta_3.\text{Dummy}_3\right) * R_{t-1} + \varepsilon$$

where: R_t is return on day t; and $\text{Dummy}_1 = 1$ iff $R_t < (\mu_R - 6 * \sigma_R)$, $\text{Dummy}_2 = 1$ iff $R_t > (\mu_R + 6 * \sigma_R)$, and $\text{Dummy}_3 = 1$ otherwise. The distribution of R_t is described by μ_R and σ_R.

The results of my analysis of the relationship above for the period 1950–2014 are shown in the following table, and confirm conclusions from the previous figure. The significant negative co-efficient on the large fall dummy, β_1, shows that much of each fall is reversed the following day; the smaller, but still significant, negative co-efficient on the large rise dummy, β_2, shows they are partially reversed the following day; while the significant positive co-efficient following lower moves, β_3, shows that smaller rises and falls tend to persist. Although not shown here, similar – but less significant – results come from using other multiples of standard deviation above and below the mean (Table 6.1).

The following charts depict another view of short term clustering of S&P 500 returns using overlapping 250 day data periods since 1950. The left hand chart plots the slope of the regression of tomorrow's return versus today's return for the previous 250 days, which is a measure of changing serial correlation of returns. The right chart shows the sum of squared returns for the previous 250 days, which is a measure of volatility (Fig. 6.3).

Two points stand out. The first is that there has been a change in character of the S&P 500 since about 1970, with a steady decline in autocorrelation of returns and steady rise in volatility. The second point is the pronounced cyclicality in autocorrelation and volatility of returns, with both displaying 5–10 year waves. The significance of this is that key parameters in equity distributions are time varying, and cluster or move monotonically until the

Table 6.1 Regression of S&P change on prior day's return

Variable	Regression parameter
Constant: α	0.029***
Large fall dummy: β_1	−0.348***
Large rise dummy: β_2	−0.094**
'Normal' prior day return: β_3	0.067***
Adjusted R-squared	0.014

***<0.01; **<0.05

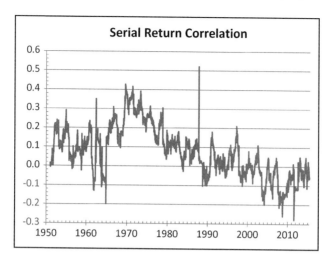

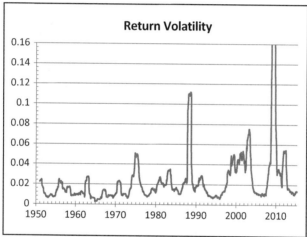

Fig. 6.3 Regime shifting in S&P 500 Index returns

pattern dissolves or reverses, which adds further to the explanation of why it has proven impractical to econometrically forecast mean and variance beyond trivial periods (Ghysels et al. 2005).

6.2.2.4 Tendency of Prices to Trend

Another pronounced feature of equity returns is their tendency to trend, which is sufficiently strong to justify momentum as a systematic factor in equity returns (e.g. Carhart 1997). Prices display persistence over the short term which is revealed as clumping; or mimic creeping equilibrium by moving in a

96 Applied Investment Theory

straight line before changing direction. Trends generally form in the absence of a clear trigger, persist over the medium term (months to a few years), and are only partially explicable even on an ex post basis.

A common justification of monotonic price drift that can follow corporate events such as stock splits, seasoned equity offerings, and dividend changes is under-reaction by investors (Subrahmanyam 2007). Whilst this is sometimes dismissed as irrational because – on an ex post basis – investors fail to meet the test of pricing information in a timely and unbiased fashion, there are rational explanations. Investors, for instance, rarely comprehend the full impact of any new information because initial announcements tend to be brief, and full detail is released much later, with tangible progress even further delayed. Incomplete information exposes investors to uncertainty, so they will discount its full value until the outcome becomes clearer.

If buyers and sellers have equal access to information, they will reach comparable estimates of securities' fair value based on current operations and value to be added or lost by initiatives and operating improvements. The difference between these – the equity's value only with assets in place and its future value with expected improvements – is, however, subject to information asymmetry, disruptions during implementation, and exogenous firm-specific factors (such as competition or market shifts). Where investors are equally informed, buyers will not be willing to pay the full future value of the equity, and sellers will settle for less: the negotiated value – which becomes current market price – will reflect the uncertainty of buyers and sellers, and lie between fair value without and with future improvements in place. Similar logic applies to security attributes or systematic factors (such as size, price-to-book, and price momentum) that determine, or proxy for, value or uncertainty. Thus prices bounce around as new data arrives and old data is re-interpreted which opens up gaps between market prices and fundamental values, and this noise stimulates trading for speculation or arbitrage that helps align prices and fundamentals. Because full future values are uncertain, prices will only incorporate them over time, which inevitably sets up drift in prices.

Clear illumination of the basis of under-reaction can be seen by reference to acquisitions and mergers, which are the highest profile and most economically significant corporate transactions. One finding is that announcement of an acquisition between listed bidding and target companies is followed by a slight fall in their combined market value (Roll 1986), which indicates negative synergies are expected from the merger. This is a surprise given that even a modest rationalisation of fixed costs would justify a combined share price rise of at least 15%.[9] It is, however, consistent with studies of announcements

---

[9] Corporate fixed costs (SG&A) average around 25% of revenue (e.g. Weiss 2010). Conservatively assume a saving of 10% of combined SG&A, with pre-tax earnings equal to 15% of revenue and a 30% tax rate:

6 Structure of Equity Prices 97

of other corporate strategic initiatives which show they do not have much impact on share price. As examples, the cumulative abnormal return during three days following announcement by US firms of layoffs in the 1980s and 1990s was −0.3% (Farber and Hallock 2009); and it was just 0.3% following announcement of major sports sponsorships (Reiser et al. 2012). In similar vein there is little financial impact from announcement of company-wide strategies such as better ESG or sustainability.

The poor performance of firms after making major announcements reflects investor concern that benefits may have been over-estimated and/or doubt that they may not be fully captured due to delay or sub-optimum execution. This is consistent with acquisition announcements where the share price of the acquirer – which bears a disproportionate portion of wealth lost or fore-gone – falls relative to that of the target; and also with investor under-reaction discussed earlier.

Price trends can also arise from monotonic secular influences (such as immigration), or slow adjustment to unexpected regime shifts (such as realignments of global monetary policy after 1980). Other staggered flows of price-sensitive information come from the sequential nature of data series such as official interest rates, economic growth and corporate profits which can trend for extended periods.

Another contributor to trending is that many investment decisions are procyclical, including investor flows that follow prices (e.g. Warther 1995), decisions based on technical trading rules (Park and Irwin 2007), and the tendency of institutional investors to herd and follow trades of competitors (Sias, 2004). Another procyclical influence falls on leveraged investors because a rise in portfolio value allows them to increase their holdings whilst keeping leverage constant (and *vice versa*) (Adrian and Shin 2008). In similar fashion, a change in security prices affects investor confidence by confirming the success or otherwise of their decision and pro-cyclically interacts with the wealth effect to affect their willingness to make further investments.

Trending arises, too, because virtually all value-sensitive information is under human control, with much of the most important corporate data – such as announcements of strategy or investment – subject to discretion in timing their release. As examples of where human control can promote trends, institutional investors will prefer to split large transactions, and transact smaller parcels when volume is heavy (Admati and Pfleiderer 1988);

---

this gives additional pre-tax revenue of 2.5% of revenue, which at a constant price:earnings ratio would justify a combined share price rise of one sixth.

98   Applied Investment Theory

firms make financial decisions such as dividends and leverage in light of previous decisions, and will execute one-off transactions such as stock issues and mergers at the most propitious time (Brown 2011); and analysts revise their published opinions of securities in increments (Cronqvist et al. 2009). The result is that much price-sensitive information does not emerge at random nor instantly reach the market, but trickles out over time.

Another human contributor to trending is that the market order imbalance, or level of buy orders less the level of sell orders, persists from one day to the next (Chordia et al. 2002). The imbalance also contributes to reversal of large price moves through high buying after market crashes and increased sales after market rises.

Prices themselves can promote trending because investors monitor market transactions for possible indications of other investors' insights. Even in the absence of new security-specific information, fundamental valuations will change because of trading activity in the security and related securities and shifts in other markets (particularly debt and currency). Thus price changes induce unplanned trading, which continually adjusts the fundamental value of a security and accelerates any trend so that security demand and price co-move.

Trending prices throw into question one of the best established assumptions in economics, which is that demand curves slope downwards (or are flat): that is, as the price of a product rises, it steadily moves above potential consumers' hedonic or fair value based on marginal utility from consumption, and so fewer people choose to purchase it, leading to a decline in demand. Extended to markets, traders who see a security's price rise will passively reduce their demand, so that the price and volume of a product move in opposite directions. All this is so certain that a positive relationship between security demand and price was described by Thaler (1989) as "heresy".

Even so, an upward sloping supply curve is accepted in the case of Veblen goods, which have luxury features so that rising prices signal greater attraction and increase buyers' preference and demand (Leibenstein 1950). It is easy to envisage just such a process leading to an upward sloping demand curve for equities. Most obviously, investors interpret a price rise as resulting from buying by better informed investors, and so place a higher value on the security, which further lifts price. The opposite applies, of course, during periods of market decline. One finance study using the assumption that equities are a luxury good was able to explain the equity risk premium (Aït-Sahalia et al. 2004).

6.2.3 Macrodrivers of Equity Returns

While security prices are set within markets, transactions are but part of a complex chain that is subject to influence from exogenous influences in the broader economy and from the actions of corporate executives and other agents. Like many of the drivers discussed above, these can be involuntary and induce changes in price that are independent of fundamentals.

Probably the most important macrodriver of equity returns is global liquidity which has led to bouts of asset price inflation since the 1990s. One source is central banks which – in most countries – adopted an easy liquidity policy, and resulting bank lending flooded the world with cash at low interest rates. The official line is that this encourages business and consumers to support economic growth, but much of the cash flowed straight into speculation.

A second source of liquidity has come involuntarily through demography. The most important is a wall of money that started flowing when governments began to sponsor retirement savings programmes. These first emerged in the United States with the Revenue Act of 1978 that introduced tax incentives to save for retirement, and made 401 (k) plans commonplace during the 1980s. The trend soon became global. In Australia, for instance, a minimum of 9% of all employees' wages is now compulsorily directed to superannuation (retirement savings). The amounts involved are huge. By the end of 2010, Americans' retirement assets totalled $17.5 trillion, with 27% in mutual funds and another 20% in direct equities. Retirement savings already represent close to half the value of US listed equities, and another $1 trillion is saved each year, with much of that going to buy more equities (US Census Bureau 2014).

Another demographic influence on liquidity is the population profile, whose effect is shown in the following figure which plots the proportion of the US population aged between 15 and 34 years, along with the US ten-year government bond yield. The intuition is that consumers' life cycle influences their expenditure, and the 15–34 age bracket is important because it comprises three key groups: those in their mid 'teens and early 'twenties who have high discretionary expenditure, including significant influence over household spending; the middle group which is setting up their own homes and filling them with durables and cars; and the older cohort of young families who kick off another wave of consumption (Fig. 6.4).

The chart shows the financial sway of history's most prominent cohort which was the baby boomers who were born during 1946–1964 (and hence were aged 15–34 during 1961–1998). As the baby boomers' influence began to be felt after the late 1960s, demand for durables and housing grew and manufactur-

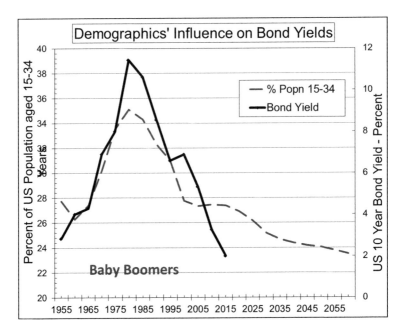

Fig. 6.4 US bond yields and 15–34 year old population

ers reacted by building additional production capacity. Demand lifted inflation, and competition for increased borrowing by corporates and households further lifted interest rates. The second phase began around 1980 as the early boomers moved into middle age: durables demand peaked, and this ushered in a period of manufacturing overcapacity that saw jobs and profits decline, and loss of pricing power which led interest rates down. The third phase came as the last of the baby boomers streamed out of the 15–34 year old cohort in the 1990s: overcapacity tripped re-engineering; savings rose as boomers moved into their high earnings phase (the first turned 45 in 1991); and inflation and interest rates plummeted. The result is that US bond yields have moved in lockstep with ageing of the baby boomers. Looking ahead, the Census Bureau's 2014 population projections show a monotonic decline in relative size of the 18–34 year old cohort out to 2060 (available at: www.census.gov).

Other macrodrivers of equity prices arise through investment decisions that have significant involuntary influences from automation or exogenous drivers. For instance, in the case of managed investments, investors notionally control flows in and out, but their discretion is effectively limited to allocation of contributions. Most inflows and redemptions are involuntary because they tend to come through mandated or tax-promoted retirement savings (e.g. compulsory superannuation, fixed contributions to retirement savings accounts); are intended to cover contingent events such as loss of employment; or else securitise an expense stream such as house purchase (Attanasio et al. 2005). Net flows, then, are related to income and life cycle (including marital status, family size, and years to retirement); and to fiscal policy because retirement savings substitute for social security.

6.2.4 Other Market Behaviours

A characteristic of complete markets is that there is such a variety of different securities within each principal asset class that those of any size have close substitutes. This continuum homogenises alternative securities so that returns at the margins are similar, and realised returns of interchangeable securities converge.

Homogenization of investments is most obvious from long term data with minimal survivorship bias. As one example, the annual real return of 20 equity markets with continuous history from 1900 to 2012 was $-0.1 \pm 2.1\%$; and the capitalisation-weighted return from a global index was 0.9% (Dimson et al. 2013). Similar performance is seen across a diverse range of assets: commodities' returns during 1911–2010 were in the range $-0.2 \pm 1.1\%$ (Reid and Burns 2010); and famous artworks had a real annual return during 1635–1987 of 1.9% (which needs to be netted of significant holding costs such as insurance, storage and maintenance) (Frey and Eichenberger 1995).

Two points stand out: over available market history, returns from a range of asset classes have been roughly equal, and little above zero in real terms. For equities, this arises from the standard assumption in financial economics that the stock market is a claim on aggregate consumption (e.g. Whitelaw 2000). Global real GDP has grown over the last century at an average of around 3% per year (Krausmann et al. 2009), which is an upper limit for stock returns on the assumption that listed firms capture all growth. To the extent that the entrepreneurial unlisted sector takes a disproportionate share of real growth and there is slippage within listed firms from agency costs and cyclical closures, then returns to equities will be somewhat less.

Another interesting characteristic of equity markets is the co-existence of multiple prices. This is a surprise because efficient markets would ensure that at least major investors share comparable information about each stock, and rationality of buyers and sellers should establish an equilibrium price, with

102   Applied Investment Theory

gaps closed by arbitrage (Lamont and Thaler 2003). The classic example of a violation of this 'law of one price' relates to relative prices of shares in the Royal Dutch Shell group. Its owners, Netherlands-listed Royal Dutch and UK-listed Shell, received fixed proportions of identical cash flows from, but their share prices diverged from equivalence for quite long periods. A second example is the closed end mutual funds discount where mutual funds trade below (and sometimes above) their net asset value. Other examples come from private equity investors who have been able to buy listed or unlisted firms, execute a rapid restructure, and then list them at far higher price: the original owners with superior knowledge of the firm should have been able to do even better.

Most apparent violations of the law of one price arise when securities are held in different forms, or trade in different physical settings, which suggests there may be rational explanations, such as higher frictions in one setting, involvement of adverse agents, or investor uncertainty. Frictions in markets have a variety of guises, with obvious examples in transaction costs and tax, sovereign risk, illiquidity, and weak information or reputation. Moreover, uncertainty will be affected by confidence in the reliability of intermediaries or agents in the market, and managers of the holding company that distributes the earnings, which reflects the quality of firm governance. Another factor that leads to violations of the law of one price is the clientele effect where particular attributes of a firm or security market are valued differently by investors in different settings. Higher relative price can also proxy in some investors' minds for reliability of returns, and they will prefer the higher-priced security instead of arbitraging the premium away.

In fact, it is common to find that near identical products or services actually have different features that affect buyers' confidence and valuation, and this leads to frequent violations of the law of one price. Consider Coca Cola, which is probably the world's most standardised good. Supermarkets in modern shopping centres in every country have a refrigerator inside the door that dispenses cans of Coke and a plastic cup for a dollar or two. Alternatively, within a few minutes' walk, consumers can pay up to five times as much for the identical serve at fast food outlets, cafes and restaurants. Price differentials between seemingly identical products are common in many other areas such as consumer goods (high end retailers vs. discount warehouses) and services (involving both leisure – such as accommodation, entertainment, bars and restaurants – and services ranging from babysitters and barbers to doctors and lawyers). Even wages for near-identical work differ between industries (e.g. Krueger and Summers 1988). A simple example shows that this, too, has a rational explanation. Take the role of personal assistant to the senior

6 Structure of Equity Prices 103

executive in a law firm and at a mine site: notionally the two jobs are the same. But consider other factors that could markedly affect the relative supply of labour: location and commute to work; physical environment and type of people that pass through the office; and job security.

It is common to purchase goods and services above their opportunity cost, which means that – unless notionally rational decision makers do not minimise their expenses – their valuations are affected by some combination of non-price factors, or they believe that higher priced goods and services give lower overall expense and so price proxies for unobservable factors such as quality, durability and personal satisfaction. These two explanations are analogous to agency costs (where agents do not maximise principals' profits) and the management concept of efficiency wage models (where employee output increases with pay). The law of one price is a chimera across the economy because consumers, including investors, jointly value both the product or service *and* its presentation and setting.

Another set of important market behaviours relate to illegal insider trading. This is common, especially ahead of mergers and acquisitions where up to a third of transactions are potentially illegal. As examples, a large scale study of stock price changes around acquisition announcements concluded that insiders made positive returns in at least 30% of transactions (Bris 2005); and detailed records of trading in a takeover firm during the month before its acquisition found insiders bought 29% of the stock (Cornell and Sirri 1992). Another study examined cases of insider trading detected by the Securities and Exchange Commission, and concluded that insiders were responsible for most of the abnormal trading volume prior to announcements, and caused about half of pre-announcement price moves (Meulbroek 1992).

The opposite of insider trading occurs when regulators or exchange operators over-ride legal transactions and reverse gains or losses by investors. A good example arose whilst writing this chapter during mid-2015 when the prices of Chinese shares fell by over 30% within three weeks, and the China Securities Regulatory Commission announced that shareholders with holdings in excess of 5% of a company's stock could not sell any shares for six months. Successful investors can be more directly punished, with the best known example dating to 1979 when the Chicago Board of Trade cruelled the Hunt brothers' attempt to corner the silver market by requiring all traders to reduce their holdings to below 600 silver futures contracts, which pricked the speculation-fuelled price bubble. Exchanges frequently impose temporary trading halts after significant price changes; and regulators in numerous countries imposed restrictions during sharp market falls in 2008, including bans on short sales.

6.3 Explanations of Equity Prices

A central question in investment is why returns differ between stocks, or how a stock's expected abnormal return can be evaluated.[10]

The answer is far from obvious. Although supply and demand match for each transaction, prices never reach equilibrium. Moreover, prices are too volatile to be explained by fundamentals, and even their largest moves often cannot be explained by information (Sect. 6.4). This mirrors opacity in individual trades, where less than a quarter of transactions are explained by identifiable characteristics of investors (Grinblatt and Keloharju 2001), or firm (Ferson and Harvey 1997). With weak understanding of factors that drive transactions, it is generally accepted that shares trade in a wide band around their true value. Fisher Black (1986: 533), for instance, said prices in an efficient market lie in the range of half to twice their value. This sustains expectations of analysts that stock mis-pricings can be traded (Kothari 2001).

The typical explanation of prices dates at least to Adam Smith (1776), who argued that prices in physical markets for houses, livestock, commodities and so on adjust to establish equilibrium between the flows of orders to buy and sell, and thus clear. This is still sometimes suggested as the driver of financial markets, too, along the lines that "prices of stocks traded on the NYSE are determined through supply and demand" (Jones 2010). In practice, though, most finance researchers do not think that supply and demand set the value of securities (see, for instance: Harford and Kaul 2005; Maher et al. 2008).

Let us examine what is known about valuation in equity markets.

6.3.1 Smart Beta: Systematic Influences on the Cross Section of Stock Returns

The standard finance paradigm allows systematic factors to affect the cross section of equity returns. In CAPM, for example, excess return for an asset is proportional to the covariance of its return with the market portfolio (the asset's beta). This, though, explains only a small part of asset returns, while other factors prove relevant. For instance, returns are negatively related to firm size and positively related to book-to-market ratio in US markets (Fama and French 1992) and elsewhere (Ferson and Harvey 1997), which points to outperformance by small capitalisation and value stocks, respectively.

---

[10] For a summary of studies into factors affecting the cross-section of equity returns see Dai (2015).

These factors are systematic, in that they have similar impacts on all firms. In the case of firm size, for instance, cash flows of smaller companies are exposed to higher information asymmetry due to limited analyst coverage and media scrutiny. Small firms have other unique risks, too, such as less liquidity and weak co-insurance from minimal diversification. As a result, expected cash flows in a small firm are either under-estimated or more heavily discounted than those in a large firm.

Another robust systematic price effect arises because many institutional investors have little or no capacity to short stocks or leverage their portfolios, and they seek to achieve a similar result by incorporating high beta stocks (Frazzini and Pedersen 2014), whose price is bid up and contributes to the longstanding low beta anomaly (Jensen et al. 1972). Systematic bias in stock selection can also come from a preference for portfolios that generate abnormal returns during weak market conditions by including stocks with low downside beta, or reduced co-movement with the market during downturns (e.g. Estrada 2006).

A second set of systematic factors relates to persistence in performance, or momentum. Thus previous winner stocks continue to outperform previous losers (Jegadeesh and Titman 1993; Hong and Stein 1999); and the market can under-value the prospects of stocks with favourable traits including ratios of income and cash flow to assets, leverage, and margin (Piotroski 2000). Stocks with these features can continue to outperform, particularly in periods of slow market growth that encourage a search for quality.

Another manifestation of systematic influences is through the implied cost of capital, which is the discount rate that equates current share prices with analysts' forecasts of future cash flows (e.g. Guay et al. 2011); and through perfect foresight pricing, which calculates the discount rate that will equate realised ex post cash flows to share price (e.g. Arnott et al. 2009). These conclude that investors overproject the relative over and under-performance of stocks and so over pay for winners and underpay for losers, which is consistent with evidence of medium term reversal of return trends.

These findings have allowed investors to seek greater or less exposure to specific systematic risks. Once this was termed arbitrage, but now a lot of these attributes have been grouped under the heading of smart beta, which selects stocks on the basis of market-wide factors, including: firm size, measures of value, price momentum, stock quality, and low beta. The aim is to sell out of falling values and buy into rising values. Because these factors are minimally correlated, a benefit of smart beta strategies is to promote diversification.

6.3.2 Influence on Returns of Firm and Security Traits

Turning to firm-specific parameters that predict profit or return, a common assumption underpinning finance research and practice is that equity prices respond in predictable ways to transient economic and financial data. As an example, they rise on favourable outlooks for monetary and economic conditions (e.g. Chen et al. 1986). This has become one of the most popular research topics in the accounting, finance and management literatures, and literally hundreds of empirical studies have found causal links between financial performance and lagged firm or security characteristics, often providing pointers to their theoretical basis.

Typical analyses study the relationship between returns up to a year or so ahead and the lagged values of fundamental variables (e.g. Ou and Penman 1989), commonly by regressing the return of firm i after time t, $R_{i,t\rightarrow t+1}$, on a publicly available signal, X_{it}, and a variety of controls (Green et al. 2013: 701).

Evaluations typically use an expression similar to the following (Ferson and Harvey 1991):

$$r_{i,t} = \lambda_{0,t} + \sum_{j=1}^{K}\lambda_{j,t}.\beta_{i,j,t-1} + \varepsilon_{i,t}$$

where: $r_{i,t}$ is excess return on equity i in month t; $\lambda_{0,t}$ is the intercept; $\lambda_{j,t}$ is the slope co-efficient on K instrument βs, whose values are conditional on publicly available information at $t-1$.

This study used monthly US stock and bond data during 1959–1986, and regressed monthly excess returns on six beta co-efficients for economic and financial moderators, which were calculated by regressing excess return on variables during the 60 months to $t-1$. The model explained about 10% of the variation in returns, and led the authors to conclude that "measures of economic risk that have been identified with average risk premiums can also capture predictable variation in asset returns."

Other studies are similarly able to explain at least a portion of stock returns with hindsight (see Fama 1991). As examples: about 7% of year ahead annual returns can be explained by lagged dividend yield, and explanatory power improves with horizon (Cochrane 2008); historical earnings (that is audited financials) explain up to around a quarter of the cross-section of returns (Ferson and Harvey 1993); and analysis of international markets shows that around 10–20% of price variation can be explained by market variables and economic factors (Ferreira et al. 2012). These regressions have been extended into models: one using earnings yield, capital investment and two accounting-based measures explain around 20% of year-ahead future returns (Chen and Zhang 2007).

The huge volume of published results obviously needs consolidation, and this has encouraged their synthesis through summary catalogues. As examples: Green et al. (2013) compiled a database of 330 signals; Harvey et al. (2014) identified 230 individual factors that have been proposed by researchers as explanations for patterns in returns; and Jacobs (2015) evaluated 100 long-short anomalies in the cross-section of expected equity returns. Such reviews conclude that higher future returns are associated with good financial performance (ROA, prior returns), measures of value (low PER, high BTM), and greater efficiency (higher leverage, R&D expense). Conversely, lower returns are associated with beta, size and indicators of growing size (such as growth in assets, employees, and sales). As an aside, it is not surprising that so many measures of firm operations are related to future profitability given that firm traits change slowly and returns persist in the medium term.

The following table draws on references cited above to list parameters whose lagged values have been shown as related to profit or return. It includes only variables that can be observed, or directly calculated from observable data such as accounting ratios (Table 6.2).

In summary, retrospective analysis has identified hundreds of factors that can explain up to about a quarter of the cross-section of equity returns, although – with interlinkages – they probably comprise a much smaller number of principal factors. These include macroeconomic variables, measures of value, security attributes, firm characteristics and numerous econometrically-derived relationships. What, though, is the practical relevance of these findings?

6.3.3 Can Lagged Variables Really Predict Returns?

Despite the spread of studies showing statistically significant relationships between return and lagged firm factors, some scepticism is prudent about the findings.

Most obviously, it is not certain that analyses are sufficiently rigorous to eliminate the possibility that results are merely transient products of data mining. Doubts about methodology are common across the literature: one study concluded "that most claimed research findings in financial economics are likely false" (Harvey et al. 2014); a test of models that predict returns of individual securities and various portfolios found they could not outperform a simple, constant estimate

108   Applied Investment Theory

Table 6.2 Common firm-specific variables whose lagged values explain returns

Lagged firm variable	Definition	Relationship with future return
Firm traits		
Accounting accruals	Change in non-cash current assets less change in current liabilities and depreciation, all divided by total assets	–
Age	Years since first listing	+
Asset growth	Percentage change in total assets over one year	–
Current ratio	Current assets divided by current liabilities	+
Distress risk	Default probability	+
Employment	Change in number of employees	–
Investment	Change in PPE and inventories divided by total assets	–
Issues	Change in shares outstanding from year prior	–
R&D expense	R&D expense divided by sales	+
ROA	Income before extraordinaries divided by total assets	+
Sales growth	Annual change in sales	–
Size	Turnover	–
Market-based variables		
Beta	Calculated from market model	–
Dividend yield	Total dividend divided by market cap	+
Leverage	Total liabilities divided by market cap	+
Return	Stock return in prior year	+
Sales: Market cap	Revenue divided by market cap	+
Size	[log] Market capitalisation	–
Value	Book value of equity divided by market cap (book-to-market ratio)	+
	Market cap divided by income (Price-to-earnings ratio)	–

equal to the average market return (Simin 2008); and an examination of the influence of macroeconomic factors found they were no better than random numbers in explaining equity returns (Chan et al. 1998).

Further support for the doubtful statistical validity of many investment relationships is their disturbing tendency to disappear shortly after being identified. As examples, anomalies relating to size, value, weekends and dividend yield weakened or disappeared after publication of papers describing them (Schwert 2001).[11] As already discussed, a similar fate befell the equity premium puzzle (Sect. 4.2).

---

[11] My favourite example is the Super Bowl stock market predictor which says that if the Super Bowl (the championship of American football that was first played in 1967) is won by a team from the old National Football League then the US equity market will be up that year; and vice versa. After a string of successful predictions in the competition's early years, the indicator was installed as a piece of market wisdom,

An equally important concern over capital market anomalies is their relevance for investors. Even studies with statistical significance invariably have low explanatory power and thus limited economic merit. Most leave open the nature and contributors to over 80% of cross-sectional variation in stock returns, with hard to quantify manager and firm fixed-effects probably playing a significant role. Moreover, intertemporal relationships vary widely in intensity and duration through cycles in the macroeconomy and in individual firms' performance. Signs on parameters are usually not constant for more than a year, so models typically break down soon after their development: in short, a comprehensive depiction of asset pricing has proved elusive (Sala-i-Martin et al. 2004).

This opens up the question of whether the analyses perform as claimed and actually test for lagged variables' *predictive* power. As noted earlier, the typical approach regresses historical returns against a set of explanatory variables at the start of each return period or in the prior period. The intuition is that predictability stems from a positive relation between future return and lagged variable (e.g. Richardson et al. 2010: 421).

This style of analysis certainly *explains* the link between return and lagged value through an historical period, but parameters are only discoverable *after* the end of the sample period. To be of practical use, the influence of variables must be identifiable ex ante, which requires that relationships be relatively stable over a medium term time horizon (so there is sufficient time for them to be identified and then implemented). Unfortunately relationships rarely persist out of sample: thus during 1976–2011 there was a significant decline in the explanatory power of eight out of twelve well-studied equity market anomalies (Chordia et al. 2014).

To amplify the instability of parameters, let us conduct a simple analysis of the type that supported the conclusion that "returns at five-year horizons seem very predictable" (Cochrane 1999: 44). Annual data for 1927–2014 from the website of NYU Professor Aswath Damodaran (http://pages.stern.nyu.edu/~adamodar/) are used in the following model for ex post OLS regression over a horizon of k years of annual excess return of the S&P 500 minus T bills against the S&P 500 price/dividend ratio:

---

secured further prominence in a 1978 column by New York Times sportswriter Leonard Koppetta, and featured in a *Journal of Finance* article which found it delivered a return double that of a buy-and-hold strategy (Krueger and Kennedy 1990). Although the Super Bowl predictor entered researchers' quiver of market biases, a review covering the next two decades shows the predictor now almost exactly matches results of a buy and hold strategy (Kester 2010).

$$\text{Return}_{t \to t+k}^{S\&P500} - \text{Return}_{t \to t+k}^{TBills} = a + b. \left(\frac{S \& P \, 500 \, \text{Index}_t}{S \& P \, \text{Dividends}_t} \right) + \varepsilon$$

Panel A of the table shows that – over 90 years of annual data – parameter values in the relationship are similar across horizon. It also confirms the usual finding that returns over longer periods are more explicable by price/dividend ratio (that is, R-squared increases with horizon). A surprise in panel B, though, is that the parameters and strength of the relationship over five years change markedly within sub-periods, with a sharp monotonic weakening. The link, then, is unstable (Table 6.3).

The following figures amplify the time varying nature of the relationship between S&P 500 excess return and the price:dividend ratio during overlapping ten year periods. The left chart plots the slope and R^2 for OLS regression of five-year returns against price:dividend ratio. It confirms that the magnitude and even sign vary: depending on the period chosen, ex post regression derives a slope of between -1.7 and $+1.1$; and its explanatory power waxes and wanes erratically. This puzzle is explained by the right plot which shows that the price:dividend ratio was low until about 1990, after which a long period of unusually high price:dividend ratio significantly changed the link. Because the relationship between excess return and price:dividend ratio varies so markedly over the medium term, it would obviously be of little value when used ex ante by investors (Fig. 6.5).

Another test of the practical ability of lagged variables to predict returns uses data published by Professor Ken French (http://mba.tuck.dartmouth.edu/pages/faculty/ken.french). The following figure plots annual values of the two best known systematic factors: SMB is the average return on portfolios of small capitalisation stocks minus that from portfolios of big stocks; and HML is the return on portfolios of high value stocks (low price-to-book) minus the return

Table 6.3 Regression of excess S&P 500 returns on price/dividend ratio

Horizon (k)	Data period	a (constant)	b (slope)	R^2 (%)
Panel A				
1 year	1927–2014	15.9	−0.27*	4.3
3 years	1927–2014	14.8	−0.24***	10.3
5 years	1927–2014	14.6	−0.21***	16.9
Panel B				
5 years	1927–1955	42.7	−1.51***	53.6
5 years	1956–1984	17.7	−0.49***	33.3
5 years	1985–2014	20.4	−0.28***	53.8

***$p<0.01$; *$p<0.10$

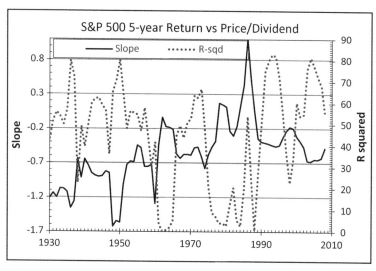

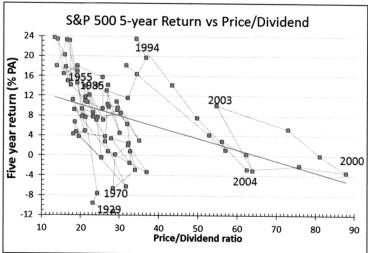

Fig. 6.5 Five-year ahead return vs. price/dividend ratio

on low value, growth portfolios. Both series in the figure obviously mean revert within a short period. Systematic factors lack the consistency in value required to make them useful for investors with a medium term horizon (Fig. 6.6).

These analyses may appear simple, but their illustration of the weak predictive power of lagged variables is consistent with results from more detailed studies. One, for instance, by Vanguard examined a dozen popular variables using US data during 1926–2012. Their test was the value of R-squared in a regression of each variable and the one-year ahead return: none was above 0.12 (Davis et al. 2012).

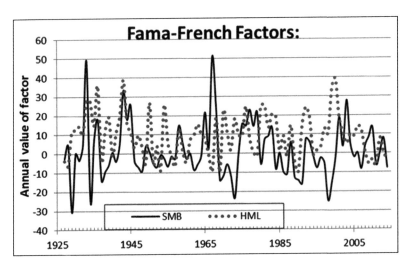

Fig. 6.6 Fama-French size and value factors

A similar study regressed monthly and yearly S&P 500 returns during 1948–2007 on 16 common predictors, and then used the parameters to predict return (Ferreira and Santa-Clara 2011). Values of R-squared lay in the range of −1.8 to 0.7%, and only four variables were significant at the 5 % level. Finally, of course, instability matches the well-recognised time variation in beta (Ferson and Harvey 1991).

The conclusion from analysing common relationships proposed as predictors of equity returns is that they are unstable in explanatory power, magnitude, and even sign. Whilst each may provide an interesting retrospective explanation of what seems to have *caused* returns, none has any practical ability to *predict* returns over investors' horizon.

6.4 Unpacking the Practical Value of Price-Sensitive Information

Probably the most common assumption amongst investment researchers and practitioners is that information is fundamental to equity valuations. As an example, Boudoukh et al. (2013) state: "A basic tenet of financial economics is that asset prices change in response to unexpected fundamental information". The centrality of this assumption to my topic of equity investment justifies examination of its merits.

6 Structure of Equity Prices   113

Consider first the nature of value-relevant information. It comes in four forms: observable, quantifiable data relating to macro factors in the economy and markets, and more granular data that is specific to firms including accounts, market transactions, and constructed variables such as price-to-book ratio and put:call ratio; news about a firm or its industry and broader environment; non-quantifiable data such as analyses, opinions and reports that interpret current conditions; and data relating to future conditions.

Another aspect of public information is that little of it fully reaches all investors at the same time: exceptions are limited to a few public events that are equally apparent to all observers, such as live telecasts of sporting contests. Every other piece of information must be prepared (such as economic data releases, or corporate announcements), or identified and reported (including shock events such as industrial accidents or CEO deaths). This means that – prior to being announced by the firm or reported by the media – virtually all price-sensitive information has been available privately (possibly to many people, including employees, customers, regulators, lawyers and other advisors), before it spreads to others along multiple pathways according to the immediacy of their data monitoring, and eventually becomes public. Even when events occur in public, preparation by humans can mean that the probable outcome is already known, either from prior trials (such as tests of new technologies), or as the result of an agreement (votes in board ballots).

Moreover, there is an unknowable volume of price sensitive private information never becomes public and only circulates within a limited pool of investors so that outsiders can only discover it indirectly by observing transactions. Examples include documents restricted to in-house use such as those prepared by a firm on its operations and strategy, and analyses by institutional investors. Other information may be of uncertain value (much opinion and private commentary seems closer to scripts prepared by bucket shops than the content of Warren Buffett's shareholder letters), or spread erratically through conversations, meetings and so on.

In short, price-sensitive information has multiple forms ranging from hard data on markets or firms to less substantial commentary or analysis. Moreover, it can be kept private for varying periods. Identifying information is complex, which is why astute investors seek out private price-sensitive information that is bartered by insider sources such as company executives (Barker 1998).

A second important question is what impact information has already had on equity valuations. This is obvious with scheduled data releases where prices move immediately, and virtually all abnormal return is earned in the first 15 minutes

114   Applied Investment Theory

(e.g. Greene and Watts 1996). For virtually all other information, though, there is typically a much less robust response. In the case of announcements of corporate results and strategies, for instance, equity prices typically take months or years to price in the full benefit (Chan 2003).

More broadly, doubts are common in the literature about the practical relevance of new public information because few announcements about valuation fundamentals bring any price reaction (Cutler et al. 1989). Literally thousands of event studies of news which should intuitively have significant permanent impact on stock prices (see: Corrado 2011) show that it usually brings a cumulative abnormal return of no more than a few percent that rarely lasts more than a day or two (Brown 2011). The small statistical signals of information's price impact soon disappear, even after a wide variety of unanticipated corporate shocks (Coleman 2011) and other surprising events (Brooks et al. 2003).

Another reason to be sceptical about the impact of new public information is that it usually cannot explain even the largest moves in equity prices. For example, a study of large jumps in the price of individual stocks during the 2000s (a one-minute return exceeding three standard deviations) found they typically occur in the absence of new public information (Bouchaud et al. 2009). A similar situation applies with indexes, and a study of the US S&P 500 futures contract between 1982 and 1999 identified 1,159 moves of greater than 0.75% within any five minutes (about seven standard deviations above average), but – after searching newswires at the time – found that 90% of the moves had no identifiable cause (Fair 2002). At least three quarters of significant price moves in indexes and individual stocks cannot be attributed to new information.

The obvious corollary is true, too, as few announcements of intuitively price-sensitive information bring significant price reaction. Thus a US study during 1941–1987 examined what the *World Almanac* described as "important world events" and which the *New York Times* ran as the lead story and noted a likely market impact. Examples included military engagements such as the Japanese bombing of Pearl Harbour, political events such as Presidential shootings, and legislative initiatives. Overall, they brought a trivial average absolute change in the S&P Index of just 0.6% (Cutler et al. 1989).

To summarise the findings above, information may intuitively be the driver of prices, but it is limited in availability and credibility, and cannot explain the largest moves in market indexes and individual share prices. Conversely, it is interesting that – while the *flow* of new public information does not move prices – the *stock* of information has relevance to valuation, so that historical data such as statutory accounts explain around a quarter of the cross-section in returns (Ferson and Harvey 1993).

This pattern has two explanations. First, even the most intuitively valuable innovation about any security is dwarfed by the stock of information already available. Thus significant, long-lived abnormal returns come only after true paradigm changes such as industry deregulation or similar 'Schumpeterian shocks' (Pettus et al. 2009), and to targets of changes in control such as acquisitions (Moeller et al. 2005). Second, much information is of uncertain value and requires understanding the mechanism(s) involved. No data points unequivocally to fundamental equity values, much less to future returns and their uncertainty: each must be interpreted, and conflicting conclusions reconciled. This takes time, during which obscure decision stimuli interact with other unobservable data to confound the effect of any single piece of information.

My own interviews with fund managers confirmed that they see little price-sensitive data in new information because of their large inventory that changes only slowly and swamps most 'news'. A London equity manager told me: "News is just noise. Most of it is already known and has no impact on price" (Coleman 2015). New public information has only transient and marginal impact on prices which are set by much broader influences. No matter how much information arrives, forward-looking materials remain subject to the same level of uncertainty about their execution and are exposed to instability in the environment, especially marketplace conditions.

6.5 Factor X: The Recurrence of Unknowable Events

A permanent feature of financial markets is event risk, or the recurrence of unknowable shocks. With this in mind, Don Stammer, a popular economist in Australia, talks about Factor X, or powerful market influences that had not even been considered a year earlier. Examples include sharp moves in equity markets and commodity prices, various currency slumps and spikes, the extent of corporate fraud in 2002 and 2007, 9–11 terrorist attacks and the Iraq invasion of Kuwait. Don points to high gains and losses associated with such shocks, and – because of their centrality to investor returns – canvasses possibilities in his forward-looking newspaper columns. His predictions have had varying degrees of success, but they perform a critical function in encouraging people to think about the impacts of seemingly improbable events.

This makes it interesting that a lot of notionally unknowable events are made to appear obvious in hindsight. One analysis entitled "Predictable Surprises: The disasters you should have seen coming, and how to prevent them" points

116   Applied Investment Theory

to shock events that were preceded by obvious indicators, including 9–11 terrorist attacks on the USA and Enron's collapse (Bazerman and Watkins 2004). The implication is that financial shocks can be predicted, and thus should be eliminated by central bank strictures, regulatory intervention, and other circuit breakers.

Predictability of Factor X finance events gains credence because many examples were clearly evident at the time. George Soros, for instance, is said to have made two fortunes by betting on the Deutschmark following German reunification in 1990, and betting against the pound sterling in 1992. A famous historical example is economist David Ricardo's purchase of heavily discounted British war bonds just before the Battle of Waterloo, which netted him a then staggering one million pounds.

None of these events was a thunderclap, and each was played out in full public view: literally anybody could have participated. The events were, however, unique, or at least extremely uncommon; and each required skill and foresight (plus independence of thought) to accurately anticipate the outcome. This is in stark contrast to many notionally unique events – such as elections or corporate acquisitions – which are merely variations on a regularly recurring theme and thus allow investors to build skill that can capture rent.

This points to three types of financial surprise. The first is typified by terrorist attacks: although each particular occurrence may be part of a high intensity, low frequency set of events, its nature and timing is not predictable in a meaningful sense. Investors need to factor in a generic disaster, and be alert to trading opportunities when they arise. The second type of surprise is one of a series of regular occurrences – whether corporate takeover or industrial disaster – which is individually unexpected, but has a typical outcome that can be traded. For instance, there is a rise over several days in the share price of most companies whose CEO dies suddenly (e.g. Salas 2010). The third type of financial surprise plays out over months in full sight, but has an uncertain time line and endpoint: return is contingent on events that have hard to predict outcomes.

These financial Factor X events fit neatly into the thick tailed distributions that are characteristic of financial markets. They provide regular opportunities (possibly annually if you believe Don Stammer) to make substantial gains. Success requires not only the courage of one's convictions but a degree of insight that is uncommon. Conversely, it can be hard to trade the outcomes of shock events because they have illiquid markets, arguably because few investors are comfortable dealing with such complexity.

In closing out on Factors X in finance, it is salient to note that they pose true Knightian uncertainty: it is not practical to develop even a rough distribution of outcomes, so fundamental value cannot be calculated. Rational investment is not feasible, and the concept of arbitrageurs pushing prices to fair value is moot. Because of the importance of this issue, we return to it later in discussion of investment education.

6.6   Conclusion

Analysis of equity returns in this chapter shows that they are not random, but subject to predictable behaviours based on prior return, date and time, and exogenous factors. The combination of involuntary influences and regular cycles and patterns can make prices partially deterministic, so that the structure of equity markets is relevant to fund manager conduct, or decisions. This explains use of heuristics ('sell in May and go away') and technical analysis.

Evidence indicates that equity returns are not symmetrical. Prices follow a sawtooth cycle with medium term periods of small upward moves punctuated by infrequent sharp falls to rest prices closer to fundamental value. This gives a negative skew to distribution of returns; and the left tail is thicker than the right tail. Moreover, bull markets rise faster and last longer than bear markets. Equity returns, then, appear biphasic.

Markets are also very efficient in processing information. Scheduled announcements are impounded in prices within seconds; even unexpected events that tend to occur in private (such as sudden CEO deaths) or out of media scrutiny (such as industrial accidents) are reflected in prices within a few trading hours, which is well before the first media release (Coleman 2011).

Efficient processing, though, does not mean that prices will always reflect ex post estimates of fundamental value. This is because of market shortcomings, especially the inability to ensure that all information is revealed. Because information asymmetry abounds, many investors avoid illiquid markets and expert counterparties. In addition, markets cannot ensure costless enforcement of contracts, so counterparty risk is a significant consideration for investors. Moreover, speculation has grown rapidly with emergence of huge derivatives markets, and their activity can trigger bubbles in prices that spill over into the real economy.

Just as speculation is not benign, equity markets are not passive conduits of investors' transactions. First, their operational features shape investor choices, and so – independent of fundamental supply-demand factors and hedonics – contribute to price determination. As an example, variations between markets in everything from trading hours to listing requirements are valued differently by different investors and this establishes a clientele effect. Markets can also affect

118   Applied Investment Theory

the conduct of intermediaries through attributes such as lack of information, illiquidity, and reputation. Thus markets have unique participants, such as counterparties with higher reliability or integrity that reduce uncertainty in the evaluation and purchase/sale of securities. As a result, it is not a surprise to find examples of multiple prices for securities across different, efficient markets.

Another important structural feature of markets is price momentum or trending, which can become self-fulfilling because less-informed investors interpret a price rise as resulting from buying by better informed investors, and so place a higher value on the security (e.g. Warther 1995), while others use technical trading rules, especially for short term investment decisions (Park and Irwin 2007). These strategies' Bayesian perspective establishes procyclical price patterns that make equities act as Veblen goods which have luxury features so that rising prices signal greater attraction for possible buyers that increases their preference and demand, and leads to an upward sloping demand curve. The opposite applies, of course, during periods of market decline. In addition, moves in equity prices systematically alter investors' wealth, which leads to changes in risk propensity and willingness to invest that alters the attractiveness of individual securities.

Although equity markets appear rich in data through their continuous provision of transactions' price and volume, they are frequently inexplicable because of high turnover and price volatility, formation and duration of trends and cycles, and sharp price changes. Moreover, they never stabilise, but seem to have multiple possible equilibria at any time. Thus a shock can knock a market out of equilibrium and into a higher or lower price level for hard to identify reasons, which is why jumps bring descriptions such as madness of crowds (Devenow and Welch 1996). This suggests an analogy with electrons inside an atom which move between orbits by giving up or receiving energy as photons.

Given that valuations reflect time-varying outcomes of unobservable choices by investors whose paradigm and decision stimuli are unknowable, it is not surprising to find that well-accepted valuation truisms can prove wanting.

One example is that findings which suggest lagged variables can predict equity returns actually have only limited ex post explanatory power, and many appear spurious (Lewellen et al. 2010; Harvey et al. 2014). The sign of market-level factors is often not stable for long, and statistically significant relationships have little economic merit or ex ante predictive capability (Ferreira and Santa-Clara 2011). Even ex post, over three quarters of the cross-section of equity returns cannot be explained by identifiable security and firm features (Ferreira et al. 2012). Moreover, little support comes from the advice of experts. In particular, economists' forecasts of macroeconomic and financial markets variables are often little better than those of naïve models (Fildes and Stekler 2002); and analysts and advisers who make recommendation on stock selection also have a weak record (Kothari 2001). This conclusion is consistent with widespread scepticism in the literature of return predictability, with authors such as Harvey et al. (2014) and Chan et al. (1998) concluding that most predictive variables are little better than random numbers.

An allied conclusion relates to the value of information, which standard investment methodologies assume drives equity prices. Empirical analyses, however, show that few announcements of intuitively price-sensitive information bring price reaction (e.g. Cutler et al. 1989), and 90% of major moves in markets and equity prices occur in the absence of information innovation (e.g. Fair 2002; Bouchaud et al. 2009). Moreover, studies of events that intuitively should permanently affect stock prices usually find that most bring cumulative abnormal return of no more than a few percent that rarely lasts more than a day or two (Brown 2011). Investor judgements, then, are based largely on unobservable information. Some of this could be re-interpretation of the large stock of existing information through building complex themes that take time and so are remote from observable information flows. Other information would be obtained privately.

This limited ability is consistent with the observation by Richard Roll (1988: 541) that "even with hindsight, the ability to explain stock market returns is modest", and his conclusion that "notoriously unpredictable" stock returns illustrate the immaturity of the science of financial economics. Because finance is all about the future, weak foresight undermines normative tools that evaluate investments. First, it becomes impractical to follow the common assumption that security prices represent the present value of future cash flows expected by the security holder, discounted at a rate set by alternative investments, adjusted to take into account relative risks. This style of valuation requires accurate projections of future cash flows and the appropriate cost of carry, neither of which is available.

Second, even the best forward-looking materials are subject to uncertainty: for instance, it is much easier to announce a new strategy than it is to implement one; and the environment is rarely stable. Forecasts of cash flows, yields and similar are invariably stymied by unexpected events, so that the most important influences on firm and security prices are unpredictable beyond a few weeks. It is a bit like driving in a thick fog using a GPS system: you are fairly confident that you know where you are, but you cannot see anything ahead, and are blind to crashes, obstacles on the road and other threats. We really know relatively little about markets' inner workings.

In closing, the obvious point about equity markets is the extent of price-insensitive, discretionary and time-varying human involvement. Transactions result from humans' buy and sell decisions, which reflect their liquidity, value estimate and trading strategy. Liquidity of funds and individuals is largely involuntary with stable mechanical drivers (such as regular savings) and non-linear sentiment influences. Value estimation is the outcome of complex naturalistic decisions with multiple stimuli, many of which trend or are under human control. The process is largely unobservable.

Moreover, equity returns feed back into decisions. First, they change investor wealth. Under Prospect Theory, risk propensity moves inversely with wealth; through the wealth effect, investment moves procyclically with wealth. Second, transactions data are the most frequent source of investment information and the most important for the insights they provide into other investors' thinking. Intuitively, one would expect that equity returns are not random, and should display patterns that reflect human control and reaction.

7

The Mutual Fund Industry: Structure and Conduct

> **The Key Takeaways of This Chapter Are**
>
> - The mutual fund industry has developed as a global oligopoly
> - Mutual funds' business model relies on commissions related to funds under management (FUM), so that fund managers do not have the sole, or perhaps even most important, goal of maximising return for clients.
> - Clients choose mutual funds for reputation and peace of mind as much as performance. Few investors react to subsequent performance
> - There is too much business risk for mutual funds to move far from the index or towards performance-based remuneration. Fund fees are typically unrelated to performance
> - Most observers of the industry are captives, and fund operations are opaque and characterised by information asymmetry. This leaves funds free to self-regulate
> - Funds can abuse the trust of their clients.

This chapter starts with a description of structural aspects of the mutual fund industry, which come from exogenous forces, the nature of the industry, and relatively stable features of funds. This establishes a framework that shapes the conduct of mutual fund managers, which is described in the next chapter.

© The Author(s) 2016
L. Coleman, *Applied Investment Theory*,
DOI 10.1007/978-3-319-43976-1_7

7.1 Exogenous Structural Forces on Mutual Funds

A powerful set of structural influences on mutual funds come from bodies outside the industry. The first is central banks whose common policy since 1990 of easy liquidity brought asset price inflation. This is memorialised as the Greenspan put (Miller et al. 2002), which reflects decisions by the US Federal Reserve to ratchet down interest rates following every tremor in equity markets and thus provide an effective floor to equity prices.

Another structural liquidity driver has been changes in the population profile as the baby boomer cohort initially brought a wave of inflation, which was followed after the early 1990s by a decline in bond rates that reduced yields on financial assets (see Sect. 6.2). Other trends that impact equity prices include globalisation of markets and reduced restrictions on trade and investment flows, which bring co-ordinated inflation and increased co-movement of asset prices, even for those that are not tradeable such as housing (Agénor 2003). This has been accompanied by systemic weaknesses in regulatory and governance frameworks that – since the 1980s – have brought widespread market and corporate collapse on a roughly seven year cycle (Coleman 2014b).

Legislators are the second exogenous body with influence on the managed investments industry, and have imposed direct restraints which – until recent years – included bans on performance-based fees for mutual funds (Alpert et al. 2015: 21). Other common restrictions prevent mutual funds from incorporating leverage in their portfolios, short selling assets, and investing in assets below investment grade rating (Golec 2003).

Securities regulation and equity market listing rules are also influential because of their onerous reporting requirements. For example, the US SEC regulation FD ('Fair Disclosure') extends the concept of firms' continuous disclosure to require that investors have equal access to price-sensitive data. Such policies render most information a public good, which forces fund managers to take innovative measures to secure insights that given them an investment advantage.

Another impact of legislation is that – across finance – it actively promotes moral hazard, which induces higher risks in firms and investors than they would take if left alone. Moral hazard is seen in easy liquidity that encourages greater investment in equities and other risky assets, the propensity of governments to bail out mismanaged financial institutions that promotes corporate risk-taking, and the cavalier attitude of exchange operators who will suspend or even over-ride legal transactions and reverse large gains or losses by investors.

7 The Mutual Fund Industry: Structure and Conduct 123

A contributor to moral hazard by mutual funds is the poor record of punishing illegal behaviour by corporations' executives. For instance, although more than 270 US companies with assets in excess of $1 billion went bankrupt between 1980 and 2006, not a single director was prosecuted for breach of their duties (Black et al. 2006). Similarly, illegal insider trading by investors seems common, and is on a detectable scale in a third of large UK and US acquisitions (Morgenson 2006). Despite that, the US Securities and Exchange Commission (SEC) files just 50 charges each year for insider trading.[1]

Other external influences on mutual funds come from rating agencies such as Lipper and Morningstar because their reports are relied upon by financial advisors who prefer to base their advice on objective performance measures (Jones et al. 2005). Ratings agencies can be loss averse and intolerant of idiosyncracity, which promotes conformance in the data and techniques that fund managers use, and can limit innovation. Another important set of industry stakeholders are consultants such as Russell and Towers Watson, which play an influential role as gatekeepers to funds' large clients.

7.2 Structural Features of the Managed Investment Industry

Within the managed investment industry, structural features are important influences on the conduct of mutual funds.

The industry's principal structural feature can be traced to government promotion of retirement savings in most developed economies. Because people contract out services where they lack the requisite skill and confidence such as care of their cars and health, most savers invest with managed funds. Thus their growth has been rapid, for example managed investments in Australia have increased at an annual rate of 12% (ATC 2010).

The mutual funds sector is now huge. In 2014, there were 80,000 separate mutual funds around the world which held FUM totalling $US31 trillion. About 85% of funds and their FUM are domiciled in just a few countries, principally the United States ($16 trillion), Luxembourg ($3.2), Australia ($1.6), Ireland ($1.5), France ($1.4), and United Kingdom, Brazil and Canada (each with just over $1 trillion) (ICI 2015: tables 65–66). Roughly 85% of mutual funds are actively managed (Morningstar 2012).

Despite strong historical growth, most managed funds come from mandated or tax-incentivised retirement savings, and – because virtually

---

[1] See: www.sec.gov/news/testimony/2011/ts120111rsk.htm.

124   Applied Investment Theory

all taxpayers and employees are now savers – future growth is limited to the number of investors and the size of their income, which are both slow in developed economies. FUM stagnation is placing pressures on mutual funds' profits.

In the United States the proportion of listed shares that is held by mutual funds has risen from 5.0% in 1985 to 20.4%, which ranks them third after households and private pension funds in the holdings of 17 investor categories (Board of Governors of Federal Reserve System 2014: table L213). Similar developments occurred in other developed economies, and mutual fund ownership of equities is above 30% in Britain, Canada, France, Norway, and elsewhere (Aggarwal et al. 2011). Given that other financial institutions (banks, insurance companies, ETFs and so on) also have large share holdings, the majority of equity investors have changed since the 1970s from individuals to highly trained, well-motivated institutional investors competing in a global oligopoly.

Despite its size, the managed funds industry displays many of the hallmarks of an oligopoly. First, it is very concentrated: in the United States, a study by *Barron's* (2015) identified 65 mutual fund families, of which the top five held 57% of total assets under management. Concentration is similar in Australia, where there are 131 investment management firms, but the top five share 40% of the market (ATC 2010). There are also large fund complexes in other major economies such as Austria, Canada, Germany, and the U.K, so that the five largest portfolio managers hold about half the market in most countries (Ferreira and Ramos 2009).

It is not only funds' market share that is concentrated, but also their location. Money managers tend to cluster in a handful of cities led by London and New York, where there and elsewhere they laager in financial enclaves. As if to emphasise their conformance, most mutual funds occupy impressive buildings with similar open foyers, cloned security processes, and be-flowered meeting rooms with dewy carafes of iced water, good coffee, and – especially in New York and Pacific Rim financial hubs – outstanding views.

The most important consequence of the oligopolistic nature of mutual funds is that no fund can control the industry, while each is exposed to impact from competitors. This intensifies the importance of credibly signalling non-price factors such as skill and reliability, and of closely monitoring competitors to detect emergence of possibly damaging strategies. This should be seen as a backdrop to dynamism in funds and fund managers: the ten-year survivorship rate of mutual funds is about 65% (Bu and Lacey 2007); and the average manager's tenure is under five years (Tuckett and Taffler 2012).

7 The Mutual Fund Industry: Structure and Conduct   125

Funds' oligopoly establishes other strong points of alignment, such as producing all but identical products, which innovate at glacial pace. There are also high barriers to entering the industry because of onerous government licensing requirements, including financial capacity; and the importance of reputation, which makes it hard for outsiders to gain traction.

An interesting structural feature of the managed funds industry is that – like banking and other finance sectors – it suffers little external scrutiny. This was noticeable during the 2008 Global Financial Crisis when newspapers, airwaves and government lobbies were filled with the opinions and prescriptions of bank economists who were firm that only government bail outs could prevent meltdown of the financial system. Industry groups and independent think tanks were silent, regulators floundered, and no more than a handful of academics made meaningful input to discussion on appropriate policy responses. Few asked why representatives of those who had caused the GFC had such a stranglehold on interpreting it, and whether their recommended solutions that favoured banks were credible. The only exception I could find is a paper by New Zealand academic Todd Bridgman (2010) who summarised his opinion in the title: 'Laughing all the way to the bank: How New Zealand's banks dominated public debate on the Global Financial Crisis and why it matters'.

Another structural aspect of the mutual fund industry is that the intuitively obvious assumption that fund investors seek highest risk-adjusted return may be overly simplistic. Most savers who lack the skill or confidence to manage their investments hand them over to experts, and their most important criteria in selecting a fund manager are subjective, including trust and investment manager attributes (Foster and Warren 2015), as well as measureable traits such as performance track record, reputation and number of funds in the family (Capon et al. 1996). The importance of trust and reputation to fund choice reflects investor concern over security of their investments (or avoidance of downside risk due to governance issues), and matches one fund manager's comment to me that investors are 'buying peace of mind'.

Even for the minority of clients with an interest in management of their savings, information asymmetry obscures the quality of investment management, and most funds are so opaque that their activities are virtually impossible to monitor (Mehran and Stulz 2007). In addition, fund clients tend to be disengaged from management of their retirement savings, so that a four year study of retirement accounts held by a panel of 7,000 US investors found that over 87% of participants did not adjust their balance or trade (Agnew et al. 2003). This limited interest presumably arises because most contributions are involuntary from either employer contributions or government mandate. Overall, investments are 'sticky', and only withdrawn from the worst performing funds (Del Guercio and Tkac 2002). Industry opacity and uninterested clients leave mutual funds essentially free to self-regulate, and they are limited only by voluntary constraints (Almazan et al. 2004).

Finally, in keeping with a typical oligopoly, the investment sector has proved highly profitable. A global survey by the Boston Consulting Group found that asset managers' profits are around 40% of net revenues and concluded that "asset management continues to rank among the most profitable industries" (BCG 2015). This is consistent with data for the United States where the finance industry accrues a third of profits made by all domestic companies even though it only generates 20% of GDP (Bureau of Economic Analysis: www.bea.gov).

7.3   Mutual Fund Conduct

The conduct of mutual funds is shaped by two structural features of their industry noted above: it operates as a typical oligopoly; and competition is built mostly around reputation, process and investment strategy rather than price and performance (Golec 2003).

In their oligopoly, funds avoid price-based competition, develop strategy in light of competitors' activities, and find it risky to diverge from the industry norm. This not only promotes convergence of processes, but also co-location of funds which spawns extensive social networks between investment managers, corporate executives, advisers such as sell-side brokers, ratings agencies, regulators, and other observers. These multiple drivers lead to a variety of game-theoretic behaviours by intelligent, rational fund executives that revolve around competition and signalling, conflict and cooperation.

Another feature of mutual funds' conduct is the extent to which they are poorly managed. Many mutual funds are run like mini kingdoms, with tolerance of non-performing staff, constant interchange of kickbacks with suppliers and clients, and total disdain for clients (Goldman Sachs executives called them 'muppets': see Smith 2012: 296). Perhaps this reflects the quip by Sir John Hicks (1935) that "the best of all monopoly profits is a quiet life".

An interesting question about mutual funds' business model is why they don't compete around performance. Even though performance-based fees are legal everywhere except China, India and Korea (although some countries, including the United States, require them to be symmetrical, with penalties for underperformance), they are "exceedingly rare" in the US and uncommon elsewhere (Alpert et al. 2015: 21). Certainly funds voluntarily participate in performance tables that are compiled by Lipper, Morningstar and similar third parties wherever mutual funds operate; but this is largely because ranking in tables is important to financial advisors who are used by a majority of investors and prefer to base their advice on objective measures (Jones et al. 2005). Otherwise, funds downplay performance.

The principal barrier to performance-based fees is the difficulty that most funds have in replicating performance (Carhart 1997), and so switching fees to a share of relative out-performance would bring two problems. First it leaves mutual fund revenues open to random fluctuation because market moves are unpredictable and returns cannot be managed. This would frequently pose a serious quandary given that equity market returns are negative during at least one year in three.[2] Second, an emphasis on performance (which would become inevitable if that became the basis of competition between funds) would highlight mutual funds' poor returns and encourage investor interest, which would probably bring unwanted attention for most actively managed funds.

Mutual funds' reliance on FUM-based fees ties their income to scale, which is doubly important because cost structure is similar funds across funds, irrespective of FUM. This raises a concern for investors that funds' commercial imperative to grow FUM might motivate fund managers to build funds under management (which determine their employer's income) at the expense of fund performance (which is investors' reward) (e.g. Brown et al. 2001). Some funds exacerbate this agency conflict by linking employee compensation to capital inflows, which can divert fund managers' focus towards promotion of investment processes (e.g. Brown et al. 2001). Thus fund managers may allocate effort to pursue FUM though client meetings, preparing reports on investments, and attendance at conferences. Other unwanted responses from inappropriate FUM-based incentives for fund managers are growth of FUM beyond a level that can produce optimum return, and a level of investment risk that may not be optimised because of a tendency to either bank good results early or take on greater risk after poor results in an effort to recover ground (Clare et al. 2014). Funds can also cater to non-investor clienteles, for instance by selecting securities that favour service providers and investee firms, or assisting institutions to issue securities.[3] At the extreme, managers literally bet the firm, as evidenced by collapse of Bear Stearns, Lehman Brothers and Merrill Lynch in 2008 (see, for instance, McLean and Nocera 2010).

---

[2] During the 16 years since 2000, the year-end close of the US S&P 500 was below its prior year value at the end of six years: 2000, 2001, 2002, 2008, 2011, and 2015.

[3] These groups may provide soft commissions through equipment such as information terminals and risk management systems, free research materials, or kickbacks in exchange for business. By one estimate, the resulting costs annually exceed one per cent of funds under management (Steil 2004).

128   Applied Investment Theory

As a result of agency conflicts, performance optimisation is not necessarily the sole, or even principal, objective of fund managers, despite its importance to clients. The last facilitate fund managers' possibly damaging conduct by being disengaged from funds' process and performance. Agency issues arise from fund managers' typically broad discretion over investment decisions, and because of moral hazard arising out of the industry's structure, opacity of fund activities, and disengagement of clients (Mahoney 2004).

One strategy adopted by funds to manage this complex set of potential agency conflicts is to compensate managers for performance of funds under their management relative to an index (Ma et al. 2013). This, though, is generally limited to a relatively small part of total compensation, so that only a third of fund managers report that results relative to a benchmark have 'a lot of impact' on their bonus (Farnsworth and Taylor 2006). Research into motivations that arise from the mix of fund managers' compensation is still skimpy, but the limited importance of option-like payoffs linked to performance of funds under management is consistent with conclusions from studies of executive compensation which suggest that excessive risk can accompany potentially lucrative performance inducements (Feng et al. 2011). Fund managers are also subject to the formal procedures and controls common to financial organizations, and most protect their human capital by acting as stewards and working to optimise value for investors (Tosi et al. 2003).

The best funds acknowledge that success depends on their social licence to operate, and shore it up through a responsible, comprehensive approach to address concerns that they may not act as unconditional value maximizers or may ignore preferences of investors (Athanassakos 1992). Funds will self-select into low cost ways of signalling their favourable return and risk prospects by upgrading the quality of their communication and reporting. They enhance governance through adoption of style labels and appointing fund managers with external characteristics that build investor confidence such as education, experience and appearance. This explains why most fund managers hold Chartered Financial Analyst (CFA) accreditation, which signals investment competence and reliability, and thus helps clients offset information asymmetry and avoid the lemons problem (Riley 1975).

Funds also mitigate risks by voluntarily constraining their investment strategy to prevent borrowing, short positions or derivatives (Almazan et al. 2004). Funds will avoid investing in companies with attributes that proxy for uncertain strategies through ethical and similar investment criteria; and avoid firms with business models that incorporate threats to sustainability of society, the environment or the economy, including markets. This extends to positive signals of social responsibility against environmental, social and governance criteria (ESG) and other corporate social responsibility (CSR) measures, and led to development of the United Nations Principles for Responsible Investment (www.unpri.org).

Voluntary constraints are more pronounced in funds that have fewer monitoring mechanisms embedded in their governance structure such as not being part of a large family (which facilitates peer monitoring), and having fewer independent directors. Serendipitously, constraints that serve as substitutes for monitoring do not adversely affect performance (Almazan et al. 2004).

Finally, funds have a preference to self-limit their property rights and remain passive in relation to investee firms, which explains why institutional shareholding is not related to firm performance (e.g. Bhagat et al. 2004). However, they monitor investee firm performance, and – if it drops below the industry average – will use their influence to reduce firm free cash (Coleman 2014a).

7.4 Conclusion

Consistent with the SCP paradigm, structural features of funds' industry discourage them from competing on price, and structural features of markets discourage them from competing on performance.

The mutual fund industry is a true global oligopoly, where a handful of large families control between a third and half the market in most countries and sell near identical products. Funds are essentially free to self-regulate because clients show little interest in management of their savings. Typical of an oligopoly, funds avoid competing on the basis of price; and – because their performance is not replicable – only rarely offer performance-based fees.

Revenue is largely from fees as a proportion of funds under management, which sets up strong agency conflict between mutual funds whose imperative is growth in FUM and clients whose objectives are security of funds and optimised performance. Mutual funds expend considerable effort on mitigating agency conflicts, but many practices prove inimical to investor interests.

8

Fund Managers' Conduct: The Story of How They Invest

> **The Key Takeaways of This Chapter Are**
>
> - Structural features of markets and the funds management industry determine fund manager (FM) conduct, including: market attributes, configuration of the funds management industry, prevalence of moral hazard and agency issues, and state of the economy
> - Empirical evidence shows that investors cannot meaningfully predict financial inputs to standard valuation models, and few rely solely on them.
> - FMs follow an intuitive modelling process according to macro themes within their own unique paradigm. The most important information is privately sourced, and search for it supports the industry's extensive socialisation.
> - Fund managers assume that equity values are contingent on state of the world; and see risk as uncertainty and possible loss in value.
> - Fund managers' utility functions incorporate historical security price, and hedonic features of the security and its market.
> - FMs look to the current cross-section of equity values rather than expected return, and rank alternatives in light of opportunity cost by combining information available at the time.
> - Fund managers are strongly influenced by colleagues, competitors, clients and others so that their investment decisions arise at least in part as a social construct.

© The Author(s) 2016
L. Coleman, *Applied Investment Theory,*
DOI 10.1007/978-3-319-43976-1_8

131

132   Applied Investment Theory

The objective of this book is to re-engineer the existing investment paradigm to better match investor behaviour and thus improve understanding of investment practices, particularly those of mutual fund managers. The starting point has been to describe the existing neoclassical investment paradigm, and then amass real-world evidence. This chapter presents what is known with empirical certainty about the investment process followed by fund managers. I experimented with several formats to find the best way to present the large volume of information, and settled on the obvious linear depiction with theoretical support.

An important caveat in the following discussion is that we really know relatively little about investment processes. Although equity prices axiomatically result from equilibrium between marginal supply and demand, it is difficult to unravel determinants of these transactions, and how they reconcile valuations of buyers and sellers. Moreover, as already noted, even retrospective analyses explain less than a quarter of the cross section of equity returns, and most large moves in equity prices and indexes occur without apparent justification. This mirrors opacity in determinants of individual trades where the personal characteristics, holdings and trading activity of investors and firm attributes explain less than about a quarter of transactions. Gaps yawn in every depiction of fund manager investing and much of the basis of security prices can only be inferred.

8.1   Fund Manager (FM) Decision Making

Fund managers share many similarities because they are overwhelmingly male (85+%), invariably university educated, often with a finance specialty or CFA accreditation (40+%), aged around 40 with at least 10 years industry experience across several firms, and work 50+ hours per week.[1] It is not a surprise, then, to find limited heterogeneity in fund managers' investment decisions.

The psychology and personal characteristics of fund managers shape their conduct. Most are confident, and also experienced, well-trained, well-resourced and motivated. Understandably, they rebuff a cookbook style of valuation which leaves limited room for personal skill, in favour of personalised investment models that require judgement and reinforce the value of their human capital (Chevalier and Ellison 1999). This fits within the tournament literature because fund managers work in a competitive setting (Schwarz 2011).

---

[1] For demographic profiles of fund managers, see, amongst others: Beckmann et al. (2008), Brown et al. (2014), Drachter et al. (2007), Farnsworth and Taylor (2006), and Tuckett and Taffler (2012).

8 Fund Managers' Conduct: The Story of How They Invest   133

The intuitively reasonable expectation that fund managers behave rationally does not mean that their decision making is always demonstrably scientific. Structural aspects of markets render the investment outlook largely uncertain, and not amenable to quantification. The environment FMs face is a complicated, ill-understood mix of secular and industry forces, market microstructure, industry pressures and their employers' strategy. Fund managers assume that equity value is shaped by time-varying systemic factors including technology, politics, economics, financial conditions and behaviour of other markets, and so is contingent on conditions at the time of sale.[2] The multiple non-linear determinants of security prices mean investors cannot make economically meaningful predictions of variables that normative valuation models require, and so cannot use them.

Obviously, too, investment decisions can only be made using information available at the time, and are subject to bounding. In fact, restrictions on the quality and flow of information in even the most efficient markets mean that news is not instantly obvious to all investors nor equally shared between them, and so most fund managers assume that shares are not fairly valued (Arnswald 2001). They seek to identify and capitalise on information asymmetries, of which the most important are between the buyers and issuer of securities, and between market insiders (traders, and those supplying services to investors such as banks and investment funds) and outsiders.

Investment is characterised by weighty stresses and cognitive constraints, which makes it typical of complex naturalistic decision making. Here information is ambiguous, and success depends on judgment, which forces simplification of decisions and promotes use of experience-based mental models that are rich in heuristics and stories that reflect personalized prejudgments (Kahneman 2011). This is exactly what is observed in fund managers (Tuckett and Taffler 2012), who structure the investment process by developing a paradigm that sets out assumptions on the determinants of equity valuations (Bodie et al. 2011). A drawback of using stories and heuristics as decision tools is that their coarse editing of prospects is a common source of systematic biases (Kahneman and Tversky 1979). In addition, fund managers will follow the practice applied in their other decisions and incorporate non-economic considerations.

8.1.1 Fund Managers' Valuation Paradigm

Fund managers typically begin the investment process by populating their paradigm with assumptions and expectations about the global economy

---

[2] It is sometimes suggested that security returns comprise a chaotic system (e.g. Hsieh 1991), which is a common depiction of many natural and man-made systems. The evidence for this, however, is weak (Barnett and Serletis 2000).

134   Applied Investment Theory

and political situation to build a macro view (Bodie et al. 2011). This experience-based mental model is usually a narrative, or set of linked stories, that identifies investment themes and indicators of superior return (e.g. Olsen 2002). The tops down perspective describes how industries and sectors will play out, identifies proxies for future return and uncertainty, and details value-relevant measures and heuristics that can identify and help edit prospects. It is an intuitive modelling process that applies fund managers' unique paradigm to process an eclectic mix of publicly available information, insights gained from company visits, and anecdotes gleaned from their network of industry experts, company insiders and colleagues.

Tops down or thematic investing has much in common with scenario planning, which tells stories of the future that describe developments, milestones and expected occurrences (Ringland 1998). The net is to link investment outlooks to a small number of personalized value drivers, which simplifies the process of eliminating inferior opportunities, reduces alternatives to a meaningful number in promising areas, and provides focus for monitoring decisions.

Within their themes, investors document a conforming thesis for each investment that links to their personalized value drivers, and simplifies the process of eliminating inferior opportunities. It starts with observable variables such as historical cash flows or price-to-earnings ratio, which are then adjusted to future values. Also, investors face bounding because their resources are limited and it is not practical to analyse all the available data and every factor driving returns (Chap. 6 indicated up to 300). This encourages them to edit prospects using heuristics, which do not require forecasts and simplify the process. The best reliably signal high future returns, and – to reduce the possibility of loss – low uncertainty. Fund managers also seek advantage through proprietary information by searching for qualitative data across their social networks.

This is fundamental valuation, which Kothari (2001) describes as "the use of information in current and past financial statements, in conjunction with industry and macroeconomic data to arrive at a firm's intrinsic value … [which is] the guiding principle of most mutual fund managers." The process also serves as a powerful tool to communicate investment rationales and strategy to colleagues and clients as a seamless set of consistent expectations within a convincing argument. And construction of an impressive investment narrative highlights fund managers' skill and intuition and enhances their hard-to-replicate human capital.

As fund managers work through the investment process, they think of share values in terms of their price (rather than return) (Hellman 2000) that is contingent on state of the world (Arrow 1964). They also tailor investment techniques by horizon. Over the short term, perhaps a few days, historical returns are used for prediction: technical analysis is useful. Over the medium term, months to a year or two, trends form and prices move monotonically, although patterns' formation and dissolution have no theoretical basis and cannot be predicted. Over horizons beyond a business or market cycle, security prices mean revert and can be explained using value measures such as dividend yield (Cochrane 2008). At best, FMs think in terms of a roughly two year terminal value, possibly constructed by truncating the future to the reasonably foreseeable next year and a serially-related subsequent year (Hellman 2000).

The following figure provides a schematic depiction of fundamental determinants of share price (Fig. 8.1).

The price of a share is based on the firm's relatively stable inherent value, which is a function of historical and projected cash flows, and can be tested by relative valuation. This is overlain by more fluid factors such as actions of competitors, and changes in perception of value and uncertainty; and is then priced in accord with prevailing market and financial factors. The implication is that economics, investor sentiment and systematic variables drive value (Chen, Da and Zhao 2013).

This depiction is consistent with the structure-conduct-performance paradigm: structure lies in markets' institutional arrangements and firms' culture that drive decisions over the long term; conduct varies between decisions in response to more transient news and judgements with varying influence on investor perceptions and market valuations; which all lead to financial performance of the firm.

Within the firm, non-human influences arise from its assets (size, composition and location), structure (both capital and organisational), and operations (technology and organisation); while organic influences include strategy, governance, knowledge and culture. Investors also use proxies for

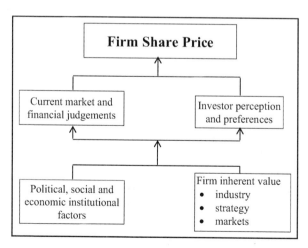

Fig. 8.1 Model of a firm's share price

136   Applied Investment Theory

high return and/or low uncertainty to indicate fundamental value such as ratios of price to free cash flow and to book value. Other investment criteria relate to the firm's probability of survival under adverse conditions as evidenced by fixed cost measures such as ratio of EBITDA to external liabilities, and its competitiveness as indicated by better than industry median costs, productivity and other operational measures. Finally, investors expect that factors such as business model and management quality proxy for firm performance (both high returns and low risk).

While valuing equities using these measures requires skill and judgement, each is readily observable and they provide an alternative to DCF techniques that require reliable forecasts of hard-to-predict future cash flows and financial conditions. The fact that qualitative data can sometimes seem to dominate theoretical approaches led Treynor and Black (1973: 66) to observe that the typical product of a security analyst is "subjective, judgmental work", which leads to laments along the lines that "we as a profession [may] have overestimated the rationality of investors" (Elton et al. 2004: 262).

Financial decisions are not the only ones that investors make, and their investment process will incorporate techniques used in non-financial transactions. Most purchases – whether for a car, house, or ingredients for dinner – arise because of a need, and available choices are narrowed according to their hedonics (Ford or Porsche?) and price: few incorporate calculations of intrinsic value through detailed financial analysis. This is true even in settings that are similar to markets with strong competition (think of the metres-high price boards outside retail petrol outlets), or many buyers and sellers (e.g. eBay or Airbnb). Thus it is not surprising to see that equity supply and demand respond not just to economically rational parameters, but also to qualitative financial attributes and qualitative and quantitative non-financial information.

Apart from endogenous influences, fund managers need to meet expectations of large clients, which reflect stakeholder objectives and help bolster funds' social licence to operate. Thus funds adopt a moral compass, and voluntarily constrain their investment universe to exclude companies with uncertain strategies such as excessive leverage or a dangerous technology, or which exhibit behaviour that might damage the reputation of their firm. Many influential clients have embraced sustainable or socially responsible investing (SRI) and impose more specific requirements in relation to environmental, social and governance criteria (ESG) and other corporate social responsibility (CSR) measures.

Although SRI is usually depicted as a philosophical objective or contributor to psychic shareholder reward, it is rational when it favours firms with low risk business models and strategies that avoid value destruction, or provides insurance against loss by preferring firms that promote good will amongst stakeholders (see: Godfrey et al. 2009). As an example of value-adding SRI, Generation Investment Management is a London based LLP with about $US3 billion in FUM, which makes sustainability issues central to investment selection in the expectation that this will force a long term view that delivers superior risk-adjusted return (www.generationim.com).

SRI is consistent with the conclusion in Chap. 4 that sustainability and governance seem positively related to financial performance, although the effect is uncertain and of varying size. Its financial implications justify funds in accepting the real and opportunity costs of voluntarily going beyond compliance, and counters criticism of uncosted investment that aspires to meet social responsibilities (e.g. Friedman 1970).

8.1.2 Fund Managers Share Common Information and Analytical Techniques

Once fund managers establish an overall strategy, portfolios must be populated from the bottom up with favourably priced securities by overlaying historical data with qualitative judgements about key components of future financial performance. This requires superior information and insights about investee firms.

In practice, though, it is difficult to obtain superior information because contemporary corporate governance and securities regulation require that firms provide investors with equal access to data. Moreover, insights are complicated because most information is non-standardized and unprocessed, and must be interpreted, and conflicting conclusions reconciled. The number of employees and book value of assets, for instance, are accurately reported by firms but tell little about how they are deployed, or how their capability compares with that of competitor firms. More granular measures of performance such as product quality, safety and equipment reliability are not normally made public and so must be inferred. It has become increasingly important to understand measures of varying quality and intangibles given their growing importance to valuations.

Although fund manager outperformance is expected to come through superior evaluation of data, no information points unequivocally to current security values, much less to future returns and their uncertainty. Thus fund managers continually seek ways to enhance data's uncertain quality. Some follow public investment signals: about half grant a price premium to socially responsible companies (Luo et al. 2015); and many use sell-side analysts' reports to direct their own analyses (Frey and Herbst 2014).

Overall, there is reason to doubt FM's practical ability to obtain information advantage as – given requirements for fair disclosure – most corporate

138 **Applied Investment Theory**

information is available to any interested investor, and managers probably have few truly proprietary sources of information. There is similarly limited variety to be found in the analytical techniques available to fund managers, which contributes to one of their industry's most striking features which is the sameness of strategy: most equity managers describe their own strategy as little more than buying well-run companies with a good business model at a price below their fair value (Coleman 2015).

8.2 The Role of Prices in Investor Utility Functions

As discussed in Sect. 6.4, intuitively price sensitive information has a low rate of innovation, whilst FMs need to regularly update expectations. They achieve this through observing market transactions whose price and volume provide all but continuous data.

Transactions are important to FM valuation because non-public data and analysis are not evenly shared, and so prices can signal superior skill or information about either the state of the world or firm cash flows. A trend in the price vector (rate and direction of price change) can follow unfolding secular influences, or slow adjustment to regime shifts. A price trend can also warn of the onset of one of the financial crises that sweep in with little warning every seven or so years, wreak their havoc like some meso-American religion that kills its followers, and then move off quietly as if satisfied. Thus equity price can indicate the arrival of unseen value-sensitive data, point to expectational errors where valuations have become biased away from good forecasts, indicate other investors' better knowledge, and warn if an investor's paradigm or information base has become less relevant (Baker and Wurgler 2006).

Another role of price is to serve as a point of reference against historical highs and lows, and to convey insights into return in absolute terms and against the market. Investors can add value over the medium term by optimally timing their purchase through price-based heuristics such as historical highs and lows. For those expecting a trending framework, current price indicates future direction. Thus price indicates the extent to which the market has already incorporated investors' insights: for instance, a substantial recent rise to the top of its historical range indicates limited upside potential.

Another way that investors incorporate transactions data in their utility function is through technical analysis. A study of fund managers across five countries found that the vast majority use technical analysis or some form of charting based on historical prices to predict future prices. For decisions with horizons up to a month, it is the most important form of investment analysis

(Menkhoff 2010). This is confirmed by fund managers that I have spoken to, with one admitting he did not believe in technical analysis before starting to manage money, but has since learned that he cannot ignore it.

A structural feature of equity prices which encourages technical analysis is their roughly lognormal distribution. This explains trading using Fibonacci numbers which have an exponential structure where each is the sum of its two predecessors, giving a sequence of: 0, 1, 1, 2, 3, 5, 8, 13, ... , $n_{x-1} + n_{x-2}$, ... A typical 'rule' expects reversal of a downward trend after a fall of 61.8% from a high, which is consistent with mean reversion of lognormally distributed prices where over 80% of values fall within 62% of the top of the range. Another contributor to use of technical analysis is that equity prices trend over the medium term, which encourages momentum trading. This, too, is rational given that economically significant returns (10–30 bp per week) come from momentum trading in stock market indexes (Chan et al. 2000).

Fund managers will also use mean reversion to construct seemingly crude anti-cyclical heuristics. When facing the need to liquidate some securities, they will sell winners and hold losers because they are expected, respectively, to drop and rise on reversion to the mean (e.g. Da Costa Jr. et al. 2008). This last explains the disposition effect, although it is more commonly attributed to loss-averse investors' preference to avoid crystalizing a loss (e.g. Shefrin and Statman 1985).

Mean reversion also sees FMs overload on well-priced securities at the bottom of their historical range, trim holdings after a run up in prices, and take profits around historical highs (Beckmann et al. 2008). Fund managers also trade around the extremes of dimensionless measures that do not have an absolute scale or unit of measurement, but mean revert within a range, which explains use of the classic valuation measures, particularly ratios of stock price-to-book value, price-to-earnings and price-to-dividends.

It is not just fund managers who trade around price bounds. Historical highs are a significant influence on timing of sales by individual investors (Grinblatt and Keloharju 2001). Sophisticated investors behave similarly, as shown by the price where executives exercise employee stock options (Heath et al. 1999) and offer prices in acquisitions (Baker et al. 2012), both of which cluster around stocks' highest price in the previous 52-weeks. That is, the best estimate of fundamental value of a firm by those who know most about it – its executives and potential acquirers – is the recent price high.

Fund managers' scrutiny of transactions data for signs of better informed investors is a staple of Bayesian decision making, which can trigger reflexive responses that have complex non-linear impacts with different effects across time. Reliance on price signals for investment decisions is another rational response to patterns in prices that are a structural feature of equity markets, despite the managed fund industry's typical fine print warning against doing so.

8.2.1 Using Proxies to Rank Relative Valuations of Equities

Structural features of markets mean that investors cannot make economically meaningful forecasts of future equity performance, which directs fund managers away from expectations and towards equities' current prices, particularly relative to alternatives (Hellman 2000). Thus FMs consider the cross-section of prices of possible investments, and think of fair value in terms of their opportunity cost: buying one means holding less of another.

Fund managers rank candidate investments using proxies for firms' performance or uncertainty. Those indicative of future performance include: value measures such as ratios of price to book or cash flow, trends in performance and industry growth, and signals of managers' ability to increase cash flow (such as qualifications and skill).

In terms of proxies for uncertainty, FMs' principal focus is endogenous to the firm. It reflects concern at operational shortcomings that destroy value, and failure of the firm's strategic initiatives to improve cash flows. These are best proxied by historical performance and reliability, including: poor reputation and governance; past unreliability evidenced by surprises and failure to meet objectives; high operational and financial leverage; and risky business models or technologies. Given the poor record of managers' decisions (see Sect. 4.3), restrictions on their strategic opportunities serve as inverse measures of uncertainty. Relevant proxies include scale (large size imposes inertia), slow industry growth (with few opportunities), good governance (which prevent management entrenchment), and sustainable or ethical performance criteria.

Thus investors develop estimates of relative value from historical data, hedonic features of the security, and market conditions. Cohesive application of these indicators leads to preference for firms that rank well against proxies for good strategy such as reputation and governance.

8.3 Socialisation of Investment Decisions

A consistent feature of oligopolistic industries is that firm behaviours are conditioned by the actions of competitors and other industry stakeholders, which leads to convergence of organisational structures, business models and operational processes. The most prominent behaviour that this brings to investment management is fund managers' extensive socialisation with competitors, executives of investee firms, ratings agencies, advisers such as sell-side brokers, and – less frequently – clients. Fund managers build a social economy of institutions and

8 Fund Managers' Conduct: The Story of How They Invest

communications channels that are formal through meetings and conferences, less formal as co-location in a handful of cities led by London and New York and in recognised financial enclaves (which promotes information sharing: Bell and Zaheer 2007), and – through what one lawyer described to me as "the drumbeat of Wall Street" – almost ephemeral via tips, whispers and rumours.

Based on evidence from studies of other networks (e.g. Stein 2008), the rapid, seamless transmission of information across fund managers relies on hubs and spokes. Hubs are the few fund managers who either intensely study data flows or distribute it widely, and information flows to spokes, or less connected FMs. This linked community becomes pervasive in shaping the information FMs receive, what factors they consider to be important to investment decisions, and their preferred techniques to analyse data and present conclusions (Henningsson 2009).

This complex of clients, colleagues, competitors and industry observers – whose study is termed economic sociology (e.g. Fligstein 2001) – engulfs market participants who become subject to social constraints on utility maximization. It also channels a large volume of opinion and expectations between managers, which shapes their investment themes and can lead to informational contagion (Arnswald 2001) that has such strong affects on markets as to bring comparisons between investor social networks and epidemics (Shive 2010).

We discuss these game-theoretic interactions in following sections. The fascinating result is that investment decisions arise at least in part as a social construct.

8.3.1 Sourcing Information from Social Networks

The most important competitive resource for fund managers is information. Most information, though, is a shared, public good with little value because contemporary corporate governance and securities regulation require that firms provide investors with equal access to data. Nor is information of much use in its raw form. A lot is historical and hard to make forward looking; only the most closely audited data is complete and reliable, and the rest is subject to uncertainty in its quality and needs to be validated. Moreover, it is difficult to detect whether even value-sensitive information has been incorporated in prices.

The net is to place importance on proprietary information. Access, though, is difficult even for well-resourced institutions because value-relevant information does not have a market and so must be developed privately or exchanged through barter. Fund managers also face information asymmetry because of better informed firm managers, other investors who are more skilled or knowledgeable, and an inability to view the full chain of securities' supply and demand.

142 Applied Investment Theory

To reduce the difficulty in acquiring and validating knowledge, funds build a social economy of contacts and communications channels whose sole purpose is to obtain superior investment information (White 2002). This is held by insiders such as executives of investee firms, regulators and advisers; better informed or more insightful investors, including competitors; and others with knowledge of industry, economic or political developments (see: Malkiel 2005). As a result, much of the behaviour of intelligent, rational fund managers can only be understood in the light of attempts to address inefficiency in their marketplace through social interactions.

One of fund managers' most important social links is with executives of investee firms. Private information is the common mixing variable, and FMs expect that relationships with company executives will provide insight into industry trends and deliver superior investment performance (Holland and Doran 1998). The information exchange allows corporate executives to create favourable impressions amongst fund managers of their firm's strategy and outlook, which they expect will be reciprocated by fund managers' support for their share price through investment in the firm (Barker 1998). Executives follow two strategies: persuasion which uses their superior, relevant knowledge of the firm to exploit knowledge asymmetries; and ingratiation which uses their resources and prestige to induce positive affect in fund managers through favours, flattery and opinion reinforcement (Westphal and Bednar 2008). Consensual information flows allow executives to influence fund managers' decisions, whilst managers build trust with executives to obtain information and deal with uncertainty in the quality of information they collate (Hellman 2000).

This private data exchange allows fund managers to evaluate less quantifiable influences on firm performance. The executives have insights into corporate data which can help fund managers validate and amplify shared, but uncertain, public firm data; and they can provide proprietary private information and feedback on FMs' conclusions. Interactions inevitably reveal insights into executives' attributes that indicate their level of skill in managing firm resources which proxies for future performance, and narrow gaps in information such as the quality of firm's strategy formulation, knowledge development and other intangibles (which usually make up more than half of market capitalization). This qualitative evaluation is becoming more important as rising price-to-book ratios show greater importance of these hard to evaluate firm features (Roberts et al. 2006), and listing of inherently higher risk firms has placed a premium on insightful firm-specific data (Brown and Kapadia 2007).

Value that fund managers place on information sourced from executives is consistent with other evidence of executives' knowledge, including the success

8 Fund Managers' Conduct: The Story of How They Invest

of investment strategies that follow insiders' announced trades (e.g. Friederich et al. 2002), and the significance of executive fixed effects in explaining variation in firms' financial decisions (Brochet et al. 2011).

Fund managers' socialisation with information sources overcomes their inability to observe the path followed by important invisible, private information, no matter whether it is authoritative (government data, corporate accounts), proprietary analysis (broker reports), or not (gossip, tips, speculation). Socialisation also gives some understanding of the extent to which any information might already be built into prices, and the value that other investors will place on it.

8.3.2 Impression Management

Normative investment techniques – such as discounted cash flow analysis and the capital asset pricing model – play a conflicted role in fund manager valuations. On one hand, fund managers realise these techniques have little practical use because it is impractical to forecast their key inputs such as cash flows and discount rates, and relationships between equity returns and lagged firm traits are too unstable to be of much use (Ferreira and Santa-Clara 2011). Nor do fund managers believe there is any nexus between equity return and risk because it has no empirical basis (see: Anderson et al. 2009; Bali 2008; Scruggs 1998).

Thus, even though fund managers are rational in that they have stable, well-defined preferences and make optimal choices, they prefer to use intuitive skill and qualitative data rather than normative theoretical approaches. Support for this conclusion comes from surveys that show fund managers are fully conversant with the standard investment paradigm, but make little practical use of it (the many examples include: Amenc et al. 2011; Coleman 2014c; Holland 2006). This is also consistent with findings that as many as half of all financial analysts never rely on traditional, rational pricing.

This makes it a surprise to see that normative investment techniques are a staple inclusion in fund managers' investment narrative: it is unusual to see any investment proposal – whether originating from a corporation, mutual fund or other financial institution – that is not accompanied by an impressive analysis that incorporates core elements of modern portfolio theory, discounted cash flows and risk evaluation. Thus Peleg (2014: xii) opines that the "cash flow model is deemed by all modern financial experts to be the correct one for appraising the value of a financial asset"; and the influential textbook *Investments* by Bodie et al. (2011: 299) says "explicitly or implicitly, practitioners do use a CAPM".

144   Applied Investment Theory

How is it possible to reconcile this marked inconsistency between what investment practitioners say they do and how they report their conclusions? The answer lies in fund managers' social network. Despite a preference for qualitative techniques, FMs face pressures from asset consultants and influential clients who expect to see traditional theory supporting investment decisions. In the real investment world, fund managers face high business risk in not meeting expectations of important stakeholders, and they outwardly conform by following a Treynor and Black (1973) style process with analytical techniques that match industry norms.

Fund managers complement their qualitative, intuitive recommendations with normative, quantitative analysis in order to influence clients and other groups in their social network. This is termed impression management (Schlenker 1980). It follows signalling theory to show conformance with investment industry culture, and is another example of where objectives that are unrelated to maximising fund performance can seem to dominate fund managers' investment decisions.

Unfortunately, industry culture can be so strong as to compel analysts to support their recommendations with normative analyses (Abhayawansa and Guthrie 2012). Evidence that many quantitative analyses are a charade to manage impressions of influential stakeholders comes from examination of investment reports which show that analysts' recommendations are often unrelated to accompanying quantitative analyses (e.g. Barniv et al. 2010).

Conversely, if done properly, the overlay of quantitative analysis required for fund managers' impression management strengthens their qualitative judgement and provides empirical support for the investment narrative. Cash flow projections and relative valuation are also particularly useful vehicles for communicating assumptions behind the investment process.

8.3.3 Herding

The most striking consequence of socialisation of the managed funds industry is herding where institutions follow prior trades by competitors (Sias 2004), which elicits the common complaint over crowded trades. Herding reflects a mechanism that co-ordinates decisions. This can be organic through the influence of conforming worldviews and paradigms, and shared data such as corporate news and analysts' forecasts (Arnswald 2001). It can be more mechanical, too, following a common decision stimulus such as price change, new public information, or observation of others' decisions (Devenow and Welch 1996). Rating agencies also promote conformance via their role as gatekeepers to large clients of funds.

Somewhat counter-intuitively, competition will promote herding. Fund managers can be encouraged to replicate competitors' behaviours (Chiang and Zheng 2010) because they are competing for common pools of investible assets that follow performance (e.g. Warther 1995), or to avoid the risk that a divergent strategy poses to their reputation and compensation (Bikhchandani and Sharma 2001). Herding would be consistent, too, with a recognised hierarchy of fund manager skills, where successful investors assume the leadership role (Cohen and Levinthal 1990). As a caution against myopic herding, however, misinterpretation of determinants of success can see irrational decisions of leading firms mimicked by less successful competitors (DeMarzo et al. 2011).

An extreme of herding is contagion, where sentiment spills widely across investors. Perhaps motivated by greed, feedback between sequential price moves can become pronounced; and investors are increasingly sucked in by success of speculation (which is the usual explanation of delusional price bubbles). It is sobering to recognise that speculative bubbles typically stem from emergence of new technologies with the prospect of huge profits. Examples in the United States have been as varied as railroads during the second half of the nineteenth century and oil early in the following century, or TMT (technology, media and telecoms) in the 1990s and CDS (collateralised debt securities) in the mid-2000s. International examples include tulips in seventeenth century Holland, and trade expeditions to newly discovered lands during the eighteenth century.

Somewhat perversely, uncertainty about innovations' true potential makes it impossible to rule out the possibility of a massive run up in price and gives these speculative securities high value as options. Each, though, has so many risks and uncertainties that financial outcomes are unknowable and traditional valuation techniques are inapplicable. Sensible analysts avoid technological wonder, ask fundamental questions, and demand favourable cost-benefit ratios (Schnaars 1989). This prevents being trapped by over optimistic advocates and helps debunk forecasts that represent prevailing orthodoxy, rather than fact.

8.4 Investor Reflexivity and Market Evolution

Discussion in previous sections of the varied contributors to fund manager conduct makes the seemingly obvious, but usually over-looked, point that fund managers' behaviour is not mechanical but organic. In particular, they constantly monitor price-sensitive information in transactions as possible signals of competitors' superior information and/or realignment of market

146   Applied Investment Theory

sentiment (Ackert et al. 2008), which can bring precautionary response where each manager's actions affect other investors' decisions and thus prices.

The intuition that investor decisions affect the conduct of other investors supports the Austrian school of economics that was discussed in Chap. 2, and has been extended by George Soros (1994) in his *Theory of reflexivity*. The latter's intuition is that markets help shape their future because their thinking participants respond to other investors' decisions and market transactions, and so induce feedback and non-linearity in prices. The role of investors is similar to that of players in a football game where physics accurately predicts the trajectory of a ball when kicked, but fans appreciate that its actual path will be subject to unpredictable disruption by other players which depends on their proximity, psychology, reaction time and so on. Importantly, too, players' actions are related not just to their location and ability, but also to their desire to influence the score (e.g. Wolfers 2006).

Alternative perspectives on reflexivity are given by game theory and the beauty pageant analogy. Game theory won John Nash (1950) a Nobel Prize, and sees investment like a game of poker where players' strategy must respond to the expected reactions of other players. Lord Keynes (1936) developed the beauty parade analogy to point out that successful investors do not choose the objectively best investments, but those that other investors (i.e. the beauty parade judges) decide are best. He joined other luminaries in pointing out that there are a lot of factors in addition to fundamentals that drive equity prices, and went further by describing markets as casinos.

Another influence that humans have on markets is to act in anticipation, which has the interesting consequence of sometimes reversing intuitive cause and effect. A simple example arises ahead of a firm's scheduled profit announcement: correct anticipation of its content by traders will see prices move accurately ahead of the announcement which thus brings no price change. In this way, traders produce an effect (say higher prices) in anticipation of the cause (profit increase) à la Keynes' beauty parade. Another reversal of cause and effect sees information lag prices, so that price falls bring on bad news, and *vice versa*. For example, analysts typically downgrade firms after they release bad news, which exacerbates the price decline (Cornell 2001).

While the structures of markets and investors are often assumed to be in a consistent, steady state, there is considerable evidence that they experience gradual evolutionary influences. A relevant concept is the adaptive markets hypothesis which extends evolutionary principles – including competition, reproduction and natural selection – to the development of market structures (Lo 2004). This envisages that bounded rationality and competition for the best return across multiple classes of investors leads to trial and error over

8 Fund Managers' Conduct: The Story of How They Invest   147

multiple decisions so that natural selection optimizes investors' heuristics. It is easy to envisage evolution occurring within the high volume of iterative transactions between agents and as a result of development in market scale and technologies.

An example of where the fittest markets survive can be seen in development of features such as trading hours, tick sizes and index construction that do not have any *a priori* optimum. Over time, traders mutually construct an acceptable structure, which is expected to change with markets' traits. One example is the rapid rise in trading activity (with a five-fold increase in turnover by value on the NYSE in the 25 years to 2008), which was largely driven by institutional investors and has been accompanied by a reduction in transaction costs and bid-ask spreads (Chordia et al. 2011). Other examples can be seen in the change of investors from largely individuals to largely institutions, introduction of new products and trading platforms such as derivatives and on-line order systems, new marketplaces such as dark pools, and earlier listing of more risky firms (Brown and Kapadia 2007).

Non-market institutions can be forced to evolve, too. One example is the growing importance of intangibles to firm valuations, which is best evidenced by higher market to book ratios (e.g. Edmans 2011). Intangibles largely comprise factors that are not yet economically proven such as knowledge, patents and strategy, and so are particularly difficult to value, which has forced an increase in disclosure of non-financial information by firms (Coram et al. 2011).

Reflexivity and evolution rely on the power of interaction between investors. Reflexivity involves constant, quick feedback from investors into market prices which implies that equilibrium is not possible in an active market. Evolution is much slower, but also sees feedback from changes in technology and scale that modify structures of investors and markets. In short, equilibrium and a steady state are unlikely in any financial market.

8.5   Conclusion

This chapter used the framework of structural forces in markets and the mutual fund industry to tell the story of fund managers' equity investment. The grounded description is consistent with real-world evidence and familiar finance theories, and is comprehensive in depicting the full chain of fund manager conduct. In essence, fund managers develop fundamental valuations in light of their own experience-based paradigms, match their analytical techniques to prevailing methods (Hellman 2000), and take account of other market participants' views. Overall, their decisions are minimally encumbered.

148 Applied Investment Theory

Certainly FMs must manage liquidity in open ended funds, stay true to label, and be aware of benchmarks and competitor strategies. In addition, most are salaried employees and subject to the formal procedures and controls common to financial organizations. But they are essentially unfettered by history, unlike (say) corporate executives who must match assets and liabilities and take account of prior choices in decisions on dividends, corporate structure and the like (Coleman 2014a).

The depiction to date of markets and fund managers provides some comfort for neoclassical finance theory by affirming several core precepts: despite some pockets of short term predictability, security prices are minimally forecastable; markets are efficient to the extent that informed experts cannot best others across a range of measures; and idiosyncratic risk is not priced. On the other hand, the conclusions negate theoretical tenets: securities trade in very wide ranges rather than close to (an unknowable) fundamental value, and arbitrage is not effective in ensuring a single price; the slope of demand curves varies so that markets do not achieve equilibrium; quantitative asset pricing and mean-variance optimisation cannot be applied; and systematic influences on returns are unstable and unpredictable.

Another challenge to normative theory is the extent of socialisation within the managed funds industry, so that fund manager decisions reflect social dynamics. Investment is not amenable to normative techniques, which are relegated to paying lip service to manage client and firm impressions. Reliance on qualitative judgement suits investment professionals because it displays their hard-to-replicate skill, and – as one fund manager told me over a drink in Istanbul – means they are "not just a pilot for the research reports or analytical process" (Coleman 2015).

This complements a desire by fund managers to make their intuitive investment process hard to replicate to put the investor in charge of valuation, which is a convenient support for the argument of finance industry professionals that less experienced investors should employ their skills. But, nobody can make reliable forecasts of cash flows and market yields, and the only accurate price-related information is historical with transient predictive power. Our understanding of capital market behaviours remains limited, and predictive capability is minimal.

Fund managers' investment process typically starts with a macro view of the global economy and political situation, and then drills down through countries and industries to select investments. FMs identify attractive investments in a sort of intuitive modelling process that applies their own unique paradigm and heuristics to process an eclectic mix of publicly available information, insights gained from company visits, and anecdotes gleaned from industry experts, company insiders and colleagues.

8 Fund Managers' Conduct: The Story of How They Invest 149

Within their models, managers think in terms of security prices rather than returns. They consider equities' opportunity cost, and rank alternative investments through a combination of fundamental value (which is a subjective estimate of the present value of future cash flows and qualitative judgement about their uncertainty) and non-priced based hedonic features of the security (e.g. industry, ESG, management), socialisation factors (including peer actions, interactions and communications), and the transactional setting (jurisdiction, physical location). This leads to marked heterogeneity in buyers and sellers which means that securities can have multiple equilibria and sell at different prices in different settings.

A complementary set of contributors to disequilibria in markets arise because of their thinking participants. Even though individual transactions may approach equilibrium, they never clear the market. That is because each transaction alters investors' wealth and hence risk propensity which reshapes investor perceptions and relative valuations that changes the supply-demand balance and triggers further transactions. This leaves asset prices subject to multiple, non-linear responses by investors to new information and transient influences, which render prices indeterminate. As Lord Keynes (1936: 153–154) observed: "day-to-day fluctuations in the profits of existing investments, which are obviously of an ephemeral and non-significant character, tend to have an altogether excessive, and even absurd, influence on the market."

In summary, few fund managers use neoclassical finance theory, largely because of the inability to develop forward looking data to populate its models. Few believe in core concepts such as that security prices equal discounted future cash flows, security demand curves are flat or downward sloping, and return reflects expected risk. Most find that publicly available information has limited price impact, and it is impractical to forecast security prices to a useful level of accuracy. Conversely, they believe that markets trend in the short term, but are stationary around a real mean over the long term, which leads to predictability and some merit in technical analysis.

On the assumption that FMs' qualifications, expertise, and oversight lead to a rational set of behaviours, their conduct reflects optimised performance within the current mutual funds framework. Thus fund portfolios are essentially self-selected and comprise FMs' preferred choices. The implication is that improving performance requires external intervention.

9

Performance of Mutual Funds

> **The Key Takeaways of This Chapter Are**
>
> - Net return of the average mutual fund in most countries and periods is below benchmark. Any fund manager skill is offset by fund expenses and fees.
> - At best, outperformance by mutual funds occurs at the margins and in specialist applications
> - Incentives for fund managers and other investment analysts are weakly directed towards maximising fund return
> - Profits by mutual funds and finance firms are high relative to their economic contribution
> - Investors' agents contribute to emergence of financial scams, so that finance is the only sector where leading firms have received multi-billion dollar fines for defrauding their customers. The industry may face an ethical crisis.
> - The mutual fund sector can be interpreted through the structure-conduct-performance (SCP) paradigm:
>   - A structural feature of markets is investors' inability to predict returns, which leads mutual funds to base their revenue around funds under management.
>   - Thus fund employees and agents are compensated for growing FUM, which diverts their efforts away from maximising client returns.

© The Author(s) 2016
L. Coleman, *Applied Investment Theory,*
DOI 10.1007/978-3-319-43976-1_9

- Fund clients are disengaged, information asymmetry obscures the quality of investment management, opacity of fund activities prevents close scrutiny, and observers and regulators provide weak oversight. This leaves mutual funds virtually free to self-regulate.
- Moral hazard induced by fee-based commissions leads agents with a weak ethical compass to exploit the trust and indifference of their client principals.

This chapter closes out the synthesis of what we know about the structure-conduct-performance of mutual funds by examining their performance. Surveys of mutual funds' clients show that return is important to them when selecting a fund manager, but so are other subjective criteria, including trust and investment manager attributes (Foster and Warren 2015), along with reputation and number of funds in the family (Capon et al. 1996). Thus it seems reasonable to expect that performance of mutual funds should be judged by both their return relative to an appropriate benchmark, and by the integrity of their role as investors' agents.

9.1 Return of Managed Funds

Although mutual funds are large, they own under half of most equity markets' stocks. Thus outperformance is intuitively feasible if fund managers have superior skill in selecting stocks, and are motivated to identify and buy these stocks. It is a surprise, then, that most analyses find mutual funds' mean return after expenses and fees is about 1% below their benchmark (for a review see: Cuthbertson et al. 2010).[1] In a typical dissection of this conclusion, Wermers (2000) found that the average fund picked stocks which outperformed the broad market index by 1.3% per year, but this became a net of −1% after deducting transaction costs and expenses of 1.6% and underperformance of 0.7% from holding cash.

Mutual funds' underperformance seems to be one of the best accepted investment facts, and the following table reports just a few of the many studies reporting that fund managers on average display little or no skill (Table 9.1).

---

[1] It should be noted that fund returns result not just from decisions on which securities to buy or not buy, but how the portfolio is structured and that has not been part of this study.

9 Performance of Mutual Funds 153

Table 9.1 Recent analyses of mutual fund performance

Author(s)	Sample	Conclusion
Wermers (2000)	1788 US funds during 1975–1994	Value-weighted return versus S&P 500 of 1.5% PA gross, and –0.8% PA net
Pastor and Stambaugh (2002)	2609 US mutual funds in CRSP during 1963–1998	Net risk-adjusted return of –2.13% PA using the market model, and –1.07% PA using a three factor model (market, size, value)
Cuthbertson et al. (2008)	842 UK funds during 1975–2002	Net risk-adjusted return of –1.5% PA using a four factor model
Busse et al. (2010)	6040 domestic US funds during 1979–2008	Value-weighted return net of fees from a four factor model of –0.04% PA
Fama and French (2010)	Funds in the CRSP database during 1984–2006	Value-weighted return net of fees from a four factor model of –1.00% PA

Analyses of mutual fund performance began in the early 1960s (e.g. Friend et al. 1962). One of the first tests against the market was by Jensen (1968), who studied 115 US mutual funds during 1955–64 and found that they delivered a risk-adjusted net return, α, of −1.1% PA. Studies since then of institutional investors have consistently reached a similar conclusion. This is true across time periods, and is a global phenomenon given that the average equity mutual fund in 27 countries underperforms its benchmark by 20 basis points per quarter net of fees (Ferreira et al. 2012). In addition to poor performance of the average mutual fund, differences between funds in performance are not predictable from historical data, except that the worst-return funds continue to under-perform (Carhart 1997). That is, most funds do not replicate their performance.

9.1.1 Unpacking Funds' Poor Return

Intuition would suggest that fund managers should outperform the market, and that the best should consistently deliver significant alpha. However, the evidence is clear that – no matter how impressive are the resources, attributes and incentives of professional investors – these play no consistent role in the quality of decisions: that is, fund managers' investment process is no better than making random choices, and perhaps even worse than random if an investor can strike out manifestly unsuitable prospects.

This is one of the more puzzling findings from finance research given that funds and their employees enjoy high compensation and other rewards that should reflect production of significant rent (Elton et al. 2003). Moreover,

154 Applied Investment Theory

the result reflects the outcome of decisions by investment professionals who are well trained in finance theory with most holding finance MBAs and/or accreditation as chartered financial analysts (CFA).

The puzzle has three obvious explanations: fund managers are unable to select outperforming investments, so that their performance matches a random sample equal to the average investment return less costs; fund managers' principal objective is something other than generating superior return, which compromises the latter objective; or the methodology underpinning the conclusion is inappropriate.

In relation to the first possible explanation, it is hard to identify why fund managers might lack skill because data are not sufficiently detailed to examine their full decision making process (although some researchers are working to fill this gap, including www.essentia-analytics.com and www.sybenetix.com). However, there are published studies of the performance of professional groups along the chain leading to investment decisions, and these should provide proxies for fund manager ability in key investment steps. At the very least, if expertise cannot be identified in those providing inputs to various elements of investment decisions, then the skill of fund managers can reasonably be called into doubt.

Investment professionals fall into five groups. The first two provide inputs to formation of return expectations, namely economists who forecast state variables and research analysts who forecast securities' cash flows. Two further groups combine decision stimuli to predict or explain equity returns, namely industry investment analysts who value equites and academics who research into equity valuation. The final group, of course, is fund managers who invest for clients and whose weak average performance is already clear.

Starting our search for investment skill with financial economists, their most important equity valuation inputs are predictions of macroeconomic variables, principally GDP and inflation. Post audits show that economists' forecasts systematically underestimate the strength and weakness of cycles in the economy and prices, and they rarely forecast recessions and inflation surges in advance. The typical conclusion is that forecasts by economists of key inputs to investment are little better than those of naïve models (Fildes and Stekler 2002).

Further support for a lack of economists' skill comes from shock occurrence of major financial events that highlight how obviously misinformed were those who should have had a much clearer understanding. Thus a retrospective of the 2007–8 global financial crisis damned financial economists around the world as simply failing to identify the build up of huge risks to the financial system (Besley and Hennessy 2009). A more general indication of poor forecasting skill is the five-to-seven year cycle of unexpected bankruptcies, market collapses and sovereign debt crises that rage unchecked through global economies and markets (see the discussion in Chap. 1). The regularity of their recurrence does not instil any confidence in the ability of even the most powerful actors to predict the trajectory of economic systems.

A second set of expert input to investment comes through analysts' earnings forecasts, which again prove little better than naive estimates such as no change (e.g. Guedj and Bouchaud 2005). To be fair, corporate executives – who should be much better placed to predict their firms' cash flow – are no more successful (Kothari 2001). This, of course, confirms that nobody has skill in forecasting the cash flows that are central to conventional security valuations.

Another group of putative investment experts is advisers who make recommendations on stocks to buy and sell. The most prominent group is sell-side analysts, and their lack of skill is reflected in consistent bias, especially towards glamour stocks with positive price momentum, higher valuation multiples and higher volume (Jegadeesh et al. 2004). Nor do researchers in academia and elsewhere display expertise in predicting equity returns. Although they have linked hundreds of factors to future returns (Harvey et al. 2014), even ex post these are unable to explain at least 80% of the variation in month ahead stock returns.

Apart from fund managers, investment decisions by other financial institutions delivery equally poor results (e.g. Lewellen 2011), as do finance decisions by executives making acquisitions and launching major corporate strategies (Henry 2002). Perhaps the strongest reason to doubt the existence of skill is that it is not being used as a point of distinction by investment firms or funds, which prefer to compete on other criteria such as reputation. Institutions which know most about their investment expertise do not appear confident that they have any skill that will persist.

In practice, there are so many examples across investment of failed foresight and recurring crises, disasters, and industry-wide scams that the signal-to-noise ratio is weak, and it is all but impractical to identify skill in investment. This has been true since the search for investment expertise began with an article by Cowles (1933) whose title asked 'Can stock market forecasters forecast?': his negative conclusion has stood the test of time, and investment expertise remains elusive.

Inability to forecast finance variables supports the first explanation for fund managers' poor performance which is that predictions of equity returns are little better than random choices, and so the gross return of any large sample of

156   Applied Investment Theory

equity investments such as mutual funds will not deviate much from the average. This also implies that there is no information that is not built into prices, and strengthens arguments in favour of strict market efficiency (e.g. Malkiel 1995). It is also consistent with the performance of experts outside of economics and investment – whether of social changes, sports results, or weather – where accurate prediction of future events proves impractical (Coleman 1998).

The second possible explanation for lack of investment outperformance arises from the intuition that investment expertise is only likely when explicitly linked to experts' reward. In short, fund managers may not maximise fund performance when they are incentivized to pursue conflicting objectives (e.g. Chan 2015), which makes their lack of ability quite rational (e.g. Gruber 1996). This allows for the possibility of investment skill in the average manager, but concludes it is not fully deployed.

In practice, most investment experts are compromised by the need to meet other, often conflicting objectives. The income of mutual funds, for instance, is related to funds under management (FUM), and so relative performance is of secondary importance to attracting new investments. Mutual funds reinforce the implicit pressure on fund managers by sometimes linking FUM to compensation (Farnsworth and Taylor 2006). It would not be surprising to find that mutual fund managers divert time from optimizing fund return and make time available to (say) please clients, or prepare commentary that provides novelty to the media and enhances their reputation, or otherwise supports their employer.

Fund performance would also suffer if managers structure portfolios to highlight attributes that influence investor choice such as security of funds and avoidance of large losses; and to minimize risks to their career, such as by window dressing (e.g. Brown et al. 2001). Other compromises can arise from constraints on preferred actions including funds' charter; and pressures to conform to competitors' strategies, adopt the consensus view on pertinent data and analytical techniques, and follow preferences of rating agencies and large investors (Bikhchandani and Sharma 2001).

The final explanation for mutual fund underperformance is that analytical techniques might give an erroneous conclusion. This is possible because evaluations typically follow Carhart (1997), with fund returns as the dependent variable in a regression against market factors (beta, size, value and momentum) during the period, and with fund performance as the intercept, α. This represents an unreasonable test of skill because it is ex post with the assumption that fund managers know year-ahead returns to systematic factors. While resolution of this point is beyond my scope, it matches doubts across the literature about investment methodology, with one study concluding "that most claimed research findings in financial economics are likely false" (Harvey et al. 2014). Conversely, simple comparisons between the returns from funds and indexes confirm that the average fund cannot outperform its index (see, for instance: Philips et al. 2014).

9.2 Integrity of Mutual Funds' Role as Agents

The second measure proposed to test mutual fund performance is the integrity of their role as investors' agents, given that important criteria for funds' clients involve reliability, trust and reputation.

There are good reasons to conclude that some mutual funds do not seriously consider their responsibilities as individual investors' agents. Anybody with even a casual interest in the finance industry will be aware of waves of systemic corruption and weak governance in financial institutions that bring regular Samson-like toppling of the market temple. Like clockwork, it seems that each quadrennium there is either a crisis in corporate governance, or the bond and/or equity market melts down: commonly global recession follows. Even years after the crises that rolled across northern hemisphere credit, banking and sovereign debt markets through 2008–2011, evidence of their destructive power is still evident.

A common factor in most of these crises is that financial institutions take advantage of pervasive agency relationships where financial professionals play a critical role by providing advice, managing funds and executing transactions on behalf of investors who have less skill or confidence. Thus Australian market commentator Marcus Padley observed pithily in his newspaper column: "Most financial professionals exist to connect you with a service or product" (*The Age* 12 September 2009). Evidence of agency problems abound, with everything from analysts' forecasts to IPO valuations skewed to benefit the authors, and zero valued added by those charged with management of funds. Scams are all too familiar. Even investors who are not naturally cynical should heed the obvious point made to me by a London fund-of-funds manager that "running money is a business": be alert to the motives and bias of all sources of advice, and develop a strategy to manage their agents.

Most agents' abuse of client interests can be traced to structural features of the mutual fund industry. Because funds' revenue is based on FUM, they compensate agents through commissions based on transaction volume or fund flows rather than performance. This brings moral hazard that drives a wedge between the pecuniary interests of agents and the best interests of their clients. There is also a pronounced asymmetry in skill and knowledge between agents and the individual investors whom they advise or assist, which agents with self-serving biases find easy to exploit.

158   Applied Investment Theory

Financial institutions also take advantage of their control over transactions to steal from clients (see, amongst many: Coleman (2014b) and McLean and Nocera 2010). The frequency and seriousness of their illegal behaviour is evidenced by the nine to eleven figure fines imposed on most major banks in recent years for defrauding their customers and allowing unconscionable conduct by financial planners and other bank employees towards clients. Eliot Spitzer – who was Attorney General of New York during 1999–2006 and responsible for many successful bank prosecutions – argued that "widespread illegal trading schemes" cost investors more than $4 billion a year.[2] A *Forbes* cover story discussing how financial institutions abuse their huge transaction volume at clients' expense was headlined 'The Sleaziest Show on Earth' (24 May 2004, www.forbes.com).

Another common breach of the standard investment assumption that contractual obligations inherent in stocks and bonds can be costlessly enforced is seen in the surprisingly high probability of default by principals. Standard & Poor's *Annual Global Corporate Default Study*, for instance, reports that about 1% of rated corporate bonds defaulted annually during the five years to 2014. It is no longer uncommon to see failure of even the most respected financial institutions, such as ABN-Amro, Barings Bank, Bear Stearns, Lehman Brothers, LTCM and Merrill Lynch. Many others have required government handouts to prevent collapse: in 2008 tens of billions were given under the Troubled Asset Relief Program to US banks including Citigroup and Goldman Sachs; and the UK government made comparable investment in Royal Bank of Scotland.

Another interesting test of managed funds' performance is whether they extract an unfair share of available rent. We have already seen (Sect. 7.2) that around the world "asset management continues to rank among the most profitable industries" (BCG 2015), which is consistent with high profits across the finance industry. The following figure uses data for all US finance sectors since 1950 to plot shares of national GDP and company profits (sourced from Bureau of Economic Analysis at www.bea.gov). The US finance industry's share of GDP almost doubled to just over 20%, and its share of total profits more than trebled to over a third: an industry which generates 20% of GDP consumes a third of the profits reported by all US companies. Further questioning the merits of value added by the finance industry is that its profit dropped behind GDP contribution during tough periods such as the high inflation era of 1975–1985, but rent extracted surged during easy times of the Great Moderation during 1985–2007 (Fig. 9.1).

---

[2] www.ag.ny.gov/press-release/state-investigation-reveals-mutual-fund-fraud.

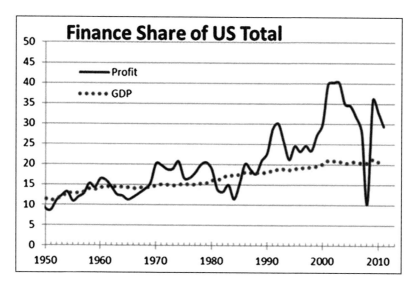

Fig. 9.1 Finance industry's share of US GDP and corporate profits

9.2.1 Is There an Ethical Crisis in Funds Management?

As discussed above, the finance industry is plagued by illegal behaviour. Alone of all industries, finance has been distinguished by huge fines for defrauding its customers (e.g. Partnoy and Eisinger 2013): settlements agreed by global banks with the US Justice Department include $US13 billion by J P Morgan Chase in 2013, and $17 billion by Bank of America in 2014.

Another aspect of the finance industry's poor conduct is that big banks do not just practice corruption on their own, but engage in complex conspiracies. A good example came to light after mid-2012 when banks were fined for by UK and US authorities for participating in a cartel to fix the LIBOR benchmark (London Interbank Offered Rate, which is a US dollar interest rate for lending between banks) their favour since at least 2006, and possibly as far back as the early 1990s.[3] Those fined include Barclays Bank (£290 million), Citibank, Deutsche Bank ($2.5 billion), J P Morgan, Lloyds, Royal Bank of Scotland, and UBS ($1.5 billion). Adding fuel to allegations by conspiracy buffs and critics of regulators, *The Wall Street Journal* (16 April 2008) had published an article years before the scandal broke questioning the reliability of LIBOR, but it prompted only cursory response from the US Federal Reserve and Bank of England. Many countries have seen scams and

---

[3] www.cftc.gov/PressRoom/PressReleases/pr6289-12.

worse perpetrated by financial advisers and planners who are employees or agents of major banks.

Such consistent, widespread evidence raises the possibility of an ethical crisis in the finance industry. Although studies of finance professionals' ethics have found them roughly comparable to values of the general population (van Hoorn 2014), forces inside financial institutions seem to have created an environment that is conducive to unethical behaviour and – according to some research – attracts psychopaths (Baddy 2011). This can be explained through the structure-conduct-performance framework, where structural aspects of the finance industry attract a disproportionate number of individuals who are prone to deceptive and illegal behaviour, and then facilitate that conduct.

The attraction of finance for less ethical people is clear: the level of savings to be managed is huge, with over $30 trillion in mutual funds around the world. The possibility of gain induces high moral hazard in financial advisers and money managers which appears as greed and abuses against investors. Nor is lack of investment knowledge a barrier to entry because hardly anybody in the finance industry displays skill, and the FUM-basis of mutual funds' revenue leads to commissions unrelated to investment performance. Investors, too, are encouraged to take additional risk by concessional taxation of retirement savings and investment earnings, and through encouragement to leverage their investment by lenders and by policy makers' explicit support of asset prices through bailout of failed institutions and implicit support through liberal monetary policy.

There is ready opportunity for scams and fraud because the absence of client scrutiny and ineffectual oversight of the industry leave funds free to self-regulate, and financial institutions and their regulators are tolerant of agency abuses. Means is provided by information asymmetry between agents and fund clients, and deceptive agents are virtually immune to consequences, even after the most egregious acts. Those of us who know the destructive consequences of the means, motive and opportunity of unscrupulous finance professionals fail the industry when we view it through a lens of moral superiority.

Whether or not mutual funds are caught up in an ethical crisis, it seems an understatement to insist that investment theory be better able to explain why finance fails the important performance test of performing its agency role with integrity.

9.3 Conclusion

Poor overall performance of the mutual fund industry means that the net return from investing in the average fund is negative. This is troubling at multiple levels. Perhaps the conclusion is not valid, which implies a huge gap in our understanding and evaluation of an important sector. Perhaps fund managers are too busy working for their own or their employers' interests, which implies a sad distortion of priorities. Perhaps it is impractical to outperform the market, which is a sad indictment of the state of finance theory and knowledge.

What does appear certain, though, is that structural features of the investment industry negate any investment skills, and thus little or no expertise is evident across the various steps involved in investment. Empirical evidence points to an all but universal inability of investment professionals to forecast macroeconomic variables and firm cash flows that are inputs to equity valuation models. Future outcomes are random, and – after fees – the average advice or effort of an investment professional is worse than random choice.

While the conclusion of the lack of replicable expertise amongst fund managers does not conflict with efficiency in markets, it has implications for mutual funds along with their clients and regulators. The conclusion that funds cannot add value through investment explains their preference for sourcing revenue primarily as commissions on funds under management. Reliance of mutual funds on FUM-based revenues is an unfortunate outcome for investors because most evaluations show that the optimum outcome for them comes from fund manager compensation through a symmetrical, performance-based fee (see: Clare et al. 2014). Mutual funds have structured the industry in a way that is inimical to the interests of their clients.

The second conclusion of this chapter that funds abuse their role as investors' agents to the extent of huge financial scams is also troubling. But it, too, can be explained by the SCP paradigm as an outcome of disengagement of fund clients which leaves them indifferent to performance, information asymmetry that frequently obscures the quality of funds' investment management, and opacity of fund activities that prevents close scrutiny. Along with weak oversight by observers and regulators, this leaves mutual funds free to self-regulate. Moral hazard is induced in financial advisers by the industry practice of paying fee-based commissions, and those with a weak ethical compass exploit the trust and indifference of clients.

This chapter is the last of four that summarise what we know about mutual fund investment, and show the explanatory power of the structure-conduct-performance paradigm. One clear thread is how structural features in unforecastable equity returns and an oligopolistic mutual fund industry promote a fund business model that draws revenues from FUM-based commissions, and so drives a wedge between the interests of funds (to boost FUM) and those of their clients (to optimise return). Funds' drive for FUM leads to industry compensation and commission arrangements that are related to savings flows, which induces moral hazard in clients' agents

162   Applied Investment Theory

that is chronically abused. This is an interesting feedback loop within the structure-conduct-performance paradigm: a structural feature of markets is FMs' inability to predict equities' returns; thus mutual funds avoid performance-based fees and link revenue to funds under management, which leads to revenue-based compensation for fund employees and agents and diverts their efforts away from maximising client returns. SCP makes it easy to trace the root causes of poor mutual fund performance and illegal behaviour.

Evidence that funds ignore the interests and preferences of investors and fail to act as unconditional value maximisers (Athanassakos 1992) makes it interesting that the incentives, socialisation and biases of professional investors are not seen by researchers as relevant to returns from their decisions. Thus, while agency problems are well studied in corporate finance, they are glossed over in asset pricing where funds' owners, employees and agents are assumed to be rational, unconditional value maximisers (see, for example the AFA President's Address by Franklin Allen (2001) entitled "Do financial institutions matter?").

To conclude, it seems that the FUM-basis of mutual funds' revenue enables them to avoid the uncomfortable fact that they add little or no value through investment, and leads to other industry practices that damage investors' interests. Observers could readily conclude that the funds management business needs to be made more competitive and better attuned to investors' interests.

Part III

Towards an Enhanced Theory of Investment

10

Piecing Together the Jigsaw: *Applied Investment Theory*

The Key Takeaways of This Chapter Are

- The structure-conduct-performance (SCP) paradigm explains the behaviour and performance of fund managers as a response to structural and exogenous features of the mutual funds industry, that is also influenced by agency theory and moral hazard.
- Markets evidence cycles and patterns in returns with time-varying auto-correlation, trending over the medium term and mean reversion over the longer term.
- Transactions provide continuous new information of importance to valuation. Thus investors incorporate prices in utility functions.
- Humans have significant influence over equity prices because they control the release, and often timing, of market information including some of the most important data
- Growth of institutions to dominate ownership of equities makes their market oligopolistic. This leads to a classic sawtooth price pattern of gradual rises and sharp falls with negative skew
- Investors accept a lack of predictive capability and the recurrence of large, systematic market swings that make it impractical to project returns of

© The Author(s) 2016
L. Coleman, *Applied Investment Theory*,
DOI 10.1007/978-3-319-43976-1_10

individual equities. Thus they think in terms of equity price, and rank values of candidate investments in light of their opportunity cost.

- Investor risk incorporates uncertainty and downside loss, and is caused by target return.
- Equities' relative valuations are determined in light of their three economic components: the value of current operations; a long real call option whose price depends on value improvements; and a sold real put option whose value loss depends on unexpected adverse developments.
- These relaxations of strict assumptions in the standard investment paradigm re-engineer it to be consistent with real-world evidence, and explain fund managers' process through familiar finance theories.

Material discussed so far describes fund manager motivations and how they make investment decisions. The next step is to link this material into a comprehensive theory of fund managers' equity investment, which – as initially proposed – should be a parsimonious statement of core concepts and their inter-relationships that explains observed behaviour, reconciles the most striking investment anomalies, and generates empirical implications. That is the task of this chapter.

10.1 Central Inputs to an Applied Investment Theory

The discussion so far has identified a great deal that we know as facts about investors and markets. Those that are not well accommodated by the standard investment paradigm – and hence need to be included in a re-engineered theory of investment – include the following:

- There is no consistent statistical relationship between equity return and risk (volatility of returns) (see: Anderson et al. 2009; Bali 2008; Scruggs 1998)
- New price-sensitive information is not normally associated with moves in security prices: most news is just noise (see Sect. 6.4)
- Humans have significant influence over equity returns because they control the release, and often timing, of market information including some of the most important data (see Sect. 6.2)

10 Piecing Together the Jigsaw: *Applied Investment Theory* 167

- Growth of institutions to dominate ownership of equities makes their market oligopolistic, and leads to: a classic sawtooth price pattern of gradual rises and sharp falls, with negative skew; and calendar-based window dressing (Sect. 6.2)
- Future cash flows and market conditions are not forecastable in any meaningful sense over the multi-year horizon of most investors (Sect. 9.1)
- An equity's target return determines difficulty in achieving it, and so the possibility of loss is caused by anticipated return (Sect. 4.4)
- Investors partition outcomes into predictable positives and unexpected negatives as evidenced by the hindsight bias and mental accounting (Sect. 3.1)
- In making valuations, investors:

  - develop investment themes with multiple determinants of value (Olsen 2002)
  - see equities as contingent securities, whose value is dependent on the state of the world (Arrow 1964)
  - see real option features in equities (Myers 1977)
  - value equities in terms of price not return (Hellman 2000) as the sum of several parts (Miller and Modigliani 1961).
  - rely on current data, rather than unreliable predictions
  - prefer to use proxies and heuristics to assess value and risk, rather than normative models
  - pay heed to historical prices and observable security traits (Sect. 8.2) and employ technical analysis (Menkhoff 2010). This incorporates current price and the price vector in investors' utility function
  - separately estimate the value of expected developments and how poorly they might perform under a wrong scenario (Porter 1985).
  - do not see any nexus between return and risk
  - think of risk in isolation from return as downside uncertainty (Knight 1921), which is equivalent to lack of knowledge about a firm's business model and future cash flows (Chap. 4).

- Professional investors and other skilled financial decision makers are unable to best naive decisions (Ferreira et al. 2012) (Chap. 9)
- Moral hazard is a pervasive influence on investors; and corruption is common in finance and investment (Sect. 9.2).

To explain these empirical facts within a rational theoretical framework, it is proposed to incorporate six innovations in the re-engineered depiction of fund manager equity investment:

168   Applied Investment Theory

1. Financial performance of mutual funds is described through the structure-conduct-performance paradigm where fixed features of the industry interact with transient data flows to shape fund manager decisions and determine fund performance. Agency theory and moral hazard further explain fund manager behaviour

2. Humans have significant influence over equity prices because they control the release, and often timing, of market information including some of the most important data. This leads to calendar-based window dressing. Other human control arises from growth of institutions to dominate ownership of equities which makes their market oligopolistic, and leads to a classic sawtooth price pattern of gradual rises and sharp falls, with negative skew.

3. Markets display significant inefficiency, most obviously through regular cycles of mis-pricing, and patterns in returns with time-varying autocorrelation over the short term, trending over the medium term, and mean reversion over the longer term. Flows of public information have small, transient impact on equity valuations. Because market transactions provide continuous new information of importance to valuation, investors incorporate prices in their utility functions.

4. Investor risk relates to uncertainty in wealth, especially downside loss. Possibility of loss is caused by anticipated return because a higher target return leads to greater difficulty in achieving the expected increase in equity value.

5. Investors' lack of predictive capability and the recurrence of large, systematic market swings make it impractical to project returns of individual equities. Thus they think in terms of equity price, and rank values of candidate investments in light of their opportunity cost.

6. A three component model of valuation is used which comprises: the value of current operations; a long real call option whose price depends on value improvements; and a sold real put option whose value loss depends on unexpected adverse developments.

Before showing how these innovative perspectives combine into a descriptive investment theory, consider the theoretical bases of each.

10.1.1 Financial Performance of Mutual Funds Has Structural Determinants

The first extension to the neoclassical depiction of fund manager equity investment is to describe their industry through several familiar models: the structure-conduct-performance (SCP) paradigm where fixed features of the industry interact with transient data flows to shape fund manager decisions and determine fund performance (Bain 1959; McWilliams and Smart 1993); moral hazard where lax regulation and FUM-based commissions induce risk in mutual funds' agents and employees; and agency theory where most individual investors contract out management of their savings, but opacity in fund operations and information asymmetry establish conflicts between principals' interests and their agents' actions (Ross 1973; Jensen and Meckling 1976).

SCP is a useful framework to explain the mutual fund industry. Structural features of equity markets are seen in their general unpredictability because of time varying patterns and trends; and the interface between thinking participants, which sets up feedbacks between investor actions and decisions (Soros 1994). In addition, markets and investors display evolutionary elements – including competition and reproduction – which enable natural selection to continuously optimize structures (see: Lo 2004).

The mutual fund industry also exhibits structural features including concentration and slow change in constituent funds, and in the mix and objectives of investors; a FUM-based revenue model, disengagement of mutual funds' clients from management of their funds, and ineffective oversight of the industry by regulators, ratings agencies, and other industry observers. This leaves mutual funds largely free to regulate themselves, which sees frequent unconscionable conduct towards clients.

10.1.2 Humans Have Significant Influence over Equity Prices

Humans have influence over equity prices because they control the flow of virtually all information, and equity ownership is dominated by money managers who control demand.

It is hard to think of any market-relevant information that is not prepared and/or communicated by humans, who often choose the content, provide commentary and have control over the time of its release. Even scheduled releases of economic data or corporate accounts must be prepared, and unexpected information – everything from shock events such as industrial accidents to strategic initiatives – must be identified and reported. Virtually all price-sensitive information first becomes available privately, possibly to many people, before it spreads to others along multiple pathways according to the immediacy of their data availability, and finally becomes public when announced by the firm or reported by the media. Timing of the most important corporate data – such as announcements of major strategy or investment – is at the discretion of firm management.

170   Applied Investment Theory

As examples of human control of market-relevant information, institutional investors will prefer to split large transactions, and transact smaller parcels when volume is heavy (Admati and Pfleiderer 1988); firms make financial decisions such as dividends and leverage in light of previous decisions (Coleman 2014a), and will execute one-off transactions such as stock issues and mergers at the most propitious time (Brown 2011); and analysts revise their published opinions of securities in increments (Cronqvist et al. 2009). The result is that much price-sensitive information does not emerge at random, nor instantly reach the market.

Another human influence on equity markets arises from growth of institutions to dominate ownership of equities. Compulsory or tax incentivised retirement savings establish a regular flow of essentially involuntary investments into mutual funds, which are open ended and so each additional investment leads to a slightly higher bid price, which is then matched by other buyers, and price leap frogs up. Equity returns, then, are deterministic with an upward drift. This is consistent with the fact that the highest level of the S&P 500 in seven of the 13 years to end 2015 was in December, with six of those at year end. Incremental rises eventually push price to a level where cash becomes preferable, when investors take profits, and price falls quickly to be reset around a minimum fundamental value, after which the process repeats. This results in a cycle marked by many small price rises during institutional investors' serial overbidding and infrequent large falls as the price is reset, which give a negative skew to equity returns. This classic sawtooth price pattern is characteristic of Edgeworth (1925) cycles in markets with dominant buyers or sellers (Noel 2011).

Interpreting equity prices as subject to Edgeworth cycles explains a number of puzzles. First, creeping competition between investors gives prices a serially dependent dynamic that cannot achieve equilibrium. Also, if the underlying mechanism shifts to and from competition between buyers (during bull markets) and sellers (bear markets), there would be both positive and negative skew in returns, which helps explain the thick tails in return distributions. Irregular cycles of slow climbs to a maximum realistic price followed by quick reset to near underlying value (and vice versa in established bear markets) within relatively stable limits explain the success of technical analysis, including channels, trend lines and resistance/support levels.

Fund managers also influence equity prices through anti-cyclical responses that arise from calendar-based performance pressures, with year-end results of most importance. This encourages window dressing so that funds will reduce exposure after a good interim result and bank profits or lift risk to recover ground (Clare et al. 2014).

10.1.3 Investors Incorporate Price in Utility Functions Because of Market Inefficiencies

Information seems to have limited impact on equity valuations and usually cannot explain even the largest moves in price. Thus new public information is not usually associated with large changes in the price of individual stocks (Bouchaud et al. 2009) or market indexes (Fair 2002). On the flip-side, few announcements of intuitively price-sensitive information bring significant price reaction (e.g. Cutler et al. 1989). Similarly, even ex post, less than about 20% of the cross section of equity returns can be explained by either observable traits of investors (Grinblatt and Keloharju 2001) or securities (Ferreira et al. 2012), and there is doubt over the validity of these findings (Harvey et al. 2014). Moreover, information arrives infrequently and equity prices change far too often to be explained by innovation in news.

Because information provides limited, infrequent data on equity prices, investors monitor the continuous flow of data in transaction volumes. Fund managers know that non-public data and analysis are not evenly shared, and watch transactions for signals of superior skill, which is otherwise unobservable. Another role of price is to indicate systematic conditions, and to serve as a point of reference by identifying whether price is high or low relative to history or has recently trended, and its performance relative to competitors. Thus investors can add value by timing their purchase through price-based heuristics such as historical highs and lows.

Investors also take account of price moves as indicators of human involvement in flows of data and orders, patterns in liquidity through investment flows and security issuance, extra return from holding assets during extended market closures such as weekends and holidays, and upward drift due to involuntary investor savings.

Thus equities' price vector (rate and direction of price change) can indicate the arrival of unseen value-sensitive data, point to expectational errors where valuations have become biased away from good forecasts, indicate better knowledge, and warn if an investor's paradigm or information base has become less relevant (Baker and Wurgler 2006). It is incorporated in fund managers' utility functions as evidenced by their widespread use of technical analysis (Menkhoff 2010), and tendency to follow prices and herd (Sias 2004).

10.1.4 Investor Risk Incorporates Uncertainty and Downside Loss

Fund managers are aware of empirical evidence that equity risk is not related to return on either an ex ante or ex post basis (Anderson et al. 2009), and view risk as possible loss in wealth that is impractical to titrate. This is true Knightian uncertainty, where the distribution of losses is not amenable to statistical modelling.

For investors, expected increase in a share's value causes uncertainty. As amplification, purchase of an equity that seems undervalued implies significant change in either market assessment of the equity's value, or in the value generating process of the underlying firm. Neither occurrence is guaranteed and both are fraught with uncertainty, which leads to a truism in finance and management that "large gains tend to require large risks be taken" (Sanders and Hambrick 2007: 1055). That is, ex ante return causes uncertainty; which, of course, is the mirror image of the standard finance assumption that ex ante risk causes return.

Although the possibility of loss is caused by anticipated return, an important aspect is that uncertainty can be modified by risk management. The uncertainty-return link for equities can be expressed as follows:

$$\text{Uncertainty} = \Phi \left\{ \left(\frac{\text{Expected return}}{\text{Risk management}} \right) . Z \right\},$$

where Z is a vector of equity-specific variables.

In words: because the return from any strategic objective is a function of the difficulty in achieving it, high returns come by achieving challenging outcomes that axiomatically have a high likelihood of failure, and so uncertainty is a function of expected return. Uncertainty can, however, be moderated by managing the risk (using market instruments, insurance, or techniques such as enterprise risk management), and is affected by variables specific to the firm that affect the probable success in implementation of value-generating strategies (such as size, leverage and managerial skill that proxy for capability).

10.1.5 Investors Lack Predictive Capability, and Develop Relative Rankings of Equity Value

An important structural feature of markets is that investors cannot predict valuation-relevant factors beyond the short term, which – along with recurrence of large, systematic market swings – makes it impractical to project returns of individual equites. Given limited foresight, decisions are conditional on

10 Piecing Together the Jigsaw: *Applied Investment Theory* 173

information available at the time, and the best that investors can do is to use crude heuristics to marginally improve return and constrain the possibility of downside losses. Consistent with incorporating price in their utility function, fund managers focus on security prices rather than returns. They think in terms of a roughly two year terminal value, possibly constructed by truncating the future to the reasonably foreseeable next year and a serially-related subsequent outcome (Hellman 2000).

Consideration of prices points to the cross-section of potential investments, and investors rank their relative values in light of opportunity cost. Valuation is based on current firm data and market conditions, and is adjusted in light of investor interpretation of proxies for future return and uncertainty.

These perspectives on equity valuation can be reconciled in the following expression:

$$\text{Subjective preference} = U\{\text{Relative value, Relative uncertainty} \,|I \subset \Omega\}$$
$$|\{\text{Market price, State of the world}\}$$

where I is information available at the time of decision, and Ω is total information set.

In words, investors determine the relative value and uncertainty of each potential investment by imposing their utility function on observable data and security characteristics, and make their choice in light of current market price which is contingent on state of the world.

With restricted foresight, investors rely on observable proxies, which include trends in performance; characteristics of a firm's managers which reflect skill in achieving cash flow increases; indicators of the intentions of agents such as directors and managers, regulators and legislators; and hedonics related to risk (e.g. ESG) and return (e.g. industry growth). Other proxies recognise the importance of macroeconomic factors such as conditions in the broad economy that affect cash flows for the stock's underlying firm, and in financial markets that affect relative valuations; impact from change in conditions in the firm's industry; and uncertainty in the firm's future operations, and possible failure of strategies or projects that were anticipated to improve cash flows.

10.1.6 Three-Component Model of Equity Value

The final innovation in our theoretical model of equity investment extends the point that investment success accompanies increases in the value of a firm's assets, which requires either completion of a value-generating process,

174   Applied Investment Theory

or change in the market's assessment of the existing equity's value. Neither is guaranteed. So, overlaying valuation is a further level of uncertainty in relation to negative, or wealth destroying, events following occurrence of a wrong scenario (Porter 1985).

A way to tie together disparate factors that seem important to fund manager valuation of equities is suggested by two concepts that are well-established in finance: firm value has multiple components (e.g. Miller and Modigliani 1961), and equities have features of real options (e.g. Myers 1977).

Incorporating option components in an equity's value is logical given that shareholders value flexibility in the ability to vary execution of their investment decision by altering the size and timing of trades, period that equities are held, and – by incorporating risk management – range of outcomes. Optionality also arises exogenously because the value of the equity's claim on firm cash flows is contingent on changing state of the world (Arrow 1964), which has speculative outcomes; and because investors can affect return and uncertainty through borrowing or diversification.

The proposal here is that fund managers operationalise their ranking of candidate equities by effectively considering three economic components of a share, or the sum of its parts, which comprise: the fundamental value of assets in place or current operations; a long real call option whose price reflects expected operational improvements and strategic initiatives; and a sold real put option whose price is the monetised uncertainty associated with possible value loss from unexpected adverse exogenous impacts or outcomes from firm operations and strategies.

The assumption is not that fund managers formally calculate the values of each of these three components, but that they implicitly or intuitively incorporate equivalent calculations in their valuation process. The three-component valuation model is operationalised when investors think separately of the value of the firm's assets in place, add the value of expected improvements in earnings while holding the share, and adjust for the possibility of loss through unpredictable or unexpected events. This, of course, describes fundamental valuation as reported by many authors including Kothari (2001) and Treynor and Black (1973). The model also directly incorporates three of the principal equity valuation methods, namely accounting value, relative valuation, and contingent claim valuation; and it allows use of DCF (Damodaran 2007).

The three components of equity valuation are depicted in the figure below (Fig. 10.1).

The rationale for basing equity value in part on current operations is that these are discrete, can be clearly identified and are relatively certain. They can be variously estimated as a multiple either of normalised earnings, or of measures of earnings capacity such as assets and revenues.

10 Piecing Together the Jigsaw: *Applied Investment Theory*

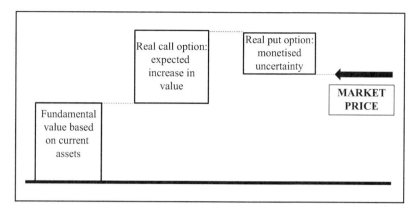

Fig. 10.1 Waterfall diagram of a share's three components of value

The real call option component of a share's value relates to return from commissioning new assets, which is qualitatively different to the return from existing assets and less certain. The call option's value is a function of earnings improvements in prospect, which is endogenous to the security. Quantification of the option is a measure of the investor's skill in stock selection, or accuracy of their expectations about probable developments in the underlying firm. The option's duration is equal to the investor's expected holding period or investment horizon; the strike price is the value of current assets; and premium is the present value of expected value enhancements.

The third component of equity value is a sold real put option that represents wealth which could be lost by the investor from occurrence of an undesirable scenario involving possible, but unexpected, adverse developments. This can arise exogenously from changes in the broad economy or at the market level such as shifts between yields on equities and risk-free securities that affect the opportunity cost of a share. Other adverse developments which affect the value of assets in place and future earnings can arise within the firm such as an operational failure, or in factors specific to the firm such as competition or industry demand.

Valuation of the real put option is a function of uncertainty, specifically the potential for downside loss: if the investor has perfect knowledge of a security's value (e.g. a 'risk-free' Treasury note), uncertainty is zero, and so is the value of the put option. Thus the put option's value is related to lack of knowledge about the firm's assets and cash flows. The duration of the option is equal to the investor's investment horizon; strike price is the value of current assets; and its premium is equal to the monetised present value of possible loss of wealth, or probability weighted value of possible wealth damaging occurrences.

176   **Applied Investment Theory**

An important feature of this three component model of an equity's value is that it does not incorporate a nexus between equity return and uncertainty, and thus explains empirical evidence that there is not a stable link between security return and risk (return volatility). Although expected incremental return causes possible loss, this can be modified through risk management by the investor and firm; and the return-risk link is further weakened by inherent uncertainty arising from unknowable shifts in state variables and the firm's environment with equally unknowable impact on current assets and improvements.

What theoretical and empirical support is there for a three-component model of equity valuation?

Although this concept has not been previously proposed, a number of researchers have successfully employed a component model of equity value. For instance, Zhang (2000) suggests that an equity's value equals the sum of the value of existing assets plus a real option related to future opportunities to vary operations. This is extended by Chen and Zhang (2007) who develop and test an options-based explanation of the predictive ability of accounting variables.

A second support for the component model comes from behavioural analyses which identify a hindsight bias in investors (e.g. Biais and Weber 2009). This sees them separately attribute successful and unsuccessful decisions, respectively, to skill in their investment evaluation and unpredictable exogenous developments. At least on an ex post basis, investors acknowledge that equity returns result from a combination of predictable improvements (which is equivalent to the real call option) and unforeseeable adverse developments (the sold real put option).

The best support for the three component model of equity valuation is a natural experiment that tests whether equity values incorporate each of the components. My simple evaluation uses dimensionless measures of equity value, namely price-to-book ratio (market capitalisation: net assets) and price-to-earnings ratio (market capitalisation: net income). The three components are quantified by proxies, so that: value of current assets is given by normalised return on equity (net income for the previous five years minus the highest and lowest values divided by average shareholders' equity); value of the real call option over future developments is given by the average annual change in revenue during the previous five years scaled by average revenue; and the real put option is given by the standard deviation of net income over the previous five years scaled by average net income. An additional independent variable, namely total assets, is added to control for size effects.

10 Piecing Together the Jigsaw: *Applied Investment Theory*

Table 10.1 Regression of value ratios against three equity components

Variable	Price-to-earnings	Price-to-book
Normalised ROE	0.325***	0.375***
Slope of revenue	7.269***	1.230***
Volatility of net income	−6.000***	−0.793***
Ln total assets	−0.172***	−0.212***
Adjusted R-squared	0.248	0.076

***$p < 0.01$

To avoid survivorship bias, the sample comprises a panel of all companies that had been included in the S&P 500 Index at any time during 1950–2014. We test the model using annual year-end data for the quarter century during 1990–2014 from the CRSP/Compustat database, which gives a sample of 1,087 firms and 19,195 observations. The last were winsorised (to be equal to, or less than two standard deviations from, the mean) and trimmed (to remove improbable data, such as negative volatility measures and value ratios).

The following table show results of OLS regression of price-to-book and price-to-earnings ratios against proxies for value of current assets and the real call and put options (Table 10.1).

This simple analysis supports the hypothesised valuation model, with highly significant parameter co-efficients with expected signs and a reasonable explanatory power. That is, both value measures are positively and significantly related to values of current assets and the real call option; and negatively and significantly related to the real put option.

These results show the cross-section of values of medium to large US firms in the quarter century to 2014 is explained in part by a three-component model comprising value of assets in place (as proxied by normalised ROE), a real call option linked to growth opportunities (proxied by recent revenue change), and a real put option linked to uncertainty (proxied by recent income volatility). Values of R-squared point to economic significance of the model.

Two points should be made about the analysis. The first is that it is ex post and provides an explanation for observed patterns in measures of equity valuation. The second is that the analysis examines the contribution of accounting variables (as proxies for the three components on the valuation model) to equity value, rather than return. Neither point detracts from empirical support for the three-component equity valuation model.

In closing, it is worth noting that the innovation of a three-component equity value was suggested by field observation, is consistent with theoretical depiction of investor behaviour, and is robust to testing in a natural experiment using market data. This use of field studies to develop theoretically-based hypotheses that are tested with real-world data epitomises the philosophy of

178   Applied Investment Theory

this book, and follows traditional asset pricing studies that use standard theory to develop hypotheses and test them using empirical data.[1]

10.2 Seemingly False Assumptions

The discussion to date has identified unequivocal facts about markets and investors that need to be comprehended in any descriptive investment theory. Just as important, though, is to identify demonstrably untrue items that the standard investment paradigm treats as facts, lest they be incorporated – even as unstated assumptions – in the re-engineered investment theory.

Already we have identified a number of assumptions that are not robust to real-world scrutiny. In terms of equities, information is far from central to equity valuation, and often seems irrelevant (see Sect. 6.4); and equity return does not have a consistent relationship with its volatility (Sect. 4.2), nor with lagged firm and security attributes (Sect. 6.3). Turning to investors, they focus on equity prices rather than returns (Hellman 2000), and make use of historical data (Menkhoff 2010) so that liquidity and transactions influence decisions (Amihud 2002).

Moreover, speculators are not passive conduits, but affect prices (Sect. 6.2). Despite assumptions of markets' efficiency and the absence of frictions and the role of arbitrage, there is evidence of manipulation (Sect. 9.2) and humans control the quality and flow of information (Sect. 10.1). Markets obviously do not offer a level playing field, so it is no surprise that most fund managers assume shares are not fairly valued (Arnswald 2001).

Perhaps the most challenging of the questionable facts supporting standard finance is its central premise that the future can be predicted with some degree of precision. To the contrary, a robust conclusion from finance research across decades and continents is that neither investors nor financial economists have much predictive ability (see Sect. 9.1). The failure of institutional investors to replicate their decisions, predict key valuation inputs, and outperform naïve rules negate the fundamental premise supporting forward looking valuation.

As cautions for redesign of the investment model, erroneous beliefs have introduced a number of unfortunate skews in standard finance. The first is the assumption that investors have sufficient skill to form economically meaningful predictions of security cash flows, economic conditions and other inputs to calculations of future value. This focusses valuation processes on the future and thus use of normative valuation techniques to calculate expected returns, which has

---

[1] Chen and Zhang (2007), for example, develop and test a model of how accounting variables explain returns; and Barberis et al. (1998), Daniel et al. (1998), and Hong and Stein (1999) test various models of how recognised investment biases could impact valuations.

downplayed the cross-section of current equity values, and ignores the need to study its mechanics. Further, the ready availability of reliable market data encourages quantitative predictions, which promotes use of statistical measures such as moments of the distribution of returns, and intuits links between quantified variables such as a positive linear relationship between return and its volatility.

In summary, research in financial economics has been herded towards ex post, quantitative analysis using remotely compiled data. Belief that investors' valuation process is obvious and the availability of good market data further diminished field research. Evidence that few of the intuited relationships have any value and real-world complications such as market frictions and non-randomness in data are dismissed as biases.

10.3 Applied Investment Theory

This section is the meat of the book and sets out the proposed descriptive model of fund manager investment decision making, which is named *Applied Investment Theory* (AIT).

Equity investment by mutual fund managers is an important topic because funds are economically significant as the largest investor groups in most developed countries (Aggarwal et al. 2011), and – as custodians of workers' retirement savings – are central to one of the most important principal agent relationships in modern economies. Fund managers around the world are also at the centre of the economically significant puzzle that – despite their skill and resources – they are one of the few professional groups that cannot best amateurs (Cochrane 1999).

AIT takes a comprehensive view of fund manager investment, and explains the performance of these skilled, well-resourced investors in terms of their motivations and exogenous forces. Under AIT, idealised assumptions of the standard investment paradigm are relaxed and real-world conditions introduced: markets are subject to frictions and so cannot eliminate information asymmetry, nor costlessly enforce security contracts; rationality is conditional on restricted foresight and constrains investment to use of available information; and risk becomes aversion to loss and Knightian uncertainty in wealth.

Applied Investment Theory has eleven core precepts.

1. The managed funds industry is a global oligopoly whose fees are typically unrelated to performance, and which has a business model built around lifting funds under management (FUM). Mutual funds are free to self-regulate because few clients react to performance, most observers are captives, and fund operations are opaque and characterised by information asymmetry.

Typical of oligopolies, the mutual funds industry does not compete on price; nor does it compete through performance-based fees even though they are all but universally legal (Alpert et al. 2015): most revenue comes from commissions as a proportion of funds under management (FUM).

Most flows to mutual funds are savings, and their growth is constrained by slow rise in the labour force and wages. This intensifies competition for FUM, which is based on the criteria that investors use to select a fund, including reputation, investment strategy and performance (Capon et al. 1996). The last is facilitated through voluntary participation in ranking tables that are compiled by Lipper, Morningstar and similar services, where position is especially important to financial advisors who are used by a majority of investors and prefer to base advice on objective measures (Jones et al. 2005).

Funds' business model is built around the principal financial objective of increasing FUM, and it is easy to envisage how return to fund clients may not be maximised. Benefits of scale can promote growth in assets beyond a level that produces optimum return; fund manager compensation is often linked to capital inflows, whereas only a third of fund managers receive significant compensation for performance of funds under their management (Farnsworth and Taylor 2006); and incentives can vary according to the fund's lifecycle stage, which can see managers neglect returns. Fund managers can also forego return by engaging in window dressing to signal better strategy (e.g. Brown et al. 2001), or altering their strategy and fund risk in light of performance by either banking good results or increasing risk propensity to try and make up for poor results (Clare et al. 2014).

Another effect of commissions is that incentives to third parties such as financial advisors are built around increasing FUM. This can encourage financial advisers to churn clients' investments, and direct them towards funds with higher incentives irrespective of risk or cost.

Whilst mutual funds' clients might be expected to monitor performance and prevent such abuses, they tend to be disengaged from management of their savings (Agnew et al. 2003), and are insensitive to performance, so they only withdraw money from the worst performing funds (Del Guercio and Tkac 2002). In addition, the quality of investment management is frequently obscured because of information asymmetry and opacity of fund activities (Mehran and Stulz 2007). Thus external observers such as industry regulators are usually not able to monitor mutual fund operations, which leaves funds free to self-regulate.

Given the obvious agency conflicts faced by mutual funds, they employ a variety of strategies to address concerns that they may not unconditionally maximize investors' value (Athanassakos 1992). Measures to enhance reputation include adoption of style labels, and appointing fund managers with external characteristics that build investor confidence such as education, experience and appearance. Funds also mitigate risks by voluntarily constraining their investment strategy to prevent borrowing, short positions or derivatives (Almazan et al. 2004). While such constraints serve as substitutes for monitoring, serendipitously they do not adversely affect performance (Almazan et al. 2004).

2. Equity prices are contingent on an unpredictable future state of the world, and are usually not related to public information nor predictable from lagged firm and security traits. Equity prices are subject to deliberate human action because people control most information flows and have discretion over timing. Dominance of investors with open-ended portfolios leads to a sawtooth price pattern in equity markets.

Two important assumptions underpin much thinking about equity prices: equities have a fundamental value that is set by information, which arrives randomly; and – apart from a few behavioural biases – prices are free of human distortion. Neither is even close to true, and the most surprising feature of equity prices is how little is known about how they are determined.

Take the role of information first. There is usually no relationship between significant price moves and identifiable value-relevant information. Thus few announcements about valuation fundamentals bring price reaction (Cutler et al. 1989); as much as 80% of significant moves in indexes and individual stock prices cannot be attributed to new information (e.g. Bouchaud et al. 2009; Fair 2002; and Pritamani and Singal 2001); and market crashes are usually unexplained (Goldstein and Razin 2015). Event studies show that most new information brings a cumulative abnormal return of no more than a few percent that rarely lasts more than a day or two (Brown 2011): the small statistical signals of price impact soon disappear, even after a wide variety of surprising events that intuitively should have permanent effect on prices (e.g. Brooks et al. 2003).

Given the limited ability to explain equity returns, it is not surprising that predictive ability is even more limited. Historical returns data has trivial forecasting power (Andersen et al. 2003). Ex ante studies of lagged firm-specific attributes using publicly available data that is available to investors show they have trivial ability to predict cross-sectional variation in year-ahead equity returns (Ferreira and Santa-Clara 2011). This arises because approximately half the return to equities comes from systematic factors (Chen, Da and Zhao 2013), which are impractical to meaningfully forecast (Fildes and Stekler 2002); and – because firm-specific factors that explain the other half of returns rarely have a stable

182   Applied Investment Theory

relationship with future returns – return-lagged variable relationships have little predictive ability over investors' horizon. Contributors to equity returns are so uncertain that Harvey et al. (2014) conclude most findings appear spurious.

Volatility is only slightly more predictable as it clusters (Ghysels et al. 2005) and econometric models are of some use out to a few days, although there is no additional predictive power in either implied volatility (Canina and Figlewski 1993) or macroeconomic variables (Engle and Rangel 2008).

A second erroneous assumption is that the only human influences on equity prices are a few, localised behavioural biases. Humans, though, have sweeping impact on markets.

For a start, no matter what channel is involved in its dissemination, most value-sensitive information is processed by humans, and much of it is subject to discretion in timing or shaped by previous decisions. Scheduled data releases are compiled and issued by humans; and all other events must be recognised and reported by humans. In addition, many decisions follow patterns. As examples, institutional investors will prefer to split large transactions so they can transact smaller parcels when volume is heavy (Admati and Pfleiderer 1988); firms make financial decisions such as dividends and leverage in light of previous decisions (Coleman 2014a), and will execute one-off transactions such as stock issues and mergers at the most propitious time (Brown 2011); and analysts revise their published opinions of securities in increments (Cronqvist et al. 2009). The result is that much price-sensitive information does not emerge at random nor instantly reach the market, but trickles out over time.

Another set of human price distortions arises in the decisions of major investors. Perhaps equity markets were once perfect and consisted of investors that were so small that none could influence price (although dealers sometimes played a role). Now, though, at least half of all equities are owned by mutual funds and other institutions, which have common objectives and timetables, socialise extensively and are pressured to conform. Financial institutions are also known to join together in elaborate conspiracies and scams. Importantly, too, fund managers run open ended portfolios of long term savings whose flows are exogenously driven, and so their investments are involuntary and relatively price-insensitive.

Mutual funds must compete to buy (or sell) equities by bidding for attractive stocks at price increments above the bids of competing institutions. Thus equity prices creep up until a maximum realistic level is reached; whereupon institutions reduce their net buying, and prices fall relatively sharply towards a low fundamental value. This leads to a saw toothed cycle of slow small, price rises with few, sharper falls, and the negative skewness in returns that is typical of virtually every developed equity market (Wen and Yang 2009).

10 Piecing Together the Jigsaw: *Applied Investment Theory*

Mutual funds also have a rigid calendar-based reporting cycle, with year-end results of most importance. This encourages window dressing so that funds will reduce exposure after a good interim result and bank profits (or lift risk to try and recover ground) (Clare et al. 2014). The net inflow from retirement savings gives equity prices an upward drift, which explains why the highest level of the S&P 500 in 7 of the 13 years to end 2015 was in December, with 6 of those at year end.

3. Modern markets are informationally efficient; but they are subject to frictions, and cannot eliminate information asymmetry, nor costlessly enforce equity contracts. Prices trend and cluster, and technical analysis is of use over the short term. Procyclical demand for equities sees them act as Veblen goods with an upward sloping demand curve

Modern markets are so efficient in processing information that prices of firms involved in totally unexpected corporate events – such as sudden CEO deaths and fatal industrial accidents – are affected within an hour, and reflect most of the new information before it begins to appear in the media several hours later (Coleman 2011). Despite this, markets suffer a number of inefficiencies.

Information asymmetry is common because data and analysis do not instantly reach all investors. Longer term, markets and investors display evolutionary elements – including competition and reproduction – which enable natural selection to continuously adapt and optimize structures (Lo 2004). Nor are markets purely mechanical, because price changes systematically alter investors' wealth and risk propensity which shift their utility functions and hence the relative attractiveness and valuations of individual securities.

Because public information is infrequent and only weakly linked to permanent revaluation of equities, investors seek more frequent source of information, and so monitor the price vector (rate of change and direction) for insights into better informed or skilled investors, or expectational errors where valuations have become biased away from good forecasts (Devenow and Welch 1996). Transactions set up feedbacks between investor actions and decisions: investors respond to a price rise either by increasing their valuation of equities, or by interpreting it as indicating buying by better informed investors (e.g. Warther 1995). In both cases they place a higher value on securities and so increase their holdings. This sets up procyclical price patterns – typically described as trends or herding – that actually arise because equities act as Veblen goods which have luxury features so that rising prices signal greater attraction for possible buyers that increases their preference and demand, and leads to an upward sloping demand curve.

184   Applied Investment Theory

This promotes momentum or trending in equity prices over the short-medium term (e.g. Carhart 1997), and guides fund managers to tailor decision choices by horizon. Over the short term, perhaps a few days, historical returns can be used for prediction because return volatility persists and extreme returns mean revert (Park and Irwin 2007). Technical analysis is useful over the medium term – a week to several months – because trends form and prices move monotonically before mean reverting (although patterns' formation and dissolution have no theoretical basis and cannot be predicted). Some techniques leverage the common assumption that security prices follow a lognormal distribution around a real mean, so fund managers apply anti-cyclical heuristics. Even simple technical trading rules can add value over the short term (see, for example: Brock et al. (1992) and Shynkevich 2012), which explains its wide use by fund managers, for whom technical analysis is their most important form of decision analysis for horizons up to a month (Menkhoff 2010). Fund managers also overload on well-priced securities at the bottom of their historical range, and take profits around historical highs; and trim holdings after a run up in prices. When facing a need to liquidate some securities, FMs will sell winners and hold losers because they are expected, respectively, to drop and rise on reversion to the mean (e.g. Da Costa et al. 2008).

Another market inefficiency is that contractual obligations implicit in equities – particularly performance of counterparties and agents such as company directors and managers – are frequently not met. On average, 1% of firms with rated bonds default annually (Standard and Poor's's 2015); and the finance industry has distinguished itself in recent years as the only one where major firms have accepted ten and even eleven figure fines for defrauding their customers (e.g. Partnoy and Eisinger 2013).

4. Mutual funds are marked by extensive socialisation and complex game-theoretic interplays with competitors, clients, investee firms and industry observers where information is the common mixing variable.

A striking feature of mutual funds is similarity in their behaviour. They co-locate in financial enclaves, share common processes and information, voluntarily participate in a wide variety of industry programmes (Coleman 2015), and frequently herd (Sias 2004). Fund managers share numerous traits because they are overwhelmingly male (85+%), invariably university educated, often with a finance specialty or CFA accreditation (40+%), aged around 40 with at least 10 years industry experience across several firms, and work 50+ hours per week.[2]

---

[2] See, amongst others: Beckmann et al. (2008), Brown et al. (2014), Drachter et al. (2007), Farnsworth and Taylor (2006), and Tuckett and Taffler (2012).

An important objective of fund managers is to build funds under management (FUM), which is promoted by sending appropriate signals to prospective and current clients. These reflect the most important influences on investors' selection of a mutual fund, which apart from performance – are reputation and size of the fund family (Capon et al. 1996) and trust and investment manager attributes (Foster and Warren 2015). Credible indicators of reliability that help offset information asymmetry and investors' lemons problem include strong governance and a focus on social responsibility through adherence to principles of responsible investment. Promoting FUM also encourages voluntary participation in industry programmes ranging from performance rankings through rating agency accreditation to ubiquitous Chartered Financial Analyst (CFA) certification of employees.

Another fund manager signal is rejection of a cook book investment formula or normative process in preference to a personalised paradigm. Thus surveys show that fund managers are fully conversant with the standard investment paradigm (e.g. Amenc et al. 2011), but make little practical use of it with as few as one in three relying on modern portfolio theory (MPT) (see: Coleman 2015), and as many as half never rely on rational pricing. In practice, though, industry culture compels analysts to support their recommendations with impressive analysis (Abhayawansa and Guthrie 2012), and FMs face pressures from firm management, asset consultants and regulators as well as influential clients who expect to see traditional theory supporting investment decisions. They conform by outwardly following a Treynor and Black (1973) style process, and it is unusual to see any investment proposal – whether inside a corporation, mutual fund or other financial institution – that is not accompanied by an impressive MPT-centered analysis incorporating discounted cash flows and risk evaluation. Evidence that much of this is a charade to manage impressions of influential stakeholders comes from examination of investment reports which show that recommendations are often unrelated to the supposedly supporting quantitative analyses (e.g. Barniv et al. 2010). Fortunately, though, MPT analyses prove a useful way to communicate complex conclusions such as contributors to value improvements.

A further objective of fund manager socialisation is information gathering. Best-practice regulation and corporate governance mean that most price-sensitive data is publicly available and so cannot play a strong role in equity valuation. Thus fund managers engage in a variety of game-theoretic interactions to access proprietary price-sensitive information held by: corporate insiders such as executives, regulators and advisers; better informed or more insightful investors; and others with knowledge of industry, economy or political developments (see Malkiel 2005).

186 Applied Investment Theory

The most important information source for fund managers comes through strong relations with executives of investee firms (Drachter et al. 2007), who provide value-relevant insights that narrow gaps in information (Roberts et al. 2006). Consensual information flows allow executives to influence fund managers' decisions and gain support for their share price, whilst fund managers validate and amplify public data, and deal with uncertainty in its quality; gain insights to executives' character and skill which proxy for future firm performance; and obtain feedback on their conclusions (Hellman 2000).

Thus signalling, impression management and the search for new information set up a complex pattern which – in combination with co-location of mutual funds and their common scrutiny by regulators and ratings agencies – establishes extensive socialisation across the funds management industry (White 2002).

5. Moments of equity returns are not related, and investors think of risk as the possibility of loss. Equities' target return indicates the difficulty of achieving any value improvement, so that return causes uncertainty.

Equity returns lack a clear nexus with statistical risk (volatility of returns) as evidenced by studies that variously report significantly positive, significantly negative and insignificant links (see: Anderson et al. 2009; Bali 2008; Scruggs 1998). This is to be expected given that there is no relationship between the mean and standard deviation of samples drawn randomly from a normal distribution (Stuart and Ord 2009). It is also part of a pattern of time variation in relationships between returns and other firm traits (e.g. Faff et al. 2000). The implication is that investment models that rely on a relationship between equity return and statistical risk or risk proxies are of no practical use (Simin 2008).

Fund managers think of investment risk as the possibility of loss at the time the security is liquidated, which is contingent on the then state of the world and developments that are numerous, multifaceted and uncertain. Possible loss arises in macroeconomic conditions in the broad economy (that affect cash flows for the stock's underlying firm) and financial markets (that affect relative investment values) because they shape the opportunity cost of investments; in factors that are specific to the firm that affect existing operations and implementation of value-generating strategies such as size and leverage, which proxy for capability; and in the results of management strategies or projects that were expected to optimise cash flows. Investment, then is uncertain (Knight 1921).

Further contributing to uncertainty in equity prices is that return is a function of difficulty in improving performance, with more challenging outcomes having a higher likelihood of failure. Thus expected return causes uncertainty, but it can be moderated by managing the risk using market instruments, insurance, or techniques such as enterprise risk management.

Thus uncertainty is a complex function of the exogenous environment and state variables, and firm-specific features that affect operations and the likelihood of successful value improvements, projects in prospect, and associated risk management strategies.

6. Fund managers price securities rationally on the basis of information available at the time, within a theme that describes their investment assumptions and ideal stocks. They are loss averse, use higher discount rates for nearer term revenues, and a higher discount rate for losses than gains. Ideal investments avoid short term loss while providing reasonable medium term return.

Fund manager investment follows the approach used with other complex tasks, which is to start by developing a story that sets out premises, themes and traits of importance to success (Kahneman 2011). Fund managers describe this as a top-down process where their macro-economic-political-social outlook points to optimum countries, sectors and asset classes, and identifies attributes of the best securities. This editing simplifies investment choice by winnowing the large universe of prospects to a manageable number for detailed consideration. Otherwise there would be too many factors driving returns and too much data to analyse, but – because editing inevitably incorporates particular tilts – it can be a source of systematic bias (Kahneman 2003).

Fund managers value equities in their pool of investment candidates using limited foresight, so their decisions are conditional on information available at the time; and their main risk is wealth loss at the time the security is liquidated. Their utility function incorporates proxies for uncertainty in future equity value.

In making decisions, fund managers are averse to significant loss. This is partly to reduce their employer's business risk, given that investors will withdraw funds after a serious loss (Del Guercio and Tkac 2002), and performance is a consideration for new investors (Capon et al. 1996). Fund managers also avoid loss to protect their human capital because they are engaged in a tournament style competition.

188   Applied Investment Theory

7. Investors are unable to form economically meaningful forecasts of returns. They look at the cross-section of equities and determine value in terms of opportunity cost and relative rank.

In valuing equities, fund managers focus on their fundamental price rather than expected return, largely because their inability to predict future cash flows or market conditions makes it impractical to develop absolute, or standalone, projections. Thus equity valuation is axiomatically conditional on information available at the time: managers assess relative attractiveness using current firm data and market conditions, which is adjusted in light of proxies for future return and uncertainty, and then interpreted through their utility function.

The process can be described as follows:

$$\text{Subjective Preference} = U\{\text{Relative value, Relative uncertainty} \,|\, I \subset \Omega\}$$
$$|\{\text{Market price, State of the world}\}$$

where I is available information, and Ω is the total information set (typically $I \ll \Omega$).

In words, investors decide rationally and recognise that equity return is contingent on an uncertain future state of the world, which is impractical to meaningfully predict. They are limited to use of information available at the time, and look at the cross-section of equity prices to determine relative value and uncertainty of each potential investment.

Under this formulation, relative valuation and uncertainty are determined separately, and as levels, not expected changes. Subsequent flows of information and changes in the state of the world will alter the relative ranking of securities.

8. Investor estimates of value and uncertainty are developed from historical data and proxies for firm performance, including: prices, valuation ratios, management ability; hedonic features of the security such as size and governance; and market conditions. Acquisition price serves as a benchmark in defining gains and losses.

The ranking process that fund managers apply to the cross-section of candidate equity investments begins with reliable current financial data, and develops expectations using observable proxies for return and future uncertainty (McFadden 1999). Some of these are quantitative and draw on historical performance such as price-to-book ratio. Other proxies are qualitative and relate to risk (e.g. ESG), and measures of management's operational and strategic capability and asset quality such as productivity and leverage. Proxies for uncertainty that might affect stakeholders indicate the quality of data and reliability of cash flows ranging from governance indicators to frequency of incidents.

Incorporation of price in investors' utility function explains a number of anomalies in investor behaviour. Attention to historical prices leads to biases based around trending, momentum and mean reversion. The price paid to acquire an equity serves as a benchmark so that subsequent moves reveal the success or otherwise of the decision. The ensuing change in investor's wealth brings psychological effects that affect risk propensity and explain decision biases including affirmation, confirmation, and overconfidence. Using prices as anchors leads to a combination of hindsight bias and mental accounting that can readily see attribution of wealth gain and loss to, respectively, the investor's stock selection skill and unexpected deterioration in the state of the world following exogenous acts-of-god or events that could not be foreseen.

9. In ranking equities, investors implicitly consider their three economic components: value of current assets; a long real call option whose value reflects expected return; and a short real put option whose value reflects uncertainty and possible loss.

Fund managers operationalise their ranking of candidate equities by separately considering three economic components of a share, or the sum of its parts, which comprise: the value of assets in place or current operations; a long real call option whose price reflects expected operational improvements and strategic initiatives; and a sold real put option whose price (and thus value loss) is the monetised uncertainty associated with unexpected adverse exogenous impacts or developments inside the firm due to operations and strategies. The intuition is that a share's price is made up of operational assets that generate current earnings, plus some portion of the increase that is expected to follow commissioning of planned enhancements, less a measure of the uncertainty associated with current operations and achieving expected improvements; all, of course, contingent on state of the world. The duration of the options is equal to investment horizon, while their strike price is value of current assets.

This conceptualisation of equity values builds on a number of well-recognised share traits. These include multiple economic components (Miller and Modigliani 1961), and real option features (Myers 1977). Investors also think of share values in terms of price (Hellman 2000), which is contingent on a future state of the world (Arrow 1964). Moreover, behavioural analyses show that investors treat gains and losses asymmetrically in that they are loss

190   Applied Investment Theory

averse, and separately account for successful and unsuccessful decisions (the hindsight bias).

As an aside, it is not suggested that FMs formally calculate values of each component, but that it is implicit in the principal fundamental equity valuation methods, namely accounting value, relative valuation, DCF analysis, and contingent claim valuation (Damodaran 2007). The three component valuation model incorporates many different investment perspectives.

The first component of a share's value is its assets in place, which is proxied by a market-related multiple of assets, normalised earnings or similar. This value component is reasonably certain because the assets are operational and analysts have experience with their financial performance. In the absence of an unexpected adverse development (which is incorporated in the real put option component), the value of current assets is reasonably well-understood.

The second component of a share's value is a real call option whose value (that is, appreciation of share price) is set by expectations of the firm's success in improving future cash flows. The value of the call option depends on the outcome of yet-to-be-implemented strategies and operational improvements, and so is endogenous to the firm. Accuracy in valuing this option is a measure of investor stock selection ability.

The third economic component of a share is a short real put option, which responds to unexpected deterioration in the state of the world. Its value (and hence wealth that would be lost by the investor) arises from an undesirable scenario that is outside the investor's expectation, and is often dismissed in hindsight as an act of god. Losses can arise exogenously from changes at the market level that alter the margin between yields on equities and risk-free securities and so affect the opportunity cost of shares. Other adverse developments can arise within the firm such as failure of value-generating actions or operations, and shifts in competition or industry demand that affect the value of assets in place and future earnings.

The real put option's premium incorporates uncertainty, specifically the potential for downside loss: if the investor has perfect knowledge of a security's value (e.g. a 'risk-free' Treasury), uncertainty is zero as is the value of the put option. Thus it is lack of knowledge about the firm's assets and cash flows that leads to uncertainty in value and possible loss of wealth. Uncertainty is determined from historical data (such as and semi-variance of previous return), indicators of information asymmetry (past surprises), and assessment of possible weaknesses in the firm's business plan and strategy (corporate culture, ESG). The premium is equal to the monetised present value of possible loss of wealth, or probability weighted value of possible wealth damaging occurrences.

10 Piecing Together the Jigsaw: *Applied Investment Theory*

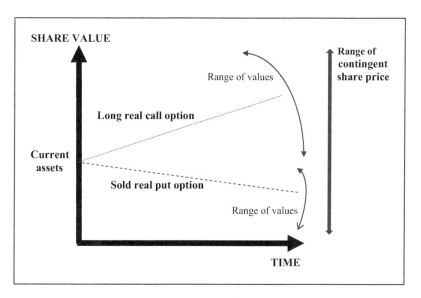

Fig. 10.2 Multi-period framework of three-component equity model

The following diagram shows contributions of the three components to share price (Fig. 10.2).

10. Fund managers do not add value for clients because it is fundamentally hard to outperform their benchmarks, their employers seek FUM growth even at the expense of performance, and they are loss averse and protect their human capital. Risk aversion, business imperatives, and transaction costs negate any fund manager skill.

Structural influences on fund managers leave them caught in a vice. On one side, equity prices cannot be established very far ahead with meaningful precision because the process of price formation is unclear and incorporates indeterminate responses by investors to new information, transient influences and feedbacks (e.g. Guedj and Bouchaud 2005). Thus a practitioner valuation primer concluded the process is so challenging that a security analyst "who is right 60 to 70 percent of the time is considered exceptional" (Hooke 2010: 9). At best, most fund managers use crude heuristics to limit downside losses, which would result in small value add for clients. Consistent, superior performance appears impractical, except possibly for an exceptional few.

On the other side, fund managers work in a global oligopoly with competition based on non-price factors which sets up strong pressures to signal skill, reliability and process to attract funds and provide the scale that boosts

192   Applied Investment Theory

their employers' profit. This can encourage FMs to divert resources and accept investment compromises that hurt performance. As a result, whilst construction of investment portfolios is the most obvious role of fund managers, it is not their only function; nor is maximizing performance their only objective.

These structural features of markets and the managed funds industry constrain fund managers to just three strategic alternatives. The few with proprietary skills will use them to advantage. A choice for less skilled managers is herding, which is a pronounced feature of the managed funds industry (Sias 2004). The third choice is to follow less ethical or even illegal approaches, which are common, too, because finance has distinguished itself as the only industry whose major players have paid nine to eleven figure fines in recent years for defrauding their customers (e.g. Partnoy and Eisinger 2013).

Fund managers contemplating the best approach know that their employers are most concerned with growing FUM, clients take limited interest in performance as long as it is reasonable (Del Guercio and Tkac 2002), compensation is only weakly influenced by performance of their funds (Ma et al. 2013), and it is doubtful they can achieve consistent outperformance (Ferreira et al. 2012). A rational fund manager who wants to protect their human capital will logically target a small margin above peers' median return with aversion to significant loss. Thus the failure of highly skilled, well-resourced fund managers to provide superior performance can be traced to their inability to make reliable forecasts and weak incentive arrangements in their industry.

11. Mutual fund performance is best explained through the structure-conduct-performance (SCP) paradigm where the stable structure of markets and the investment industry interact with more transient macroeconomic conditions to drive fund manager conduct and so determine performance. In addition, moral hazard and agency costs can be destructive of investor wealth.

A useful theoretical framework to explain fund manager behaviour is the structure-conduct-performance (SCP) paradigm (Bain 1959). Applying SCP to investment sees the stable structure of markets and the investment industry shape conduct of fund managers that interacts with transient macroeconomic conditions to drive fund performance.

Structural drivers of the industry arise because markets have consistent features relating to the way they price securities, and there is only slow change in the mix and objectives of investors. Exogenous influences on fund managers include legislation, the oligopolistic nature of their industry, and investment constraints such as the inability to accurately predict future equity prices and returns (Yan and Zhang 2009). Structural components are overlain by more transient aspects of the state of the world and investor sentiment, which are driven by continuous flow of new data (public and proprietary price-sensitive information, including transaction price and volume) whose effects can be indeterminate because many are time-varying or impractical to quantify. This leads to a variety of behaviours by fund managers that determine fund performance such as extensive socialisation with competitors, executives of investee firms and industry observers; and their personalised investment practice and decisions.

Two other factors are important. First is moral hazard which is induced by the huge scale of fees that are paid to funds and their agents (up to 1% each year of the $30 trillion in funds under mutual funds' management) and the industry's business model that links incentives to investment flows, rather than fund performance. This interacts with the second factor, namely that individual investors must deal with a variety of agents in mutual funds and financial advisers. Resulting moral hazard induces agents to take advantage of the opacity of investment operations and information asymmetry to abuse their role and exploit individual investors.

Thus SCP explains what shapes fund manager objectives, while moral hazard and agency conflicts further describe reasons for poor financial performance. The failure of mutual funds to outperform their benchmark can be traced to the distractions fund managers face which lead them to neglect the interests and preferences of investors and so fail to act as unconditional value maximisers.

In closing this description of *Applied Investment Theory*, readers should note that it is not built upon a single grand concept, but integrates many factors: investment is a chain whose smallest link is as important as the largest. Thus global behemoth banks cannot defy mean reversion buried deep in the tails of equity return distributions; and seemingly trivial ideas can build a bubble edifice that collapses for no apparent reason. The complexity and richness of AIT mimics investment life.

10.3.1 A Structural Perspective on Applied Investment Theory

The AIT model proposed above is depicted in the following figure (Fig. 10.3).

The flow chart enables a surprisingly rich interpretation of fund manager (FM) investment.

Market structure and FMs' conduct

- Public information is of limited relevance to equity valuation, and needs interpretation. To outperform, FMs seek proprietary information of direct relevance to future price, with much of it is sourced from firm executives

194   Applied Investment Theory

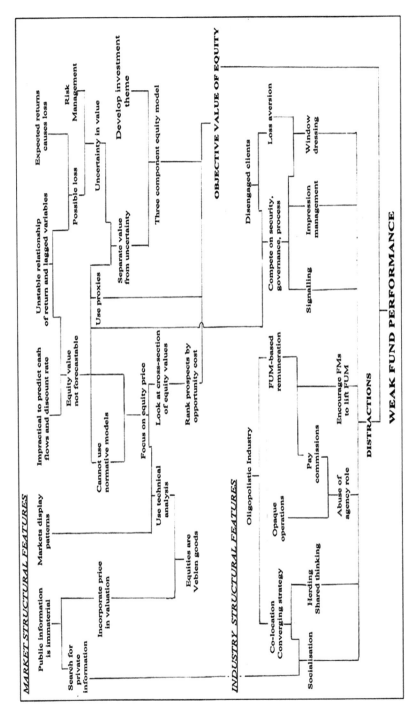

Fig. 10.3   Schematic of Applied Investment Theory

10 Piecing Together the Jigsaw: *Applied Investment Theory*   195

- It is impractical to predict future state of the world: return and equity-specific relationships are unstable, and investors cannot forecast macro-economic variables or cash flows required by normative models.
- Investors use technical analysis to capture the lognormal distribution of equity prices and identify prior valuation extremes. They monitor the price vector for possibly superior information and follow trends, so equities become Veblen goods
- The value improvement that firms target drives possible loss, which is mitigated by risk management. Target return and possibility of loss are only weakly related, so FMs separately evaluate each. Return is not related to its volatility, which has no role in valuation.
- As with other complex naturalistic decisions, fund managers start the process of equity investment by developing a narrative (which they term a theme) that sets out their paradigm, objectives and decision criteria. Structural features of equity markets then shape investment tools of practical use.
- FMs value equities in terms of three economic components: current assets; expected improvements; and possible loss.
- FMs focus on current price, and rank the cross-section of equity values according to opportunity cost using proxies for future return and uncertainty.

Industry structure and FMs' conduct

- Mutual funds' classic oligopoly encourages convergence through co-location in financial hubs and enclaves, so funds management is marked by extensive socialisation and complex game-theoretic interactions where information is the mixing variable.
- Funds are free to self-regulate due to a lack of client engagement and the industry's capture of notionally independent monitors. Fund operations are opaque and characterised by information asymmetry
- Funds' lack of reliability in performance and similar cost structure and products, respectively, promote competition through factors other than performance and price
- Funds compete on soft non-price/performance issues such as governance, security, process and reputation, which promotes signalling through voluntary participation in independent industry accreditations and rankings; and also avoids signs of risk.
- Funds pay third parties on the basis of new FUM, which compounds moral hazard from weak industry oversight and encourages exploitation of agency relationships with individual investors.

196   Applied Investment Theory

Fund manager performance

- Under structural influences, fund manager conduct converges and most incorporate a Treynor-Black overlay to an essentially qualitative investment process. Fund clients react to large losses which FMs seek to avoid, and funds seek to promote governance and reputation.
- Funds' revenue model is built around maximising FUM, sometimes to the extent of compromising performance.
- FMs are not primarily motivated or incentivised to maximise performance, so it is not their sole – perhaps not even their principal – objective.
- Rational FM strategy is to: stay close to competitor median performance; bank good results, and increase risk following a bad result; and avoid losses and risk of reputation damage.
- It is fundamentally hard for FMs to achieve positive return because of weak predictive capability, lack of value-relevant proprietary information, and shared data and processes. There are also significant transaction costs in running a fund and executing transactions.
- The net is that the structure of markets and the investment industry make it impractical or irrational for fund managers to outperform even before fees. Constraints on FMs and lack of incentives to maximise their performance offset any skill they possess.

10.4 Puzzles Resolved by AIT

An important objective of re-engineering investment theory has been to resolve some of its puzzles. AIT achieves success here.

One of the most troubling puzzles in finance which is why skilled, well-resourced institutional investors cannot add value for clients (e.g. Ferreira et al. 2012). The solution comes from applying the structure-conduct-performance paradigm to the mutual fund industry which gives a better understanding of how the structure of markets and the investment industry make it impractical or irrational for fund managers to deliver superior returns. The net is that constraints on FMs and lack of incentives to maximise their performance offset any skill they possess. Thus the average fund manager underperforms their benchmark by the value of transaction costs (e.g. Wermers 2000).

Another puzzle solved by AIT relates to behavioural biases that are known to significantly affect institutional investors (Brown and Cliff 2004). A subset of these result from the practice of evaluating decisions through ex post analyses that assume reasonable foresight by investors. Examples include over- and

10 Piecing Together the Jigsaw: *Applied Investment Theory* 197

under-reaction to news. The artificial assumption that – at the time news arrives – investors can accurately titrate its ultimate impact on a stock's fundamental value invariably proves incorrect, and investors heavily discount future value improvements that leads to creeping equilibrium as the value of news is gradually firmed up.

Perhaps the best accepted fact in investment is that an equity's fundamental value equals expected future cash flows discounted at a risk adjusted, opportunity cost,[3] and this is central to the puzzle of why well-educated finance professionals do not seem to apply DCF and other normative investment techniques (e.g. Amenc et al. 2011). The answer is that they lack the foresight necessary to develop inputs that DCF analysis requires such as future market conditions and the distribution of firm cash flows. A related puzzle is why – despite a preference for qualitative analysis – fund managers usually incorporate analyses from standard finance in their reports, although often with so little care that it does not support their conclusions (e.g. Barniv et al. 2010). This occurs because socialisation within the oligopolistic funds management industry leads to convergence of processes which requires impression management where fund managers conform to prevailing methods and meet stakeholder expectations by superficially following a fundamental investment process.

At the centre of another puzzle resolved by AIT is the widely accepted investment fact that information changes equity prices.[4] However, empirical evidence shows that it does this hold up in practice because new public information plays a limited role in equity price moves. Literally thousands of event studies of news which should intuitively have permanent impact on stock prices (see: Corrado 2011) show that it usually brings a cumulative abnormal return of no more than a few percent that rarely lasts more than a day or two (Brown 2011). Even the largest moves in equity prices often cannot be explained: large jumps in stock price typically occur in the absence of new public information (Bouchaud et al. 2009), and 90% of the largest moves in S&P futures have no identifiable cause (Fair 2002). Equally few announcements of intuitively price-sensitive information bring significant price reaction, with "important world events" followed by an average absolute return on the S&P Index of just 0.6% (Cutler et al. 1989). One reason for information's limited relevance to equity prices is its uncertain quality, whereas there is a huge amount of audited financial data, and reasonably

---

[3] The popular textbook by Brealey et al. (2012) leads its list of known finance facts with discounted cash flow analysis.

[4] As an example, Boudoukh et al. (2013) state: "A basic tenet of financial economics is that asset prices change in response to unexpected fundamental information".

198   Applied Investment Theory

standardised measures of firm performance and strategy. Thus, where new data has minimal explanatory power, historical earnings explain up to around a quarter of the cross-section in equity returns (Ferson and Harvey 1993).

Not only is new data of limited value for investors, but it is also of low frequency relative to transactions data which are continuous and provide insights into other investors' valuation. Thus – when valuing equities – fund managers look to observable data particularly prices, which explains the puzzle of why they ignore weak form market efficiency, and – in contradiction to the fine print in most finance communications – use the past as a guide to the future. Current market price tests past performance and identifies whether price is high or low relative to history, has recently trended, and how it has performed relative to competitors. This can indicate the extent to which the market has already incorporated investor insights, and a price trend can also serve as an indicator of the decisions of potentially better informed investors. Thus even sophisticated investors use technical analysis (Menkhoff 2010), follow trends and herd (Sias 2004).

Another consequence of incorporating equity price in investors' valuation is that changes after purchase confirm the success or otherwise of the decision, which induces psychological effects related to confidence and risk propensity and future investment decisions, which resolves other behavioural puzzles. Transactions also alter the wealth of investors, which shifts their utility curve and risk function that further alter their propensity to invest in equities and valuations. Price following also marks equities as Veblen goods. That is, transactions provide value-relevant information for investors. These are part of a group of impacts from transactions which explains another puzzle which is why equity prices are never stable, and do not reach anything more than short-lived equilibrium.

AIT's proposal that investors implicitly unpack equity value to comprise assets in place and two real options leads to patterns that are consistent with many puzzles from behavioural finance. A combination of hindsight bias and mental accounting can readily see attribution of wealth gain and loss to, respectively, the investor's stock selection skill and unexpected deterioration in the state of the world following exogenous acts-of-god or events that could not be foreseen. This, of course, explains the attribution bias.

Equities' multiple value components have a range of contingent prices, and price volatility is inherent in the two options. This explains how market prices have multiple possible equilibria at any time, and – like electrons in an orbit – can be shocked from one to another. As the real option components relate to contingent events with speculative outcome, they readily explain behavioural anomalies that occur without apparent justification such as price bubbles and their implosion.

AIT explains concerns of investors over uncertainty or loss of wealth (loss aversion). The monetised value of uncertainty in equity price is a complex mix of firm-specific features, risk management and the difficulty of the task involved in achieving the expected return improvement. This sees only indirect, asymmetrical links between expected return and statistical measures of risk, which explains why simple indicators such as historical share price volatility lack a consistent relationship with return (e.g. Ghysels et al. 2005). Moreover, the relationship between target return and the difficulty in executing actions to achieve it mean that expected value improvement causes uncertainty. The two option components of share value help explain the lack of a return-risk nexus because return and uncertainty are valued separately, rather than being jointly determined by the decision.

Another risk-related puzzle that AIT helps explain is uneconomic purchase of protection against loss: whether it is traditional insurance for damage and loss of life or purchase of a put option, investors pay more than its expected value (which is consistent, respectively, with high profits of insurance companies despite their overheads, and the option smirk). Loss averse investors, though, will value downside protection with an option-like premium because it involves a modest premium to offset potentially catastrophic loss of wealth from multiple poorly understood threats.

10.5 AIT and the Standard Investment Paradigm

Applied Investment Theory (AIT) qualifies, or shades, the standard investment paradigm in three ways. First, AIT envisages that markets are efficient in terms of rapidly impounding information, but they also display frictions in terms of costs, information asymmetry and inability to meet contractual obligations. Second, investors find it impractical to apply forward-looking normative models. Thus efficiency and rationality are each conditional on data available at the time and markets have institutional limitations. Third, investors think of risk as loss of wealth at the time it is needed, which renders outcomes contingent on future market conditions, and uncertain.

This re-engineering of hypotheses of the standard investment paradigm alters its assumptions and tests. It is, then, appropriate to discuss their revised nature.

First efficient markets. Under the classic depiction by Fama (1970), an efficient market is effective in capturing new information, so that prices always fully reflect available information and true value wins out in the end to provide accurate signals for firms' production-investment decisions and investors'

200   Applied Investment Theory

choices. An ideal depiction is given in the pithy observation by Samuelson (1965) that "properly anticipated prices fluctuate randomly".

AIT affirms market efficiency. It incorporates consistent evidence that markets respond quickly to new data and process it efficiently. For instance, my own studies of the market impacts of totally unexpected corporate shocks (sudden CEO deaths and fatal industrial accidents: Coleman 2011) and terrorist attacks (Coleman 2012b) show that prices are affected well before the first report appears in the media. Thus the *efficiency* of markets should not be in doubt. A second affirmation by AIT of efficient markets is the assumption that even the most professional of investors have virtually no ability to predict valuation inputs such as cash flows and market conditions. Over a typical multi-year investment horizon, returns are minimally predictable (although not totally random).

This, though, is quite different to saying that markets quickly and transparently distribute information, eliminate information asymmetry, and are passive conduits of investors' transactions. Nor can markets costlessly enforce the rights of equity and bond holders, which is evidenced by counterparty risk which is so high that it that cripples one of the largest financial institutions every year or so.[5] In addition, markets in the real world face frictions, which is the term that Clausewitz used to describe how – in war – simple things become complicated by enemy action. His perspective is illuminating, as even the simplest market transaction ('buy stock XYZ at the best price') takes place in complex settings that are subject to action by 'enemies' as diverse as tax collectors, regulators, agents affecting all level of corruption, and other investors.

A second hypothesis of standard finance is that investors have stable preferences which they use to make economically rational choices. Under AIT, rationality is conditional on the fact that even the most efficient decision can only reflect the information available, so it is unrealistic to expect that investors instantly make perfectly accurate assessments of the eventual value of information. Thus the rationality of prices and investor decisions should be judged on an ex ante basis. Fund managers will heed the financial aspects of a security, but also incorporate all available information including hedonics and firm characteristics, along with price signals and other investors' behaviour. Moreover there is no reason to expect that investors' preferences (as actioned through their individual utility functions) will remain stable in the face of changes in their wealth following shifts in market conditions and broader environment.

---

[5] In the United States since 2007 alone, major financial institutions that collapsed include: AIG, Bear Sterns, Fannie Mae, Freddie Mac, Lehman Brothers, Madoff Investment Securities, Merrill Lynch and Washington Mutual.

The third relevant hypothesis of neoclassical finance is the positive link between expected return and risk as measured by its volatility. This, too, is significantly modified under AIT where investors consider risk as the possibility of loss at the time the security is sold which is state-dependent and thus uncertain. Uncertainty cannot be measured but must be estimated by proxies such as information asymmetry, agents' involvements, and inability to project future state of the world.

This highlights two areas where the perspective of AIT differs sharply from that of standard finance. First, under AIT investment choices are made using available data to form point in time estimates of value and uncertainty; this contrasts with standard investment which relies on projecting future changes in value. Second, parameters used in AIT are expressed as levels (or historical change), not as flows or expected change. Thus AIT deals with current and historical prices, not expected returns; current relative uncertainty, not expected probabilistic risk; and current rankings of size, measures of value, and similar. This ex ante perspective that mimics real-world conditions turns established research practices on their head, points to a very different path for investors, and reaches different conclusions.

A second feature of the restatement above of investment assumptions is to allow for frictions in markets and information asymmetry between investors and agents. This points to qualitative differences between markets and counterparties, and so puts a value on the character of markets' institutional arrangements. This explains violations of the law of one price where valuations of identical assets vary when held in different structures (such as the closed end fund discount).

AIT forces re-assessment of accepted facts in standard investment by shifting evaluations of efficiency and rationality to an ex ante perspective, making return respond to uncertainty about possible loss, and incorporating a variety of non-financial parameters in investors' utility functions. Each is intuitively logical and together they have the big advantage of being able to explain many unexpected findings in investment studies. They do, however, directly contradict core premises of the neoclassical investment paradigm. Under AIT:

- Experienced investors have limited forecasting capability
- Markets violate the law of one price, and the law of demand (flat/falling demand curve)
- New price-sensitive information is rarely associated with moves in security prices
- Investors pay heed to historical prices and observable security traits that should have no value.

10.6 Conclusion

Applied investment theory fleshes out fund managers' investment process into a coherent theme. The data they need and its implications are quite uncertain, which is compounded by lack of knowledge about future developments, information asymmetry and inability to determine what has been incorporated in price. FMs concentrate on minimizing left tail investment loss and their employers' commercial exposures, with little attention to statistical risk. Managers evaluate data using observable proxies for return and uncertainty, of which the most value-relevant are their assessments of the quality of firm management and strategy because each proxies for future firm performance. They communicate their complex judgements through conventional quantitative analyses that meet stakeholder expectations.

While this depiction of fund managers' investment process is unremarkable, it has the interesting consequence of explaining funds' poor performance. The mutual funds world is one where the average educated, experienced finance professional cannot beat the market. Financial institutions routinely abuse their agency role with savers. The only realistic explanation is that the structure of markets and the investment industry make it impractical or irrational for fund managers to deliver superior performance. This, of course, again highlights how little we know about the practices of investment valuation

AIT questions the wisdom of the managed investment edifice. Reality is that the most professional investors cannot beat the market, and the most respected financial institution will abuse its authority as an agent of individual investors. A rational managed funds industry would acknowledge an absence of skill, and undertake nothing more than mechanical functions. This suggests that the optimum investment vehicle for most of us is some kind of vanilla, no-frills index fund. Those with more investment skill might add a bit of pizazz through personalized asset allocation and designer leverage.

11

Real World Application of Applied Investment Theory

The Key Takeaways of This Chapter Are

- Applied Investment Theory (AIT) proposes a framework to explain mutual fund investing, and concludes that poor fund performance has structural causes.
- AIT opens up as many questions as answers:
  - its innovations need to be thoroughly validated by developing a rigorous theoretical basis, testable hypotheses and empirical data for appropriate natural experiments
  - important gaps persist in our understanding of actual processes used by fund managers to compile and analyse data; and the nature and extent of expertise along the chain of investment.
- Although expectation of investment profit is one of mankind's oldest illusions, most investors optimise return through no-frills, low cost index funds
- Significant changes should be made to investment industry regulation.
  - Structural causes of poor returns call for increased competition between fund managers, and improvements in their focus and reporting in the industry.
  - Chronic abuse of agents' role calls for remuneration solely on the basis of fee for service or performance, and tougher penalties.

© The Author(s) 2016
L. Coleman, *Applied Investment Theory*,
DOI 10.1007/978-3-319-43976-1_11

The spur for developing applied investment theory (AIT) is that the standard investment paradigm cannot explain the emerging crisis in investment that is characterised by chronic global, financial crises and debilitating investment puzzles such as underperformance of fund managers. There is a pressing need for a better description of investors' behaviour that enjoins theory and empirical evidence, integrates research and practice, and builds an investment paradigm of value to finance practitioners, investors and researchers.

The process followed here draws on learnings from medicine, which – like investment – is an archetypal practitioner-driven discipline. It captures evidence from field research and impounds real-world data in theory through 'knowledge translation' (Straus et al. 2009). The interaction between researchers and practitioners disseminates knowledge back to research, ensures that theory does not stagnate and improves decisions.

Let us consider how *Applied Investment Theory* could promote equally productive interaction between investment researchers and practitioners.

11.1 A Research Agenda for Applied Investment Theory

Applied investment theory (AIT) logically explains what we observe in the mutual fund industry. This, of course, is a long way from detailing exactly what happens across markets, mutual funds and the investment process. Similarly, while theoretical and empirical support is provided for AIT's core premises, that is a long way from proving them to be soundly based. Thus AIT highlights gaps in our understanding of fund manager investment and its poor performance, which will support a research agenda that is somewhat different to that of traditional finance.

Although AIT identifies a nexus in financial economics between action-and-reaction or cause-and-effect that is typical of the physical sciences, it brings a different research focus. This is because – unlike scientific phenomena – investment decisions and outcomes occur at quite different times, and results are contingent on an unknowable future state of the financial world. This is typical of many predictive tasks such as forecasting weather and outcomes of contests (ranging from elections to acquisitions) where numerical inputs are available, but successful choice reflects good judgement and intuition.

A second change to the investment research agenda arises because AIT integrates observation, practice and theory within a specific framework; and then reaches the conclusion that structural features of markets and the managed

11 Real World Application of Applied Investment Theory   205

funds industry promote an investment process where returns from mutual funds are no better than their market benchmark. Certainly this structure-conduct-performance approach is standard in strategy and industry research (including banking: e.g. Hannan 1991), but it is less common in market-oriented studies which tend to assume away external structural influences and dismiss investor conduct as irrational. Thus AIT invites better understanding of the state of the world, and scrutiny of the inner workings of the investment process, rather than assuming it is mechanical and quantitative. This suggests a need to change one or more of contemporary investment techniques, structure of the managed funds industry, and financial planning advice.

A third reason why AIT changes traditional finance research is that it does not allow any foresight by investors, and assumes they use a broad spectrum of observable, value-determining factors that encompass institutions, markets, firms and investors. This requires investor decisions to be tested and examined ex ante against a mix of criteria, not just financial. Moreover, fund managers' practice of basing investment decisions on personal judgment of anecdotal evidence indicates that normative investment techniques and statutory accounting information require upgrade.

AIT relies on broad materials compiled from interviews and other qualitative studies that are suited to highly uncertain settings such as investment. Thus it has identified processes and factors that are not apparent through remote quantitative analyses, and supported them with empirical evidence and theoretically-based explanations. But it is still largely based on investor self-reports, which do not establish a clear link between what investors actually do when making investment decisions, the cash flows generated by firms, and the market returns achieved. So, because "scant attention is paid in finance to profound questions about how decision makers make sense of the knowledge that they have somehow acquired" (Bailey 2005: 65), institutional investors' actual practices are still very much a black box.

Research should be directed at improving understanding of relationships along the complex chain from investor decisions to market returns. Illumination will come from granular observation of investment decision making in the field. This should encourage the nascent discipline of the anthropology of finance, which – true to its roots – studies markets, investment and banking to understand what the natives think and do (see surveys by Baba (2012) and Maurer 2006). Another technique follows the study by Graham and Harvey (2001) entitled "The Theory and Practice of Corporate Finance: Evidence from the field" which surveys finance executives about their actual practices. Interviews and other qualitative research will be required to explore investment decision making in different markets and market conditions.

The objective is to identify stimuli leading up to decisions and tie them to subsequent documentation and actual trades, setting out how investors incorporate elements such as price and loss aversion and the role of broader influences on share values from contingency, uncertainty and optionality.

A challenge in better understanding the drivers of investment practices is that they are state-dependent and influenced by feedback from investors' performance. Investors' utility functions incorporate a multiplicity of regime shifting and time varying factors, and this heterogeneity in behaviour needs to be evaluated for the value it adds to rational decision making. Behavioural finance provides some input, but it needs an ex ante perspective because investors cannot look ahead; and needs to broaden the criteria for rationality beyond normative theory that cannot be applied.

A pressing research question is what can be done to improve the performance of managed funds, given that their net return to investors is rarely better than zero. AIT traces fund performance to fund managers' inability to predict shares' returns, and to the oligopolistic structure of their industry which diverts effort away from unconditionally maximising returns to clients' funds.

The first topic this suggests is to better understand variables that can predict equity outperformance. It is not sufficient to identify lagged variables that have historically explained returns. To add value, variables must be identified that give predictive power that is economically meaningful. Abnormal returns need to be traced back to theoretical underpinnings to give a better understand of their reasons for success and thus point to observable traits of firms and stocks that have superior performance. This allows better theoretical understanding of the nature of inter-temporal relationships between returns – which are investors' objective – and the factors that determine them. It was also identify causality, and endogeneity where variables that are jointly determined without causal relationships. Unless progress can be made in this area, it will remain hard to interpret the behaviour of asset prices, and thus to optimise investing.

More broadly, practitioners do not seem to employ tools that could be used to better manage their knowledge. Identifying a more structured approach may offer an opportunity to add value (see, for instance: Marshall et al. 1996).

Another research topic suggested by AIT comes from the conclusion that poor fund performance can be traced to the industry's oligopolistic structure and pressures to attract clients' funds which diverts fund managers' effort away from performance optimisation. This requires research into the structure and behaviour of the managed funds industry which would seek ways – including changes to regulation – to make it less inimical to client interests. Certainly reliability and stewardship of funds are critical, but this can be simply done through index investing by low cost fund custodians. What more is justifiable?

11 Real World Application of Applied Investment Theory 207

Related to this is individual savers' need for better investment advice. The latter usually falsely assumes that performance of asset classes and securities is predictable, and it is often biased by the paradigm or compensation arrangements of the adviser. Neither is likely to ensure optimum outcomes for savers. Part of this research into optimum investment advice should consider the practical objectives of investment portfolios given that their risk is unrelated to return; and also whether portfolio composition should be generic, or somehow matched to individual investors in terms of their psyche, expected and contingent liabilities, and non-financial assets such as human capital.

A further research topic arises because AIT – at least in conventional financial economics terms – is a descriptive theory that is lacking mathematical formulations. Certainly most theories started off as descriptive and were then formulated mathematically: in science examples include evolution, big bang formation of the universe, gravity, and conception; and examples in economics include Keynes General Theory, Lintner's dividend model, and finance theories such Miller and Modigliani's capital structure, agency theory, and efficient markets. Although good theories need not be purely mathematical, a rigid, quantitative formulation has the important advantages of codifying insights to enable economically useful predictions, and facilitating empirical validation.

Finally, AIT raises a number of new perspectives in financial economics which are significantly different to the precepts of neoclassical finance, principally:

1. The structure-conduct-performance paradigm, agency theory and moral hazard have together proven able to explain the behaviour and performance of fund managers.
2. Humans have extensive influence over equity prices because they control flows of most market information
3. Equity prices follow a sawtooth pattern because dominant investors are oligopolistic, price insensitive fund managers
4. Investors rebut efficiency in equity markets by incorporating prices in their utility functions.
5. Investors see risk as uncertainty and downside loss, which is caused by target return.
6. Investors cannot project returns of individual equities, and so think in terms of equity price, and rank values of candidate investments in light of their opportunity cost.
7. Equities are valued according to three economic components: the value of current operations; a long real call option whose price depends on value improvements; and a sold real put option whose value loss depends on unexpected adverse developments.

While the text provides empirical and theoretical support for each of these innovative perspectives, each provides a rich and important topic for finance research.

Applied Investment Theory appears to be superior to neoclassical investment, but it is only the start of a new finance paradigm that builds theory from observation and practice. In particular, it does not solve several fundamental questions relating to investment. The most important relates to its central feature which is that it deals with securities whose value lies in their future, which – like everything else in that strange land – is highly speculative. The task of managing this uncertainty is further compounded because the investment industry is dominated by agents who are driven by self-serving biases and have hard-to-identify information and skill. Thus AIT requires individual investors to choose an analytical paradigm on which to base selection of their portfolio, and a strategy to identify and manage their agents.

11.2 How to Teach Applied Investment Theory

Finance education anticipates students' future role as finance practitioners by teaching a core of theories and analytical techniques from modern portfolio theory (the neoclassical finance paradigm). At least in Anglophone countries, this assumes an investment world where decision outcomes and their probabilities are known. Investment practice, though, is an archetypal skill-based profession that makes complex naturalistic decisions. Practitioners compile a large amount of qualitative data (everything from opinion polls to discussions with corporate executives), evaluate it intuitively using evidence-based heuristics, and are intensely socialised by competitors and colleagues.

In short, finance education concentrates on normative theory and mathematical analysis using hard data such as market prices, with limited room for less robust firm-specific data, and virtually none for observations from field studies. Practitioners neglect normative investment techniques that are the staple of finance courses in favour of qualitative tools. Education also ignores the important practical issue of how to incorporate uncertainty or ambiguity into investment. Nor is there any description of what is unknowable and how this can be managed because finance teaching is blind to insights from other social sciences such as politics, sociology, and psychology; it often leaves only a small role even for economics and management.

Few finance schools seem aware of (or – more correctly – consider) these gaps between what finance students learn and later practice in the field. This is a surprise as the schism has been apparent at least since a survey by Smith and

Goudzwaard (1970) which reported 34% of academics felt that investment courses were 'very relevant' for successful portfolio management, but only 4% of practitioners agreed.

Guidance on how to better teach through the lens of Applied Investment Theory (AIT) comes from medicine, which is the discipline whose practices are closest to those of investment. In particular, medical education relies heavily on practitioners for clinical training, which is conducted in real-world hospital settings where students learn through feedback from their decisions. While this could be replicated in investment education, making the wholesale changes involved would be a considerable challenge. Improvement, though, could be achieved through providing students with a broader framework that describes impacts on long term equity valuations from politics, economics, technology, demography and other factors, and explains their mechanisms through case studies.

One of the most difficult elements of investment education is to incorporate meaningful training in how to identify and respond to situations of true Knightian uncertainty when there is no guidance available from similar historical situations. These are factor X events discussed in Chap. 6, and one-off major developments in politics such as re-unification of Germany in 1990 and economic developments, including market downtrends such as that of 2008, as well as technical challenges such as Y2K. It is not practical to develop even a rough distribution of outcomes of these almost unique events, so fundamental value cannot be calculated, and the concept of arbitrageurs pushing prices to fair value is moot. The fact that most investment professionals avoid this area (and dismiss those in it as speculators) says a lot about shortcomings in traditional finance education and training.

11.3 Investing with Applied Investment Theory

The third real-world application of Applied Investment Theory is to investment by individuals, where a number of observations are important.

The first is that equity markets move unpredictably, although not randomly because they exhibit upward drift that is punctuated by cycles and trends. Another is that most of what we consider as news or value-sensitive information is just noise; and is why policy action generally proves ineffectual. A third conclusion is that expertise is not common amongst finance professionals. This is borne out by widespread evidence that investment experts cannot outperform their benchmarks, and is re-inforced by every successive

210   Applied Investment Theory

global crisis, financial disaster, and industry-wide scam. Even insiders cannot identify the quality of future fund performance, which is why investment firms are not prepared to distinguish themselves or compete on the basis of skill. Finally, researchers know so little of the drivers of equity performance that – despite identifying hundreds of factors related to future returns – even ex post they cannot explain over 80% of the variation in cross-sectional stock returns. If there is expertise in investment, the signal-to-noise ratio is so weak that it is not statistically easy to find. In short, investment analysts have only limited skill which is hard to identify, and even that is built around intuitive manipulation of non-quantifiable, non-observable factors which is hard to replicate and share.

These conclusions from AIT do not counsel despair, but provide lessons for investors. A simple suggestion is to eschew the pursuit of skill in finance, which – if it exists and can be discovered – is probably small and of limited horizon. Most investors, then, should direct their portfolio towards index funds. But even that is problematic because the correct index is not immediately obvious: domestic or international; weighted equally, or by size or industry share of GDP; and how to mix different asset classes?

The solution is to tease out the outcomes that investors would most regret and put their portfolio in a passive strategy that uses an appropriate benchmark. If their worst regret would be an absolute loss, then select a conservative capital stable portfolio; if it is underperformance against an index, then select that index; or if it is significant long term underperformance, then choose a portfolio balanced across asset classes.

Advice for more active investors is that trends and cycles matter, and they might favour a regime shifting strategy where asset allocation is tactically adjusted in light of short to medium term expectations. Measures of value – such as low price-to-earnings ratio – are important stock selection tools because equity returns are stochastic and so price will eventually revert to a higher mean value. A winning strategy is to buy cheap and sell dear.

An implication of short term persistence in return generating processes is partial predictability of returns: whilst these relationships invariably prove transitory, they can advantage investors over the short term through error correction models. To see how this can be operationalised, consider the relationship between return on the S&P 500 Index and lagged changes in the state variables of industrial production and consumer price index (CPI). The predictive power of this relationship can be examined using an error correction model such as the following:

11 Real World Application of Applied Investment Theory 211

$$\text{Return}_{t\to t+1} = \alpha_t + \left(\beta_{1,t-n\to t}.\text{IndProdChange}_t + \beta_{2,t-n\to t}.\text{CPIChange}_t\right) +$$
$$\beta_{3,t-n-1\to t-1}(\text{Return}_t - (\alpha_{t-1} + \beta_{1,t-n-1\to t-1}.\text{IndProdChange}_{t-1} +$$
$$\beta_{2,t-n-1\to t}.\text{CPIChange}_{t-1})) + \varepsilon_t$$

In words, this involves two regressions over n prior periods of return on the S&P 500 Index against start period values of changes in industrial production and the consumer price index. The first expression involves regression during n prior months of return against change in industrial production and CPI. The second regression involves regression during n months to $t - 1$ of actual return less the projected return based on regression for n preceding months against industrial production and CPI. This predicts month-ahead return using observable macro factors and the latest month's error in prediction.

Monthly data for the two independent variables, namely CPI and industrial production, are released before the stock market opens on the 13th and 15th of the following month, respectively (or the following working day if the release date falls on a holiday or weekend). Thus independent variables relate to month t, and the dependent variable is the change in the S&P Index in the month following the opening on the 15th of month $t + 1$ (or the first working day thereafter). This analysis mimics what an investor can achieve, and the R-squared indicates how much of the month-ahead return can be predicted.

The following table reports results from analysis of the data (which is available from the Federal Reserve Bank of St Louis at https://research.stlouisfed.org) for the period 1990–2014 using month-ahead returns, and different values of n (Table 11.1).

Even this brief analysis shows promise in using public data because the co-efficients on CPI and industrial production are significant, and explain over 5% of the cross-section of returns.

Table 11.1 Prediction of S&P 500 Index using error correction model

	Month-ahead S&P Change	
	n = 12	n = 60
Constant	1.87	2.23
P12M change in CPI	−0.77**	−0.84***
P12 M change in Ind Prod	0.13*	0.14*
Prior month error	0.04	0.04
Adjusted R-squared	0.05	0.06

$* p<0.10; ** p<0.05; *** p<0.01$

11.4 A Better Regulatory Framework

Given the current investment paradigm's lack of worldly value, it is unsurprising to find that securities and corporations regulation is so ineffectual and toothless as to oversee a global crisis every seven years or so. The regularity and severity of global crises in governance of markets and firms do not instil any confidence in the ability of economically powerful actors to even stabilise, much less optimise, modern economic systems.[1] We are well overdue for a thorough overhaul of regulatory supervision of the structure and conduct of the finance industry.

Narrowing the focus of regulatory reform to just the managed investments industry, applied investment theory points to a number of potential improvements. One recognises the importance to valuation of qualitative firm data, and would weaken information asymmetry between firms' management and stakeholders by improving corporate disclosure. A good first step would be to mandate reporting along lines proposed in the Global Reporting Initiative which provides a range of non-financial information on firms (www.global-reporting.org). Corporate disclosure would also be improved by mandating reporting of the details of all corporate assets and liabilities, including minority holdings that can be obscured in current accounting standards. This would upgrade the reliability of qualitative material and personal judgment that is of varied quality and availability but is becoming ever more important in fund manager investment decisions.

A second improvement in regulation would come by increasing the breadth and severity of criminal penalties imposed following corporate failures. This would introduce a crime of financial negligence in line with legislation that has successfully cleaned up the environment and made workplaces safer. Recognising that the most damaging failures involve large, systemically important firms (those that are too big to fail), it would be a crime with strict liability to be a director or officer of a firm with assets above USD50 billion that goes into liquidation (files for Chapter 7 or 11 bankruptcy in the United States, or petitions for bankruptcy elsewhere). These big firms could also be prevented from engaging in practices that have led to failure such as high leverage and use of over-the-counter financial instruments and derivatives (see an extensive discussion of this proposal in Coleman 2014b).

A third regulatory improvement acknowledges that the oligopolistic nature of the mutual fund sector and the absence of performance-based fees divert

---

[1] For alternative perspectives on this tawdry scene see amongst many: Coleman (2014b), Gasparino (2009), McLean and Nocera (2010) and Murdock (2014).

11.5 Conclusion

This book was motivated by the global financial crises of 2008–2010 and set out to establish a new paradigm of investment. The approach is novel by starting with a base of core elements of the current investment paradigm, assembling empirically established facts about markets and investors, identifying theoretical explanations, and fusing it all into an integrated model of equity investment. The result meets the test set by Thomas Kuhn (1970) for a real body of knowledge which is that it offers an integrated description of what we observe and logically explains it.

This book is also novel by rejecting the notion of a representative investor and concentrating on a single group of investors, namely mutual funds that have become the largest investor group in most developed economies. Their prominence and rejection of the normative investment techniques that underpin academic and research thinking has brought important changes to market behaviours. AIT provides an integrated theory which explains much of their behaviour and explores its implications.

Although the qualitative data that fund managers use is difficult to observe and measure, it is markedly different to the quantitative, normative basis of data assumed in standard financial economics. The latter has always neglected field research, and so – like an ill-dressed emperor – is characterised by gaps between what people know and do and what they report about their motivations and actions. This arises at several levels. One is in research and teaching where normative theories – mean-variance portfolio optimisation, market efficiency, DCF investment analysis and so on – are taught and studied with the assurance that most practitioners apply these theories, despite research evidence to the contrary. The second set of conflicted evidence – which somewhat perversely supports the first – arises because investment professionals give clear impressions that they use normative theories by including such analyses as justification for their decisions, whereas the evidence is that analysis from the normative theories frequently does not match conclusions.

These conflicts reflect a theme that was established in my previous book *The Lunacy of Modern Finance Theory & Regulation* which is that rational investment is a chimera because the necessary data (future cash flows

214   Applied Investment Theory

and risks to them) are unknowable. In practice, uncertainty surrounding investment decisions makes them subject to bias in terms of the data incorporated in the decision and the weights given to decision stimuli. Decision makers are conscious of stylised facts about markets such as trending, mean reversion and unexpected moves; and every investment decision incorporates judgement, intuition and qualitative data even when the analysis is quantitative. But it is not possible to classify any investment decision as rational or not, and whether its purpose is arbitrage, speculation or gambling. Thus neoclassical investment theory, Austrian economics, behavioural finance and qualitative analysis are present in all investment decisions, no matter what the decision maker says!

This book has a challenging conclusion: consistent evidence that managed funds do not add value over index investing arises from structural determinants, principally that it is impractical to predict much of securities' returns, and the mutual fund industry's business model is inimical to the interests of fund clients. Sadly, the current investment paradigm is largely an unsubstantiated ideal, which cannot be implemented and is becoming increasingly irrelevant as large institutions come to dominate trading. Just as pre-Copernican scientists needed to acknowledge that the Earth was not the centre of the universe, financial economists need to acknowledge that their intuitive ideals are not an appropriate framework to describe markets and to optimise investment.

Improvement in investment performance will only come through targeted research and more creative regulation of the industry. There is reason, though, to doubt the extent to which investors could ever expect improved return. This is because fund managers lack much if any replicable skill, and it may not be possible to develop sufficient understanding of investment data and processes to make economically meaningful forecasts that are essential to outperformance.

These conclusions are at odds with mainstream finance where notionally independent academics and expert agents such as financial planners encourage investors to believe that fund managers have identifiable skill. Certainly some influential observers of the managed funds industry have already concluded that fund managers lack skill, most obviously those who sponsored establishment of passive, low cost retirement savings vehicles in Australia, Norway and elsewhere. Others involved in finance theory and practice, though, need to adapt to a different world because actual practice of investment is not well served by existing literature and advice.

Bibliography

Abhayawansa, S. and J. Guthrie (2012). "Intellectual Capital Information and Stock Recommendations: Impression Management?" Journal of Intellectual Capital **13** (3): 398–415.

Ackert, L. F., B. K. Church and K. Ely (2008). "Biases in Individual Forecasts." Journal of Behavioral Finance **9** (2): 53–61.

Admati, A. R. and P. Pfleiderer (1988). "A Theory of Intraday Patterns: Volume and Price Variability." Review of Financial Studies **1** (1): 3–40.

Adrian, T. and H. S. Shin (2008). "Liquidity, Monetary Policy and Financial Cycles." Current Issues in Economics and Finance **14** (1): 1–7.

Agénor, P.-R. (2003). "Benefits and Costs of International Financial Integration: Theory and Facts." The World Economy **26** (8): 1089–1118.

Aggarwal, R. (1993). "Theory and Practice in Finance Education: Or Why We Shouldn't Just Ask Them." Financial Practice and Education **3** (2): 15–18.

Aggarwal, R., I. Erel, M. Ferreira and P. Matos (2011). "Does Governance Travel Around the World? Evidence from Institutional Investors." Journal of Financial Economics **100** (1): 154–181.

Agnew, J., P. Balduzzi and A. Sundén (2003). "Portfolio Choice and Trading in a Large 401(k) Plan." The American Economic Review **93** (1): 193–215.

Aït-Sahalia, Y., J. A. Parker and M. Yogo (2004). "Luxury Goods and the Equity Premium." The Journal of Finance **59** (6): 2959–3004.

Allais, M. (1988). "The General Theory of Random Choices in Relation to the Invariant Cardinal Utility Function and the Specific Probability Function" in B. R. Munier (ed) Risk, Decision, and Rationality. Holland, Dordrecht.

Allen, F. (2001). "Do Financial Institutions Matter?" Journal of Finance **56** (4): 1165–1176.

© The Author(s) 2016
L. Coleman, *Applied Investment Theory*,
DOI 10.1007/978-3-319-43976-1

216 Bibliography

Almazan, A., K. C. Brown, M. Carlson and D. A. Chapman (2004). "Why Constrain Your Mutual Fund Manager?" Journal of Financial Economics **73** (2): 289–321.

Alpert, B. N., P. Justice, A. Serhan and C. West (2015) "Global Fund Investor Experience Study." Morningstar, https://corporate.morningstar.com/US/documents/2015%20Global%20Fund%20Investor%20Experience.pdf.

Ambachsheer, K. (2005). "Beyond Portfolio Theory: The Next Frontier." Financial Analysts Journal **61** (1): 29–33.

Amenc, N., F. Goltz and A. Lioui (2011). "Practitioner Portfolio Construction and Performance Measurement: Evidence from Europe." Financial Analysts Journal **67** (3): 39–50.

Amihud, Y. (2002). "Illiquidity and Stock Return: Cross-Section and Time-Series Effects." Journal of Financial Markets **5**: 31–56.

Andersen, T. G., T. Bollerslev, F. X. Diebold and P. Labys (2003). "Modeling and Forecasting Realized Volatility". Econometrica **71** (2): 579–625.

Andersen, T. J., J. Denrell and R. A. Bettis (2007). "Strategic Responsiveness and Bowman's Risk-Return Paradox." Strategic Management Journal **28** (4): 407–429.

Anderson, E. W., E. Ghysels and J. L. Juergens (2009). "The Impact of Risk and Uncertainty on Expected Returns". Journal of Financial Economics **94** (2): 233–263.

Ang, J. S. and Y. Cheng (2006). "Direct Evidence on the Market-Driven Acquisition Theory." Journal of Financial Research **29** (2): 199–216.

Arnott, R., F. Li and K. Sherrerd (2009). "Clairvoyant Value and the Value Effect." The Journal of Portfolio Management **35** (3): 12–26.

Arnswald, T. (2001) "Investment Behaviour of German Equity Fund Managers." Economic Research Centre of the Deutsche Bundesbank Deutsche Bundesbank Discussion Paper http://ssrn.com/abstract=266936.

Arrow, K. J. (1964). "The Role of Securities in the Optimal Allocation of Risk-Bearing." The Review of Economic Studies **31** (2): 91–96.

Arrow, K. J. and G. Debreu (1954). "Existence of an Equilibrium for a Competitive Economy." Econometrica: 265–290.

ATC (2010). Investment Management Industry in Australia. Australian Trade Commission. Canberra, Australian Government.

Athanassakos, G. (1992). "Portfolio Rebalancing and the January Effect in Canada." Financial Analysts Journal **48** (6): 67–78.

Attanasio, O. P., J. Banks and M. Wakefield (2005). "Effectiveness of Tax Incentives to Boost (Retirement) Saving: Theoretical Motivation and Empirical Evidence." OECD Economic Studies **39** (2): 146–172.

Baba, M. L. (2012). "Anthropology and Business: Influence and Interests." Journal of Business Anthropology **1** (1): 20.

Bachmann, K. and T. Hens (2010). "Behavioral Finance and Investment Advice" in B. Bruce (ed) Handbook of Behavioral Finance. Cheltenham UK, Edward Elgar.

Baddy, C. R. (2011). "The Corporate Psychopaths Theory of the Global Financial Crisis." Journal of Business Ethics **102**: 255–259.

Bibliography   217

Bailey, R. E. (2005). The Economics of Financial Markets. Cambridge UK, Cambridge University Press.

Bain, J. S. (1959). Industrial Organization. New York, Wiley.

Baker, H. K. and J. R. Nofsinger (2002). "Psychological Biases of Investors." Financial Services Review **11** (2): 97–116.

Baker, M., X. Pan and J. Wurgler (2012). "The Effect of Reference Point Prices on Mergers and Acquisitions." Journal of Financial Economics **106**: 49–71.

Baker, M. and J. Wurgler (2004). "A Catering Theory of Dividends." The Journal of Finance **59** (3): 1125–1165.

Baker, M. and J. Wurgler (2006). "Investor Sentiment and the Cross-Section of Stock Returns." The Journal of Finance **61** (4): 1645–1680.

Bali, T. G. (2008). "The Intertemporal Relation Between Expected Returns and Risk." Journal of Financial Economics **87** (1): 101–131.

Barber, B. M. and T. Odean (2001). "The Internet and the Investor." Journal of Economic Perspectives **15**: 41–54.

Barberis, N. and M. Huang (2001). "Mental Accounting, Loss Aversion and Individual Stock Returns." The Journal of Finance **56** (4): 1247–1293.

Barberis, N., A. Shleifer and R. Vishny (1998). "A Model of Investor Sentiment." Journal of Financial Economics **49** (3): 307–343.

Barberis, N. and R. Thaler (2003). "A Survey of Behavioral Finance" in G. M. Constantinides, M. Harris and R. M. Stulz (ed) Handbook of the Economics of Finance. Boston Elsevier/North-Holland.

Barker, R. G. (1998). "The Market for Information-Evidence from Finance Directors, Analysts and Fund Managers." Accounting and Business Research **29** (1): 3–20.

Barnett, W. A. and A. Serletis (2000). "Martingales, Nonlinearity, and Chaos." Journal of Economic Dynamics and Control **24** (5): 703–724.

Barniv, R., O.-K. Hope, M. Myring and W. B. Thomas (2010). "International Evidence on Analyst Stock Recommendations, Valuations, and Returns." Contemporary Accounting Research **27** (4): 1131–1167.

Barro, R. J. (1999). "Reagan vs. Clinton: Who's the Economic Champ?". Business Week. 22 February 1999. Issue:

Barron's (2015). "The Best Mutual Fund Families of 2014". Barrons. New York.

Bartram, S. M. (2000). "Corporate Risk Management as a Lever for Shareholder Value Creation." Financial Markets, Institutions and Instruments **9** (5): 279–324.

Basu, S. (1977). "The Investment Performance of Common Stocks in Relation to Their Price-Earnings Ratios: A Test of the Efficient Markets Hypothesis." Journal of Finance **32**: 663–682.

Bazerman, M. H. and M. D. Watkins (2004). Predictable Surprises: The Disasters You Should Have Seen Coming, and How to Prevent Them Boston MA, Harvard Business School Press.

BCG (2015) "Global Asset Management 2014." BCG Perspectives, www.bcgperspectives.com.

218 Bibliography

Beckmann, D., L. Menkhoff and M. Suto (2008). "Does Culture Influence Asset Managers' Views and Behavior?" Journal of Economic Behavior & Organization **67**: 624–643.

Bell, G. G. and A. Zaheer (2007). "Geography, Networks, and Knowledge Flow." Organization Science **18** (6): 955–972.

Ben-Rephael, A., S. Kandel and A. Wohl (2011). "The Price Pressure of Aggregate Mutual Fund Flows." The Journal of Financial and Quantitative Analysis **46** (2): 585–603.

Benink, H. and P. Bossaerts (2001). "An Exploration of Neo-Austrian Theory Applied to Financial Markets." The Journal of Finance **56** (3): 1011–1027.

Berk, J. B., R. C. Green and V. Naik (1999). "Optimal Investment, Growth Options, and Security Returns." The Journal of Finance **54** (5): 1553–1607.

Bernoulli, D. (1738, translated 1954). "Exposition of a New Theory on the Measurement of Risk." Econometrica **22**: 23–26.

Bertrand, M. and A. Schoar (2003). "Managing with Style: The Effect of Managers on Firm Policies." Quarterly Journal of Economics **118** (4): 1169–1208.

Besley, T. and P. Hennessy (2009). "The Global Financial Crisis – Why Didn't Anybody Notice?" British Academy Review (14): 8–11.

Bhagat, S., B. Black and M. Blair (2004). "Relational Investing and Firm Performance." Journal of Financial Research **27** (1): 1–30.

Biais, B. and M. Weber (2009). "Hindsight Bias, Risk Perception, and Investment Performance." Management Science **55** (6): 1018–1029.

Bikhchandani, S. and S. Sharma (2001). "Herd Behavior in Financial Markets." IMF Staff Papers **47** (3): 279–310.

Black, B., B. Cheffins and M. Klausner (2006). "Outsider Director Liability." Stanford Law Review **58** (4): 1055–1159.

Black, F. (1986). "Noise." The Journal of Finance **41** (3): 529–543.

Black, F., M. C. Jensen and M. Scholes (1972). "The Capital Asset Pricing Model: Some Empirical Tests" in M. C. Jensen (ed) Studies in the Theory of Capital Markets. New York, Praeger.

Black, F. and M. Scholes (1973). "The Pricing of Options and Corporate Liabilities." Journal of Political Economy **81**: 637–654.

Board of Governors of Federal Reserve System. (2014). "Flow of Funds Accounts of the United States." www.federalreserve.gov/releases/z1/current/z1.pdf.

Bodie, Z., A. Kane and A. J. Marcus (2011). Investments (9th Edition). New York, McGraw Hill.

Boettke, P. J. (1994). "Introduction" in P. J. Boettke (ed) The Elgar Companion to Austrian Economics. Aldershot UK, Edward Elgar.

Bollerslev, T., D. Osterrieder, N. Sizova and G. Tauchen (2013). "Risk and Return: Long-Run Relations, Fractional Cointegration, and Return Predictability." Journal of Financial Economics **108** (2): 409–424.

Börsch-Supan, A. and J. Köke (2002). "An Applied Econometrician's View of Empirical Corporate Governance Studies". German Economic Review **3** (3): 295–326.

Bibliography 219

Bouchaud, J.-P., J. D. Farmer and F. Lillo (2009). "How Markets Slowly Digest Changes in Supply and Demand" in T. Hens and K. Schenk-Hoppé (ed) Handbook of Financial Markets: Dynamics and Evolution Amsterdam, North-Holland.

Boudoukh, J., R. Feldman, S. Kogan and M. Richardson (2013) "Which News Moves Stock Prices? A Textual Analysis." National Bureau of Economic Research, ftp://www1.idc.ac.il/Faculty/Kobi/text_20121223.pdf.

Boulding, K. E. (1935). "The Theory of a Single Investment." Quarterly Journal of Economics **49** (3): 479–494.

Brealey, R., S. C. Myers and F. Allen (2014). Principles of Corporate Finance (11th edition). New York, McGraw Hill.

Brealey, R. A., S. C. Myers and A. J. Marcus (2012). Fundamentals of Corporate Finance. New York, McGraw-Hill Irwin.

Bridgman, T. (2010). "Empty Talk? University Voices on the Global Financial Crisis." Policy Quarterly **6** (4): 40–45.

Bris, A. (2005). "Do Insider Trading Laws Work?" European Financial Management **11** (3): 267–312.

Brochet, F., L. Faurel and S. McVay (2011). "Manager-Specific Effects on Earnings Guidance: An Analysis of Top Executive Turnovers." Journal of Accounting Research **49** (5): 1123–1162.

Brock, W., J. Lakonishok and B. LeBaron (1992). "Simple Technical Trading Rules and the Stochastic Properties of Stock Returns." Journal of Finance **47** (6): 1731–1764.

Bromiley, P. (1991). "Testing a Causal Model of Corporate Risk Taking and Performance." Academy of Management Journal **34** (1): 37–59.

Brooks, R. M., J. Patel and T. Su (2003). "How the Equity Market Responds to Unanticipated Events." Journal of Business **76** (1): 109–133.

Brown, G. and N. Kapadia (2007). "Firm-Specific Risk and Equity Market Development." Journal of Financial Economics **84**: 358–388.

Brown, G. W. and M. T. Cliff (2004). "Investor Sentiment and the Near-Term Stock Market." Journal of Empirical Finance **11** (1): 1–27.

Brown, H. S., M. De Jong and T. Lessidrenska (2009). "The Rise of the Global Reporting Initiative: A Case of Institutional Entrepreneurship." Environmental Politics **18** (2): 182–200.

Brown, L. D., A. C. Call, M. B. Clement and N. Y. Sharp. (2014). "Skin in the Game: The Inputs and Incentives That Shape Buy-Side Analysts' Stock Recommendations." Available at SSRN 2458544.

Brown, S. J. (2011). "The Efficient Markets Hypothesis: The Demise of the Demon of Chance?" Accounting & Finance **51**: 79–95.

Brown, S. J., W. N. Goetzmann and J. Park (2001). "Careers and Survival: Competition and Risk in the Hedge Fund and CTA Industry." The Journal of Finance **56** (5): 1869–1886.

Bu, Q. and N. Lacey (2007). "Exposing Survivorship Bias in Mutual Fund Data." Journal of Business & Economics Studies **13** (1): 22–37.

Bibliography

Burawoy, M. (1998). "The Extended Case Method." Sociological Theory **16** (1): 4–33.

Busse, J. A., A. Goyal and S. Wahal (2010). "Performance and Persistence in Institutional Investment Management." The Journal of Finance **65** (2): 765–790.

Camerer, C. (2000). "Prospect Theory in the Wild" in D. Kahneman and A. Tversky (ed) Choices, Values and Frames. New York, Russell Sage Foundation.

Camerer, C., L. Babcock, G. F. Loewenstein and R. Thaler (1997). "Labor Supply of New York City Cab Drivers: One Day at a Time." Quarterly Journal of Economics **112** (2): 407–441.

Camerer, C. F., G. Loewenstein and M. Rabin (Ed.). (2011). Advances in Behavioral Economics. Princeton NJ, Princeton University Press.

Campbell, J. Y. (1999). "Asset Prices, Consumption, and the Business Cycle" in J. B. Taylor and M. D. Woodford (ed) Handbook of Macroeconomics. New York, Elsevier. **1:** 1231–1303.

Campbell, J. Y. (2000). "Asset Pricing at the Millennium." The Journal of Finance **55** (4): 151–1567.

Campbell, J. Y., A. W. Lo and A. C. MacKinlay (1997). The Econometrics of Financial Markets. Princeton NJ, Princeton University Press.

Canina, L. and S. Figlewski (1993). "The Informational Content of Implied Volatility." Review of Financial studies **6** (3): 659–681.

Canner, N. N., G. Mankiw and D. N. Weil (1997). "An Asset Allocation Puzzle." American Economic Review **87**: 181–191.

Capon, N., G. J. Fitzsimons and R. A. Prince (1996). "An Individual Level Analysis of the Mutual Fund Investment Decision." Journal of Financial Services Research **10** (1): 59–82.

Capozza, D. R., P. H. Hendershott and C. Mack (2004). "An Anatomy of Price Dynamics in Illiquid Markets: Analysis and Evidence from Local Housing Markets." Real Estate Economics **32** (1): 1–32.

Carhart, M. M. (1997). "On Persistence in Mutual Fund Performance." The Journal of Finance **52** (1): 57–82.

Cesarini, D., M. Johannesson, P. Lichtenstein, O. Sandewall and B. Wallace (2010). "Genetic Variation in Financial Decision-Making." The Journal of Finance **65** (5): 1725–1754.

Chan, A. (2015). "Seeing into the Future". Chronicle of Higher Education. 5 October 2015. Issue:

Chan, K., A. Hameed and W. Tong (2000). "Profitability of Momentum Strageies in the International Equity Markets." Journal of Financial and Quantitative Analysis **35** (2): 153–172.

Chan, L. K., J. Karceski and J. Lakonishok (1998). "The Risk and Return from Factors." Journal of Financial and Quantitative Analysis **33** (2): 159–188.

Chan, W. S. (2003). "Stock Price Reaction to News and No-News: Drift and Reversal After Headlines." Journal of Financial Economics **70**: 223–260.

Chen, H., H. Desai and S. Krishnamurthy (2013). "A First Look at Mutual Funds That Use Short Sales." Journal of Financial and Quantitative Analysis **48** (03): 761–787.

Chen, L., Z. Da and X. Zhao (2013). "What Drives Stock Price Movements?" Review of Financial Studies **26** (4): 841–876.

Chen, N.-F., R. Roll and S. A. R. Ross (1986). "Economic Forces and the Stock Market." The Journal of Business **59** (3): 383–403.

Chen, P. and G. Zhang (2007). "How Do Accounting Variables Explain Stock Price Movements? Theory and Evidence." Journal of Accounting and Economics **43** (2): 219–244.

Cheung, Y.-W. and C. Y.-P. Wong (2000). "A Survey of Market Practitioners' Views on Exchange Rate Dynamics." Journal of International Economics **51** (2): 401–419.

Chevalier, J. and G. Ellison (1999). "Are Some Mutual Fund Managers Better Than Others?" Journal of Finance **54** (3): 875–899.

Chiang, T. C. and D. Zheng (2010). "An Empirical Analysis of Herd Behavior in Global Stock Markets." Journal of Banking & Finance **34** (8): 1911–1921.

Chordia, T., R. Roll and A. Subrahmanyam (2002). "Order Imbalance, Liquidity, and Market Returns." Journal of Financial Economics **65** (1): 111–130.

Chordia, T., R. Roll and A. Subrahmanyam (2011). "Recent Trends in Trading Activity and Market Quality." Journal of Financial Economics **101** (2): 243–263.

Chordia, T., A. Subrahmanyam and Q. Tong (2014). "Have Capital Market Anomalies Attenuated in the Recent Era of High Liquidity and Trading Activity?" Journal of Accounting and Economics **58** (1): 41–58.

Christoffersen, P. F. (2003). Elements of Financial Risk Management. San Diego CA, Academic Press.

Ciana, P. (2011). New Frontiers in Technical Analysis: Effective Tools and Strategies for Trading and Investing. Hoboken NJ, John Wiley & Sons.

Clare, A., N. Motson, R. Payne and S. Thomas (2014) "Heads We Win, Tails You Lose. Why Don't More Fund Managers Offer Symmetric Performance Fees?", Available at SSRN: http://ssrn.com/abstract=2525545.

Clark, P. K. (1973). "A Subordinated Stochastic Process Model with Finite Variance for Speculative Prices." Econometrica **41** (1): 135–155.

Clarkson, G. P. E. (1963). "A Model of the Trust Investment Process" in E. A. Feigenbaum and J. Feldman (ed) Computers and Thought. New York, McGraw-Hill Inc: 347–371.

Coase, R. H. (1960). "The Problem of Social Cost." Journal of Law and Economics **3**: 1–44.

Cochrane, J. H. (1999). "New Facts in Finance." Economic Perspectives **23** (3): 36–58.

Cochrane, J. H. (2008). "The Dog That Did Not Bark." Review of Financial Studies **21** (4): 1533–1575.

Cohen, W. M. and D. A. Levinthal (1990). "Absorptive Capacity: A New Perspective on Learning and Innovation." Administrative Science Quarterly **35** (1): 128–152.

Colander, D., H. Föllmer, A. Haas, M. Goldberg, K. Juselius, A. Kirman, T. Lux and B. Sloth (2009). The Financial Crisis and the Systemic Failure of Academic Economics. Kiel, Kiel Institute for the World Economy.

222 Bibliography

Coleman, L. (1998). "The Age of Inexpertise." Quadrant **42** (5): 63–66.

Coleman, L. (2006). Why Managers and Companies Take Risks. Heidelberg, Springer.

Coleman, L. (2009). Risk Strategies: Dialling Up Optimum Firm Risk. Farnham, Surrey, Gower.

Coleman, L. (2011). "An Exploratory Analysis of Factors Influencing Initial Market Response and Media Reports Following Shock Corporate Events." The Financial Review **46**: 313–336.

Coleman, L. (2012a). "Explaining Crude Oil Prices Using Fundamental Measures." Energy Policy **40** (1): 318–324.

Coleman, L. (2012b). "Testing Equity Market Efficiency Around Terrorist Attacks." Applied Economics **44** (31): 4087–4099.

Coleman, L. (2014a). "Involuntary Corporate Finance: The Dominance of History in Decisions." Applied Economics **46** (33): 4101–4115.

Coleman, L. (2014b). The Lunacy of Modern Finance Theory & Regulation. London, Routledge.

Coleman, L. (2014c). "Why Finance Theory Fails to Survive Contact with the Real World: A Fund Manager Perspective." Critical Perspectives on Accounting **25** (3): 226–236.

Coleman, L. (2015). "Facing Up to Fund Managers: An Exploratory Field Study of How Institutional Investors Make Their Decisions." Qualitative Research in Financial Markets **7** (2): 111–135.

Coleman, L. and R. M. Casselman (2016). "Optimizing Decisions Using Knowledge Risk Strategy." Journal of Knowledge Management **in press**.

Coles, J. L., N. D. Daniel and L. Naveen (2006). "Managerial Incentives and Risk-Taking." Journal of Financial Economics **79** (2): 431–468.

Cooper, M. J., H. Gulen and M. J. Schill (2008). "Asset Growth and the Cross-Section of Stock Returns." Journal of Finance **63** (4): 1609–1651.

Coram, P. J., T. J. Mock and G. S. Monroe (2011). "Financial Analysts' Evaluation of Enhanced Disclosure of Non-Financial Performance Indicators." The British Accounting Review **43** (2): 87–101.

Corley, K. G. and D. A. Gioia (2011). "Building Theory About Theory Building: What Constitutes a Theoretical Contribution?" Academy of Management Review **36** (1): 12–32.

Cornell, B. (2001). "Is the Response of Analysts to Information Consistent with Fundamental Valuation? The Case of Intel." Financial Management **30** (1): 113–136.

Cornell, B. and E. R. Sirri (1992). "The Reaction of Investors and Stock Prices to Insider Trading." The Journal of Finance **47** (3): 1031–1059.

Corrado, C. J. (2011). "Event Studies: A Methodology Review." Accounting & Finance **51** (1): 207–234.

Covall, J. D. and T. J. Moskowitz (1999). "Home Bias at Home: Local Equity Preference in Domestic Portfolios." The Journal of Finance **54** (6): 2045–2073.

Bibliography 223

Cowles, A. (1933). "Can Stock Market Forecasters Forecast?" Econometrica **1**: 309–324.

Cremers, K. J. M. and A. Petajisto (2009). "How Active Is Your Fund Manager? A New Measure That Predicts Performance." Review of Financial Studies **22** (9): 3329–3365.

Cremers, M., M. A. Ferreira, P. P. Matos and L. T. Starks (2015). "Indexing and active fund management: International evidence." Journal of Financial Economics.

Cronqvist, H., A. Low and M. Nilsson (2009) "Persistence in Firm Policies, Firm Origin, and Corporate Culture: Evidence from Corporate Spin-Offs." http://ssrn.com/abstract=954791.

Cuthbertson, K., D. Nitzsche and N. O'Sullivan (2008). "UK Mutual Fund Performance: Skill or Luck?" Journal of Empirical Finance **15** (4): 613–634.

Cuthbertson, K., D. Nitzsche and N. O'Sullivan (2010). "Mutual Fund Performance: Measurement and Evidence." Financial Markets, Institutions and Instruments **19** (2): 95–187.

Cutler, D. M., J. M. Poterba and L. H. Summers (1989). "What Moves Stock Prices?" Journal of Portfolio Management **15** (3): 4–12.

Cyert, R. M. and J. G. March (1963). A Behavioral Theory of the Firm. Englewood Cliffs NJ, Prentice-Hall.

Da Costa Jr, N., C. Mineto and S. Da Silva (2008). "Disposition Effect and Gender." Applied Economics Letters **15** (6): 411–416.

Dai, W. (2015) "A Review of the Empirical Evidence on the Dimensions of Expected Stock Returns." Dimensional, https://my.dimensional.com/.

Damodaran, A. (1989). "The Weekend Effect in Information Releases: A Study of Earnings and Dividend Announcements" Review of Financial Studies **607–623**.

Damodaran, A. (2002). Investment Valuation. New York, John Wiley & Sons.

Damodaran, A. (2007). Valuation Approaches and Metrics: A Survey of the Theory and Evidence. New York, Now Publishers Inc.

Daniel, K., D. Hirshleifer and A. Subrahmanyam (1998). "Investor Psychology and Security Market Under- and Overreactions." The Journal of Finance **53** (6): 1839–1885.

Das, P. K. and S. P. U. Rao (2011). "Value Premiums and the January Effect: International Evidence." The International Journal of Business and Finance Research **5** (4): 1–15.

Dass, N., M. Massa and R. Patgiri (2008). "Mutual Funds and Bubbles: The Surprising Role of Contractual Incentives". Review of Financial Studies **21** (1): 51–99.

Davis, J. H., R. Aliaga-Díaz and C. J. Thomas (2012) "Forecasting Stock Returns: What Signals Matter, and What Do They Say Now." The Vanguard Group, https://personal.vanguard.com/pdf/s338.pdf.

De Bondt, W., G. Muradoglu, H. Shefrin and S. K. Staikouras (2008). "Behavioral Finance: Quo vadis?" Journal of Applied Finance **18** (2): 7–21.

De Bondt, W. F. M. and R. H. Thaler (1989). "Anomalies: A Mean-Reverting Walk Down Wall Street." The Journal of Economic Perspectives **3** (1): 189–202.

224 Bibliography

De Bondt, W. F. M. and R. H. Thaler (1994). Financial Decision-Making in Markets and Firms: A Behavioral Perspective. Washington, National Bureau of Economic Research.

Del Guercio, D. and P. A. Tkac (2002). "The Determinants of the Flow of Funds of Managed Portfolios: Mutual Funds vs. Pension Funds." Journal of Financial and Quantitative Analysis **37** (4): 523–557.

DeMarzo, P. M., R. Kaniel and I. Kremer (2011). "Relative Wealth Concerns and Complementarities in Information Acquisition." Review of Financial Studies **24** (1): 169–207.

Dempster, G. M. (2011). "Austrian Foundations for the Theory and Practice of Finance." Journal of Economics and Finance Education **10** (2): 70–81.

Devenow, A. and I. Welch (1996). "Rational Herding in Financial Economics." European Economic Review **40**: 603–615.

Dimson, E., P. Marsh and M. Staunton (2013). Credit Suisse Global Investment Returns Yearbook 2013. Zurich, Credit Suisse AG.

Dostoevsky, F. (1914). The Gambler and Other Stories. Melbourne, William Heinemann Ltd.

Drachter, K., A. Kempf and M. Wagner (2007). "Decision Processes in German Mutual Fund Companies: Evidence from a Telephone Survey." International Journal of Managerial Finance **3** (3): 49–69.

Edgeworth, F. Y. (1925). "The Pure Theory of Monopoly" in (ed) Papers Relating to Political Economy. London, Macmillan and Co. **1:** 111–142.

Edmans, A. (2011). "Does the Stock Market Fully Value Intangibles? Employee Satisfaction and Equity Prices." Journal of Financial Economics **101** (3): 621–640.

Edmans, A., D. Garcia and Ø. Norli (2007). "Sports Sentiment and Stock Returns." The Journal of Finance **62** (4): 1967–1998.

Edwards, F. R. and R. G. Hubbard (2000). "The Growth of Institutional Stock Ownership: A Promise Unfulfilled." Journal of Applied Corporate Finance **13** (3): 92–104.

Ekholm, A. and D. Pasternack (2005). "The Negative News Threshold: an Explanation for Negative Skewness in Stock Returns." European Journal of Finance **11** (6): 511–529.

Elton, E. J., M. J. Gruber and C. R. Blake (2003). "Incentive Fees and Mutual Funds." The Journal of Finance **58** (2): 779–804.

Elton, E. J., M. J. Gruber, S. P. A. Brown and W. N. Goetzmann (2010). Modern Portfolio Theory and Investment Analysis (8th edition). New York, John Wiley & Sons.

Elton, E. J., M. J. Gruber and J. A. Busse (2004). "Are Investors Rational? Choices Among Index Funds." The Journal of Finance **59** (1): 261–288.

Engle, R. F. and J. G. Rangel (2008). "The Spline-GARCH Model for Low-Frequency Volatility and Its Global Macroeconomic Causes." The Review of Financial Studies **21** (3): 1187–1222.

Espahbodi, H., P. Espahbodi and R. Espahbodi (2015). "Did Analyst Forecast Accuracy and Dispersion Improve After 2002 Following the Increase in Regulation?" Financial Analysts Journal **71** (5): 20–37.

Estrada, J. (2006). "Downside Risk in Practice." Journal of Applied Corporate Finance **18** (1): 117–125.

Faff, R. W., D. Hillier and J. Hillier (2000). "Time Varying Beta Risk: An Analysis of Alternative Modelling Techniques." Journal of Business Finance & Accounting **27** (5): 523–554.

Fair, R. C. (2002). "Events that Shook the Market." Journal of Business **75** (4): 713–731.

Fairfield, P. M. and T. L. Yohn (2001). "Using Asset Turnover and Profit Margin to Forecast Changes in Profitability." Review of Accounting Studies **6** (4): 371–385.

Fama, E. F. (1970). "Efficient Capital Markets: A Review of Theory and Empirical Work." The Journal of Finance **25** (2): 383–417.

Fama, E. F. (1991). "Efficient Capital Markets: II." The Journal of Finance **46** (5): 1575–1617.

Fama, E. F. (1998). "Market Efficiency, Long-Term Returns and Behavioral Finance." Journal of Financial Economics **49** (3): 283–306.

Fama, E. F. and K. R. French (1992). "The Cross-Section of Expected Stock Returns." The Journal of Finance **67** (2): 427–465.

Fama, E. F. and K. R. French (1993). "Common Risk Factors in the Returns of Stocks and Bonds." Journal of Financial Economics **33** (1): 3–56.

Fama, E. F. and K. R. French (1995). "Size and Book-to-Market Factors in Earnings and Returns". The Journal of Finance **50** (1): 131–155.

Fama, E. F. and K. R. French (2004). "Capital Asset Pricing Model: Theory and Evidence." The Journal of Economic Perspectives **18** (3): 25–46.

Fama, E. F. and K. R. French (2010). "Luck Versus Skill in the Cross-Section of Mutual Fund Returns." The Journal of Finance **65** (5): 1915–1947.

Fama, E. F. and J. D. MacBeth (1973). "Risk, Return, and Equilibrium: Empirical Tests" The Journal of Political Economy **81** (3): 607–636.

Farber, H. S. and K. F. Hallock (2009). "The Changing Relationship Between Job Loss Announcements and Stock Prices: 1970–1999." Labour Economics **16** (1): 1–11.

Farnsworth, H. and J. Taylor (2006). "Evidence on the Compensation of Portfolio Managers." Journal of Financial Research **29** (3): 305–324.

Feng, M., W. Ge, S. Luo and T. Shevlin (2011). "Why Do CFOs Become Involved in Material Accounting Manipulations?" Journal of Accounting and Economics **51** (1): 21–36.

Ferreira, M. A., A. Keswani, A. F. Miguel and S. B. Ramos (2012). "The Determinants of Mutual Fund Performance: A Cross-Country Study." Review of Finance **17** (2): 483–525.

Ferreira, M. A. and P. A. Laux (2007). "Corporate Governance, Idiosyncratic Risk, and Information Flow." The Journal of Finance **62** (2): 951–989.

Ferreira, M. A. and S. B. Ramos (2009) "Mutual Fund Industry Competition and Concentration: International Evidence." Available at SSRN 1343096.

Ferreira, M. A. and P. Santa-Clara (2011). "Forecasting Stock Market Returns: The Sum of the Parts Is More Than the Whole." Journal of Financial Economics **100** (3): 514–537.

Bibliography

Ferson, W. E. and C. R. Harvey (1991). "The Variation of Economic Risk Premiums." Journal of Political Economy **99** (2): 385–415.

Ferson, W. E. and C. R. Harvey (1993). "The Risk and Predictability of International Equity Returns." Review of Financial Studies **6** (3): 527–566.

Ferson, W. E. and C. R. Harvey (1997). "Fundamental Determinants of National Equity Market Returns: A Perspective on Conditional Asset Pricing." Journal of Banking & Finance **21** (11): 1625–1665.

Fildes, R. and H. Stekler (2002). "The State of Macroeconomic Forecasting." Journal of Macroeconomics **24** (4): 435–468.

Finucane, Melissa L., et al. 2000. "The affect heuristic in judgments of risks and benefits." *Journal of behavioral decision making* 13.1 (2000): 1.

Fisher, P. A. (2003). Common Stocks and Uncommon Profits and Other Writings. Hoboken NJ, John Wiley & Sons.

Fligstein, N. (2001). The Architecture of Markets: An Economic Sociology of Twenty-First-Century Capitalist Societies. Princeton NJ, Princeton University Press.

Fogel, S. O. C. and T. Berry (2010). "The Disposition Effect and Individual Investor Decisions" in B. Bruce (ed) Handbook of Behavioral Finance. Cheltenham UK, Edward Elgar**:** 65–80.

Foster, F. D. and G. J. Warren (2015). "Interviews with Institutional Investors: The How and Why of Active Investing." The Journal of Behavioral Finance

Fox, C. R. and A. Tversky (1998). "A Belief-Based Account of Decision Under Uncertainty." Management Science **44** (7): 879–895.

Francis, J. C. and D. Kim (2013). Modern Portfolio Theory. Hoboken NJ, John Wiley & Sons Inc.

Frankfurter, G. M. (2006). "The Theory of Fair Markets (TFM) Toward a New Finance Paradigm." International Review of Financial Analysis **15** (1): 130–144.

Frazzini, A. and L. H. P. Pedersen (2014). "Betting Against Beta." Journal of Financial Economics **111** (1): 1–25.

Frey, B. S. and R. Eichenberger (1995). "On the Return of Art Investment Return Analyses." Journal of Cultural Economics **19** (3): 207–220.

Frey, S. and P. Herbst (2014). "The Influence of Buy-Side Analysts on Mutual Fund Trading." Journal of Banking & Finance **49**: 442–458.

Friederich, S., A. Gregory, M. John and I. Tonks (2002). "Short-Run Returns Around the Trades of Corporate Insiders on the London Stock Exchange". European Financial Management **8** (1): 7–30.

Friedman, M. (1970). "The Social Responsibility of Business Is to Increase Its Profits". The New York Times Magazine. New York NY. 13 September 1970

Friend, I. (1973). "Mythodology in Finance." The Journal of Finance **28** (2): 257–272.

Friend, I., F. E. B. Brown, E. S. Herman and D. Vickers (1962). A Study of Mutual Funds. Washington DC, U.S. Government Printing Office.

Frino, A., G. Lepone and D. Wright (2015). "Investor Characteristics and the Disposition Effect." Pacific-Basin Finance Journal **31** (1): 1–12.

Froot, K. A., D. S. Scharfstein and J. C. Stein (1993). "Risk Management: Coordinating Corporate Investment and Financing Policies." The Journal of Finance **48** (5): 1629–1658.

Garbade, K. D. and W. L. Silber (1983). "Price Movements and Price Discovery in Futures and Cash Markets." The Review of Economics and Statistics **65**: 289–297.

Gasparino, C. (2009). The Sellout. New York, Harper.

Ghysels, E., P. Santa-Clara and R. Valkanov (2005). "There Is a Risk-Return Trade-Off After All." Journal of Financial Economics **76**: 509–548.

Glaser, B. G. and A. L. Strauss (1967). The Discovery of Grounded Theory: Strategies for Qualitative Research. Chicago, Aldine Publishing Company.

Glosten, L. R., R. Jagannathan and D. E. Runkle (1993). "On the Relation Between the Expected Value and the Volatility of the Nominal Excess Return on Stocks". The Journal of Finance **48** (5): 1779–1801.

Godfrey, P. C., C. B. Merrill and J. M. Hansen (2009). "The Relationship Between Corporate Social Responsibility and Shareholder Value: An Empirical Test of the Risk Management Hypothesis." Strategic Management Journal **30**: 424–445.

Goldstein, I. and A. Razin (2015). "Three Branches of Theories of Financial Crises." Foundations and Trends in Finance **10** (2): 113–180.

Golec, J. (2003). "Regulation and the Rise in Asset-Based Mutual Fund Performance Fees." Journal of Financial Research **26** (1): 19–30.

Gompers, P., J. Ishii and A. Metrick (2003). "Corporate Governance and Equity Prices." Quarterly Journal of Economics **118** (1): 107–155.

Gonzalez, L., J. G. Powell, J. Shi and A. Wilson (2005). "Two Centuries of Bull and Bear Market Cycles." International Review of Economics & Finance **14** (4): 469–486.

Goyal, A. and P. Santa-Clara (2003). "Idiosyncratic Risk Matters!" The Journal of Finance **58** (3): 975–1007.

Grable, J. E. (2000). "Financial Risk Tolerance and Additional Factors that Affect Risk Taking in Everyday Money Matters." Journal of Business and Psychology **14** (4): 625–630.

Graham, J. R. and C. R. Harvey (2001). "The Theory and Practice of Corporate Finance: Evidence from the Field." Journal of Financial Economics **60** (2–3): 187–243.

Green, J., J. R. M. Hand and X. F. Zhang (2013). "The Supraview of Return Predictive Signals." Review of Accounting Studies **18**: 692–730.

Greene, J. T. and S. G. Watts (1996). "Price Discovery on the NYSE and the NASDAQ: The Case of Overnight and Daytime News Releases." Financial Management **25** (1): 19–42.

Greenwood, R. and D. Scharfstein (2013). "The Growth of Finance." The Journal of Economic Perspectives **27** (2): 3–28.

228   Bibliography

Grinblatt, M. and M. Keloharju (2001). "What Makes Investors Trade?" Journal of Finance: 589–616.

Gruber, M. J. (1996). "Another Puzzle: The Growth in Actively Managed Mutual Funds." The Journal of Finance **51** (3): 783–810.

Guay, W., S. P. Kothari and S. Shu (2011). "Properties of Implied Cost of Capital Using Analysts' Forecasts." Australian Journal of Management **36** (2): 125–149.

Guedj, O. and J.-P. Bouchaud (2005). "Experts' Earning Forecasts: Bias, Herding and Gossamer Information." International Journal of Theoretical and Applied Finance **8** (7): 933–946.

Gummer, B. (1998). "Decision Making Under Conditions of Risk, Ambiguity and Uncertainty: Recent Perspectives." Administration in Social Work **22** (2): 75–93.

Gupton, G. and R. S. Stein (2005) "LossCalc v2: Dynamic Prediction of LGD." Moodys KMV Investors Services.

Hannan, T. H. (1991). "Foundations of the Structure-Conduct-Performance Paradigm in Banking." Journal of Money, Credit and Banking **15** (2): 68–84.

Harford, J. and A. Kaul (2005). "Correlated Order Flow: Pervasiveness, Sources, and Pricing Effects." The Journal of Financial and Quantitative Analysis **40** (1): 29–55.

Harris, L. (2003). Trading and Exchanges. Oxford, Oxford University Press.

Hart, S. L. (1995). "A Natural-Resource-Based View of the Firm." The Academy of Management Review **20** (4): 986–1014.

Harvey, C. R., Y. Liu and H. Zhu (2014) "… And the Cross-Section of Expected Returns." National Bureau of Economic Research SSRN ID 2249314.

Harvey, C. R. and A. Siddique (2000). "Conditional Skewness in Asset Pricing Tests." The Journal of Finance **55** (3): 1263–1295.

Hasbrouck, J. (2015) "High frequency quoting: Short-term volatility in bids and offers." Available at SSRN 2237499.

Headrick, T. E. (1992). "Expert Policy Analysis and Bureaucratic Politics: Searching for the Causes of the 1987 Stock Market Crash." Law and Policy **14** (4).

Heath, C., S. Huddart and M. Lang (1999). "Psychological Factors and Stock Option Exercise." The Quarterly Journal of Economics **114** (2): 601–627.

Hellman, N. (2000). Investor Behaviour - An Empirical Study of How Large Swedish Institutional Investors Make Equity Investment Decisions. PhD Stockholm University.

Henningsson, J. (2009). "Fund Managers as Cultured Observers." Qualitative Research in Financial Markets **1** (1): 27–45.

Henry, D. (2002). "Why Most Big Deals Don't Pay Off". Business Week. 14 October 2002

Hicks, J. R. (1935). "Annual Survey of Economic Theory: The Theory of Monopoly." Econometrica **3** (1): 1–20.

Higgs, H. (Ed.). (1926). Palgrave's Dictionary of Political Economy. London, Macmillan and Co.

Highhouse, S. and P. Yüce (1996). "Perspectives, Perceptions and Risk-Taking Behavior." Organizational Behavior and Human Decision Processes **65** (2): 159–167.

Hirshleifer, D. (2001). "Investor Psychology and Asset Pricing." The Journal of Finance **56** (4): 1533–1597.

Hofstede, G. (1997). Cultures and Organisations: Software of the Mind. London, McGraw Hill.

Holland, J. (2006). "Fund Management, Intellectual Capital, Intangibles and Private Disclosure." Managerial Finance **32** (4): 277–316.

Holland, J. (2014). "A Behavioural Theory of the Fund Management Firm." The European Journal of Finance: 1–36.

Holland, J. B. and P. Doran (1998). "Financial Institutions, Private Acquisition of Corporate Information and Fund Management." The European Journal of Finance **4** (2): 129–155.

Hong, H. and J. C. Stein (1999). "A Unified Theory of Underreaction, Momentum Trading, and Overreaction in Asset Markets." The Journal of Finance **54** (6): 2143–2184.

Hooke, J. C. (2010). Security Analysis and Business Valuation on Wall Street. Hoboken NJ, John Wiley & Sons, Inc.

Hooker, N. H. and V. Salin. (1999). "Stock Market Reaction to Food Recalls." Retrieved 11 November 2003, 2003, http://agecon.tamu.edu/faculty/salin/research/nafs.pdf.

Hsieh, D. A. (1991). "Chaos and Nonlinear Dynamics: Application to Financial Markets." The Journal of Finance **46** (5): 1839–1877.

Humphrey, S. J. (2004). "Feedback-Conditional Rregret Theory and Testing Regret-Aversion in Risky Choice." Journal of Economic Psychology **25** (6): 839–857.

Hutton, A. P., L. F. Lee and S. Z. Shu (2012). "Do Managers Always Know Better? The Relative Accuracy of Management and Analyst Forecasts." Journal of Accounting Research **50** (5): 1217–1244.

Hwang, S. and S. E. Satchell (2010). "How Loss Averse Are Investors in Financial Markets?." Journal of Banking & Finance **34** (10): 2425–2438.

Hyland, D. C. and J. D. Diltz (2002). "Why Firms Diversify: An Empirical Examination." Financial Management **31** (1): 51–81.

ICI (2015). 2014 Investment Company Fact Book. Washington DC, Investment Company Institute.

International Federation of Accountants (2003). Enterprise Governance: Getting the Balance Right. New York, International Federation of Accountants.

Jackofsky, E. F., J. W. J. Slocum and S. J. McQuaid (1988). "Cultural Values and the CEO: Alluring Companions?" Academy of Management Executive **2** (1): 39–49.

Jacobs, H. (2015). "What Explains the Dynamics of 100 Anomalies?" Journal of Banking & Finance **57** (1): 65–85.

Jegadeesh, N., J. Kim, S. D. Krische and C. M. C. Lee (2004). "Analyzing the Analysts: When Do Recommendations Add Value?" The Journal of Finance **59** (3): 1083–1124.

Jegadeesh, N. and S. Titman (1993). "Returns to Buying Winners and Selling Losers: Implications for Stock Market Efficiency." Journal of Finance **48**: 65–91.

230 Bibliography

Jensen, M. C. (1968). "The performance of mutual funds in the period 1945–1964." The Journal of Finance **23**: 389–416.

Jensen, M. C. (1993). "The Modern Industrial Revolution, Exit, and the Failure of Internal Control Systems". The Journal of Finance **48** (3): 831–880.

Jensen, M. C., F. Black and M. S. Scholes (1972) "The Capital Asset Pricing Model: Some Empirical Tests." http://www.efalken.com/LowVolClassics/blackjensen-scholes.pdf.

Jensen, M. C. and W. H. Meckling (1976). "Theory of the Firm: Managerial Behavior, Agency Costs, and Ownership Structure." Journal of Financial Economics **3** (4): 305–360.

Jensen, M. C. and C. W. J. Smith (Ed.). (1984). The Modern Theory of Corporate Finance. New York, McGraw-Hill Inc.

Jones, C. P. (2010). Investment: Principles and Concepts Hoboken NJ, John Wiley & Sons.

Jones, M. A., V. P. Lesseig and T. I. Smythe (2005). "Financial Advisors and Mutual Fund Selection." Journal of Financial Planning **18** (3): 64–70.

Kaen, F. R. (2003). A Blueprint for Corporate Governance. New York, American Management Association.

Kahneman, D. (2003). "Maps of Bounded Rationality: Psychology for Behavioral Economics." The American Economic Review **93** (5): 1449–1475.

Kahneman, D. (2011). Thinking, Fast and Slow. New York, Farra, Straus and Giroux.

Kahneman, D. and A. Tversky (1979). "Prospect Theory: An Analysis of Decision Under Risk." Econometrica **47** (2): 263–291.

Kamstra, M., L. Kramer and M. Levi (2000). "Losing Sleep at the Market: The Daylight Saving Anomaly." American Economic Review **90** (4): 1005–1011.

Kamstra, M. J., L. A. Kramer, M. D. Levi and R. R. Wermers (Forthcoming). "Seasonal Asset Allocation: Evidence from Mutual Fund Flows." Journal of Financial and Quantitative Analysis.

Kee-Hong, B., L. Chanwoo and K. C. J. Wei (2006). "Corporate Governance and Conditional Skewness in the World's Stock Markets." Journal of Business **79** (6): 2999–3028.

Kester, G. W. (2010). "What Happened to the Super Bowl Stock Market Predictor?" The Journal of Investing **19** (1): 82–87.

Keynes, J. M. (1936). The General Theory of Employment, Interest and Money. London, Macmillan Press Limited (1973 reprint).

Keynes, J. M. (1937). "The General Theory of Employment." The Quarterly Journal of Economics **51** (2): 209–223.

Keynes, J. N. (1891). The Scope and Method of Political Economy. London, Macmillan & Co.

Kirzner, I. (1987). "The Austrian School of Economics" in J. Eatwell, M. Milgate and P. Newman (ed) Palgrave Dictionary of Economics. London, Macmillan.

Knetsch, J. L. (1995). "Assumptions, Behavioral Findings, and Policy Analysis." Journal of Policy Analysis and Management **14** (1): 68–78.

Knight, F. (1921). Risk, Uncertainty and Profit. Boston, Houghton-Mifflin.

Kőszegi, B. and M. Rabin (2007). "Reference-Dependent Risk Attitudes." The American Economic Review: 1047–1073.

Kothari, S. P. (2001). "Capital Markets Research in Accounting." Journal of Accounting and Economics **31** (1): 105–231.

Kramer, L. A. and J. M. W. Weber (2012). "This Is Your Portfolio on Winter Seasonal Affective Disorder and Risk Aversion in Financial Decision Making." Social Psychological and Personality Science **3** (2): 193–199.

Krausmann, F., S. Gingrich, N. Eisenmenger, K.-H. Erb, H. Haberl and M. Fischer-Kowalski (2009). "Growth in Global Materials Use, GDP and Population During the 20th Century." Ecological Economics **68** (10): 2696–2705.

Krueger, A. B. and L. H. Summers (1988). "Efficiency Wages and the Inter-Industry Wage Structure." Econometrica **56** (1): 259–293.

Krueger, T. M. and W. E. Kennedy (1990). "An Examination of the Super Bowl Stock Market Predictor." Journal of Finance **45** (2): 691–697.

Kuhn, T. S. (1970, 2nd edition). The Structure of Scientific Revolutions. Chicago, University of Chicago Press.

Kunte, S. (2015) "The Herding Mentality: Behavioral Finance and Investor Biases." https://blogs.cfainstitute.org.

Kyle, A. S. and F. A. Wang (1997). "Speculation Duopoly with Agreement to Disagree: Can Overconfidence Survive the Market Test?" Journal of Finance: 2073–2090.

La Porte, T. R. (1996). "High Reliability Organizations: Unlikely, Demanding and at Risk." Journal of Contingencies and Crisis Management **4** (2): 60–71.

Lakonishok, J., A. Shleifer and R. W. Vishny (1994). "Contrarian Investment, Extrapolation, and Risk". The Journal of Finance **49** (5): 1541–1578.

Lamont, O. A. and R. H. Thaler (2003). "Anomalies: The Law of One Price in Financial Markets." The Journal of Economic Perspectives **17** (4): 191–202.

Leibenstein, H. (1950). "Bandwagon, Snob, and Veblen Effects in the Theory of Consumers' Demand." Quarterly Journal of Economics **64** (2): 183–207.

Leipnik, R. B. (1991). "On Lognormal Random Variables: I. The Characteristic Function." The Journal of the Australian Mathematical Society. Series B **32** (3): 327–347.

Leiser, D., O. H. Azar and L. Hadar (2008). "Psychological Construal of Economic Behavior." Journal of Economic Psychology **29** (5): 762–776.

Levy, H. and M. Levy (2002). "Arrow-Pratt Risk Aversion, Risk Premium and Decision Weights." Journal of Risk and Uncertainty **25** (3): 265–290.

Lewellen, J. (2011). "Institutional Investors and the Limits of Arbitrage." Journal of Financial Economics **102** (1): 62–80.

Lewellen, J., S. Nagel and J. Shanken (2010). "A Skeptical Appraisal of Asset Pricing Tests." Journal of Financial Economics **96** (2): 175–194.

Bibliography

Lewis, M. and M. Noel (2011). "The Speed of Gasoline Price Response in Markets with and Without Edgeworth Cycles." Review of Economics and Statistics **93** (2): 672–682.

Lim, K.-P. and R. Brooks (2011). "The Evolution of Stock Market Efficiency Over Time: A Survey of the Empirical Literature." Journal of Economic Surveys **25** (1): 69–108.

Lincoln, Y. S. and E. G. Guba (1985). Naturalistic Inquiry. Beverley Hills CA, Sage Publications.

Lintner, J. (1965). "The Valuation of Risk Assets and the Selection of Risky Investments in Share Portfolios and Capital Budgets." Review of Economics and Statistics **47**: 13–37.

Lo, A. W. (2004). "The Adaptive Markets Hypothesis: Market Efficiency from an Evolutionary Perspective." Journal of Portfolio Management **30**: 15–29.

Lopes, L. L. (1994). "Psychology and Economics: Perspectives on Risk, Cooperation and the Marketplace." Annual Review of Psychology **45**: 197–227.

Loughran, T. and P. Schultz (2004). "Weather, Stock Returns, and the Impact of Localized Trading Behavior." Journal of Financial and Quantitative Analysis **39** (2): 343–364.

Lovallo, D. and D. Kahneman (2003). "Delusions of Success. How Optimism Undermines Executives' Decisions." Harvard Business Review **81** (7): 56–63.

Lubatkin, M. and H. M. O'Neill (1987). "Merger Strategies and Capital Market Risk". Academy of Management Journal **30** (4): 665–684.

Luo, X., H. Wang, S. Raithel and Q. Zheng (2015). "Corporate Social Performance, Analyst Stock Recommendations, and Firm Future Returns." Strategic Management Journal **36** (1): 123–136.

Ma, L., Y. Tang and J.-P. Gomez (2013). Portfolio Manager Compensation in the U.S. Mutual Fund Industry. Finance Down Under 2014 Building on the Best from the Cellars of Finance. Melbourne.

MacCrimmon, K. R. and D. A. Wehrung (1984). "The Risk In-Basket." Journal of Business **57** (3): 367–387.

Maher, J. J., R. M. Brown and R. Kumar (2008). "Firm Valuation, Abnormal Earnings, and Mutual Funds Flow". Review of Quantitative Finance and Accounting **31** (2): 167–189.

Mahoney, P. G. (2004). "Manager-Investor Conflicts in Mutual Funds." The Journal of Economic Perspectives **18** (2): 161–182.

Malkiel, B. G. (1995). "Returns from Investing in Equity Mutual Funds 1971 to 1991." The Journal of Finance **50** (2): 549–572.

Malkiel, B. G. (2003). "The Efficient Market Hypothesis and Its Critics". The Journal of Economic Perspectives **17** (1): 59–82.

Malkiel, B. G. (2005). "Reflections on the Efficient Market Hypothesis: 30 Years Later." The Financial Review **40** (1): 1–9.

Malkiel, B. G. and Y. Xu (1997). "Risk and Return Revisited." Journal of Portfolio Management **23** (3): 9–14.

Markowitz, H. M. (1952). "Portfolio Selection." The Journal of Finance 7: 77–91.

Marshall, C., L. Prusak and D. Shpilberg (1996). "Financial Risk and the Need for Superior Knowledge Management." California Management Review 38 (3): 77–101.

Maurer, B. (2006). "The Anthropology of Money." The Annual Review of Anthropology 35: 15–36.

Mayers, D. and C. W. Smith (1990). "On the Corporate Demand for Insurance: Evidence from the Reinsurance Market". The Journal of Business 63 (1): 19–40.

McFadden, D. (1999). "Rationality for Economists?" Journal of Risk and Uncertainty 19 (1): 73–105.

McLean, B. and J. Nocera (2010). All the Devils Are Here. London, Portfolio Penguin.

McWilliams, A. and D. L. Smart (1993). "Efficiency v. Structure-Conduct-Performance: Implications for Strategy Research and Practice." Journal of Management 19 (1): 63–78.

Mehr, R. I. and B. A. Hedges (1963). Risk Management in the Business Enterprise. Homewood IL, Richard D. Irwin, Inc.

Mehra, R. and E. C. Prescott (2003). "The Equity Premium in Retrospect" in (ed) Handbook of the Economics of Finance 1: 889–938.

Mehran, H. and R. M. Stulz (2007). "The Economics of Conflicts of Interest in Financial Institutions." Journal of Financial Economics 85 (2): 267–296.

Menkhoff, L. (2010). "The Use of Technical Analysis by Fund Managers: International Evidence." Journal of Banking & Finance 34 (11): 2573–2586.

Merton, R. C. (2003). "Thoughts on the Future: Theory and Practice in Investment Management." Financial Analysts Journal 59 (1): 17–23.

Meulbroek, L. K. (1992). "An Empirical Analysis of Illegal Insider Trading." The Journal of Finance 47 (5): 1661–1699.

Mill, J. S. (Ed.). (1874). On the Definition of Political Economy, and on the Method of Investigation Proper to It. Essays on Some Unsettled Questions of Political Economy. London, JW Parker.

Miller, K. D. and P. Bromiley (1990). "Strategic Risk and Corporate Performance." Academy of Management Journal 33 (4): 756–779.

Miller, K. D. and J. J. Reuer (1996). "Measuring Organizational Downside Risk." Strategic Management Journal 17: 671–691.

Miller, M., P. Weller and L. Zhang (2002). "Moral Hazard and the US Stock Market: Analysing the 'Greenspan Put'". The Economic Journal 112 (472): C171-C186.

Miller, M. H. and F. Modigliani (1961). "Dividend Policy, Growth and Valuation of Shares." Journal of Business 34: 411–433.

Mitchell, J. (2001). "Clustering and Pyschological Barriers: The Importance of Numbers." The Journal of Futures Markets 21 (5): 395–428.

Moeller, S. B., F. P. Schlingemann and R. M. Stulz (2005). "Wealth Destruction on a Massive Scale? A Study of Acquiring-Firm Returns in the Recent Merger Wave." The Journal of Finance 60 (2): 757–782.

234 Bibliography

Montier, J. (2007). Behavioural Investing: A Practitioner's Guide to Applying Behavioural Finance. Chichester, England, John Wiley & Sons.

Morgenson, G. (2006). "Whispers of Mergers Set Off Suspicious Trading". New York Times. New York. 27 August 2006

Morningstar (2012) "Morningstar Direct Fund Flows Update." http://corporate.morningstar.com/decflows11/FundFlowsJan2012.pdf.

Murdock, C. W. (2014) "Save the Economy: Break Up the Big Banks and Shape Up the Regulators." Social Justice, http://ecommons.luc.edu/social_justice/38.

Myers, S. C. (1977). "Determinants of Corporate Borrowing." Journal of Financial Economics **5** (2): 147–175.

Nash Jr, J. F. (1950). "The Bargaining Problem." Econometrica **18** (2): 155–162.

Niessen, A. and S. Ruenzi (2007). Sex Matters: Gender Differences in a Professional Setting. CFR Working Paper, Centre for Financial Research.

Noel, M. D. (2011). "Edgeworth Price Cycles" in S. N. Durlauf and L. E. Blume (ed) New Palgrave Dictionary of Economics. London, Palgrave Macmillan.

Noronha, G. and V. Singal (2004). "Financial Health and Airline Safety." Managerial and Decision Economics **25** (1): 1–26.

Nutt, P. C. (1999). "Surprising but True: Half the Decisions in Organizations Fail." Academy of Management Executive **13** (4): 75–90.

Odean, T. (1998). "Are Investors Reluctant to Realize Their Losses?" The Journal of Finance **53** (6): 1775–1798.

Okri, B. (2014). The Age of Magic. London UK, Head of Zeus.

Oliver, B. R. (2013) "Decision Making Under Risk in the 21st Century." FIRN Research Paper, http://ssrn.com/abstract=2286976.

Olsen, R. A. (2000). "The Instinctive Mind on Wall Street: Evolution and Investment Decision-Making." The Journal of Investing **9** (4): 47–54.

Olsen, R. A. (2002). "Professional Investors as Naturalistic Decision Makers: Evidence and Market Implications." The Journal of Psychology and Financial Markets **3** (3): 161–167.

Olsen, R. A. (2010). "Toward a Theory of Behavioral Finance: Implications from the Natural Sciences." Qualitative Research in Financial Markets **2** (2): 100–128.

Olsen, R. A. and G. H. Troughton (2000). "Are Risk Premium Anomalies Caused by Ambiguity?" Financial Analysts Journal **56** (2): 24–31.

Omenn, G. S., A. C. Kessler, N. T. Anderson, P. Y. Chiu and J. Doull (1997). "The Presidential/Congressional Commission on Risk Assesment and Risk Management" in (ed) Framwork for Environmental Health Risk Management. Washington DC.

Orlitzky, M. (2008). "Chapter 5. Corporate Social Performance and Financial Performance: A Research Synthesis" in A. Crane, A. McWilliams, D. Matten, J. Moon and D. S. Siegel (ed) The Oxford Handbook of Corporate Social Responsibility. Oxford UK, Oxford University Press.

Bibliography   235

Osborn, R. N. and D. H. Jackson (1988). "Leaders, Riverboat Gamblers, or Purposeful Unintended Consequences in the Management of Complex, Dangerous Technologies." Academy of Management Journal **31** (4): 924–948.

Ou, J. A. and S. H. Penman (1989). "Financial Statement Analysis and the Prediction of Stock Returns." Journal of Accounting and Economics **11**: 295–330.

Pablo, A. L., S. B. Sitkin and D. B. Jemison (1996). "Acquisition Decision-Making Processes: The Central Role of Risk." Journal of Management **22** (5): 723–746.

Park, C.-H. and S. H. Irwin (2007). "What Do We Know About the Profitability of Technical Analysis?" Journal of Economic Surveys **21** (4): 786–826.

Partnoy, F. and J. Eisinger (2013). "What's Inside America's Banks?" The Atlantic. Washington DC. Issue:

Pastor, L. and R. F. Stambaugh (2002). "Mutual Fund Performance and Seemingly Unrelated Assets." Journal of Financial Economics **63**: 315–350.

Peleg, D. (2014). Fundamental Models in Financial Theory. Cambridge MA, The MIT Press.

Penman, S. H. (1996). "The Articulation of Price-Earnings Ratios and Market-to-Book Ratios and the Evaluation of Growth." Journal of Accounting Research **34** (2): 235–259.

Pettus, M., Y. Y. Kor and J. T. Mahoney (2009). "A Theory of Change in Turbulent Environments: The Sequencing of Dynamic Capabilities Following Industry Deregulation." International Journal of Strategic Change Management **1** (3): 186–211.

Philips, C. B., F. M. Kinniry Jr, T. Schlanger and J. M. Hirt (2014) "The Case for Index-Fund Investing." https://pressroom.vanguard.com/content/nonindexed/Updated_The_Case_for_Index_Fund_Investing_4.9.2014.pdf.

Piotroski, J. D. (2000). "Value Investing: The Use of Historical Financial Statement Information to Separate Winners from Losers." Journal of Accounting Research **38** (1): 1–41.

Popper, K. R. (1959). The Logic of Scientific Discovery. London Hutchinson.

Porter, M. E. (1980). Competitive Strategy: Techniques for Analysing Industries and Competitors. New York, Free Press.

Porter, M. E. (1985). Competitive Advantage. New York, Free Press.

Prendergast, C. (2002). "The Tenuous Trade-Off Between Risk and Incentives." The Journal of Political Economy **110** (5): 1071–1102.

Pritamani, M. and V. Singal (2001). "Return Predictability Following Large Price Changes and Information Releases." Journal of Banking & Finance **25**: 631–656.

Quiggin, J. (2012). Zombie Economics: How Dead Ideas Still Walk Among Us. Princeton NJ, Princeton University Press.

Rabin, M. (1996). "Psychology and Economics." Retrieved 4 May 2003, 2003, http://elsa.berkeley.edu/~rabin/peboth7.pdf.

Rabin, M. (1998). "Psychology and Economics." Journal of Economic Literature **36** (1): 11–46.

236   Bibliography

Rabin, M. and R. H. Thaler (2001). "Anomalies: Risk Aversion." Journal of Economic Perspectives **15** (1): 219–232.

Rantala, V. (2015) "How Do Investment Ideas Spread Through Social Interaction? Evidence from a Ponzi Scheme." http://ssrn.com/abstract=2579847.

Rawlinson, G. (Ed.). (1964). The Histories of Herodotus. New York, Dutton.

Reid, J. and N. Burns (2010) "Long Term Asset Return Study." Deutsche Bank Global Markets Research, www.etf.db.com/UK/pdf/EN/research/researchfixedincome_2010_09_13.pdf.

Reiser, M., C. Breuer and P. Wicker (2012). "The Sponsorship Effect: Do Sport Sponsorship Announcements Impact the Firm Value of Sponsoring Firms?" International Journal of Sport Finance **7**: 232–248.

Reyna, V. F. (2004). "How People Make Decisions That Involve Risk." Current Directions in Psychological Science **13** (2): 60–66.

Ricciardi, V. (2004). "A Risk Perception Primer: A Narrative Research Review of the Risk Perception Literature in Behavioral Accounting and Behavioral Finance". Retrieved 17 February 2005, http://ssrn.com/abstract=566802.

Ricciardi, V. (2008). "The Psychology of Risk: The Behavioral Finance Perspective" in F. J. Fabozzi (ed) Handbook of Finance: Volume 2: Investment Management and Financial Management New York, John Wiley & Sons.

Richardson, S., I. Tuna and P. Wysocki (2010). "Accounting Anomalies and Fundamental Analysis: A Review of Recent Research Advances." Journal of Accounting and Economics **50** (2): 410–454.

Riley, J. G. (1975). "Competitive Signalling". Journal of Economic Theory **10**: 174–186.

Ringland, G. (1998). Scenario Planning: Managing for the Future. New York, John Wiley.

Ritter, J. (1998). "Initial Public Offerings." Contemporary Finance Digest **2** (1): 5–30.

Ritter, J. R. and I. Welch (2002). "A Review of IPO Activity, Pricing, and Allocations." The Journal of Finance **57** (4): 1795–1828.

Roberts, J., P. Sanderson, R. Barker and J. Hendry (2006). "In the Mirror of the Market: The Disciplinary Effects of Company/Fund Manager Meetings." Accounting, Organizations and Society **31** (3): 277–294.

Roese, N. J. (2004). "Twisted Pair: Counterfactual Thinking and the Hindsight Bias" in D. Koehler and N. Harvey (ed) Blackwell Handbook of Judgment and Decision Making. Oxford UK, Blackwell: 258–273.

Roll, R. (1986). "The Hubris Hypothesis of Corporate Takeovers." Journal of Business **59** (2): 197–216.

Roll, R. (1988). "R^2." Journal of Finance **43**: 541–566.

Rose, C. (2011). "The Flash Crash of May 2010: Accident or Market Manipulation?" Journal of Business & Economics Research **9** (1): 85–90.

Ross, S. A. (1973). "The Economic Theory of Agency: The Principal's Problem." The American Economic Review **63** (2): 134–139.

Ross, S. A. (1976). "The Arbitrage Theory of Capital Asset Pricing." Journal of Economic Theory **13** (3): 341–360.

Ross, S. A. (1987). "The Interrelations of Finance and Economics: Theoretical Perspectives." The American Economic Review: 29–34.

Ross, S. A. (2002). "Neoclassical Finance, Alternative Finance and the Closed End Fund Puzzle." European Financial Management **8** (2): 129–137.

Rudner, R. S. (1966). Philosophy of Social Science. Englewood Cliffs NJ, Prentice-Hall.

Ruefli, T. W., J. M. Collins and J. R. Lacugna (1999). "Risk Measures in Strategic Management Research: Auld lang syne?" Strategic Management Journal **20** (2): 167–194.

Russo, E. and P. Schoemaker (1992). "Managing Overconfidence." Sloan Management Review **33**: 7–17.

Sagristano, M. D., Y. Trope and N. Liberman (2002). "Time-Dependent Gambling: Odds Now, Money Later." Journal of Experimental Psychology **131** (3): 364–371.

Sala-i-Martin, X., G. Doppelhofer and R. I. Miller (2004). "Determinants of Long-Term Growth: A Bayesian Averaging of Classical Estimates (BACE) Approach." American Economic Review **94**: 813–835.

Salas, J. M. (2010). "Entrenchment, Governance, and the Stock Price Reaction to Sudden Executive Deaths." Journal of Banking & Finance **34** (3): 656–666.

Samuelson, P. A. (1965). "Proof That Properly Anticipated Prices Fluctuate Randomly." Industrial Management Review **6** (2): 41–49.

Sanders, W. G. and D. C. Hambrick (2007). "Swinging for the Fences: The Effects of CEO Stock Options on Company Risk Taking and Performance." Academy of Management Journal **50** (5): 1055–1078.

Sarkar, S. (2000). "On the Investment-Uncertainty Relationship in a Real Options Model". Journal of Economic Dynamics and Control **24** (2): 219–225.

Scheinkman, J. and W. Xiong (2003). "Overconfidence, Short-Sale Constraints, and Bubbles." Journal of Political Economy **111**: 1183–1219.

Schlenker, B. R. (1980). Impression Management: The Self-Concept, Social Identity and Interpersonal Relations. Belmont CA, Brooks-Cole.

Schnaars, S. P. (1989). Megamistakes: Forecasting and the Myth of Rapid Technological Change. New York, The Free Press.

Scholes, M. S. (1972). "The Market for Securities: Substitution Versus Price Pressure and the Effects of Information on Share Prices." Journal of Business **45**: 179–211.

Scholtens, B. and L. Dam (2007). "Banking on the Equator. Are Banks That Adopted the Equator Principles Different from Non-Adopters?" World Development **35** (8): 1307–1328.

Schwarz, C. G. (2011). "Mutual Fund Tournaments: The Sorting Bias and New Evidence." The Review of Financial Studies **25** (3): 913–936.

Schwert, G. W. (2001). "Anomalies and Market Efficiency" in G. M. Constantinides, M. Harris and R. M. Stulz (ed) Handbook of the Economics of Finance. Amsterdam North-Holland: 939–974.

238 Bibliography

Scruggs, J. T. (1998). "Resolving the Puzzling Intertemporal Relation Between the Market Risk Premium and Conditional Market Variance: A Two-Factor Approach." The Journal of Finance **53** (2): 575–603.

SEC (2010) "Findings Regarding the Market Events of May 6, 2010", www.sec.gov/news/studies/2010/marketevents-report.pdf.

Sharpe, W. F. (1964). "Capital Asset Prices: A Theory of Market Equilibrium Under Conditions of Risk." The Journal of Finance **19** (3): 424–442.

Shefrin, H. (2006). "The Role of Behavioral Finance in Risk Management" in M. K. Ong (ed) Risk Management – A Modern Perspective. Amsterdam, Elsevier.

Shefrin, H. and M. Statman (1985). "The Disposition to Sell Winners Too Early and Ride Losers Too Long: Theory and Evidence." The Journal of Finance **40** (3): 777–790.

Shelley, M. K. (1994). "Gain/Loss Asymmetry in Risky Intertemporal Choice." Organizational Behavior and Human Decision Processes **59** (1): 124–159.

Shiller, R. J. (1981). "Do Stock Prices Move Too Much to Be Justified by Subsequent Changes in Dividends?" The American Economic Review **71** (3): 421–436.

Shive, S. (2010). "An Epidemic Model of Investor Behavior." Journal of Financial and Quantitative Analysis **45** (1): 169–198.

Shleifer, A. and R. W. Vishny (1997). "A Survey of Corporate Governance". The Journal of Finance **52** (2): 737–783.

Shu, H.-C. (2010). "Investor Mood and Financial Markets." Journal of Economic Behavior & Organization **76** (2): 267–282.

Shynkevich, A. (2012). "Performance of Technical Analysis in Growth and Small Cap Segments of the US Equity Market." Journal of Banking & Finance **36** (1): 193–208.

Sias, R., W (2004). "Institutional Herding." Review of Financial Studies **17** (Spring): 165–206.

Siegel, J. J. and R. H. Thaler (1997). "The Equity Premium Puzzle." The Journal of Economic Perspectives **11** (1): 191–200.

Simin, T. (2008). "The Poor Predictive Performance of Asset Pricing Models." Journal of Financial and Quantitative Analysis **43** (2): 355–380.

Simmons, S. (2013). I'm Your Man: The Life of Leonard Cohen. New York, Random House.

Simon, H. A. (1955). "A Behavioural Model of Rational Choice." Quarterly Journal of Economics **69**: 99–118.

Simon, H. A. (1959). "Theories of Decision-Making in Economics and Behavioural Science." American Economic Review **49**: 253–283.

Simon, H. A. (1978). "Rationality as Process and as Product of Thought." The American Economic Review: 1–16.

Singh, J. V. (1986). "Performance, Slack, and Risk Taking in Organizational Decision Making." Academy of Management Journal **29** (3): 526–585.

Sitkin, S. B. and A. L. Pablo (1992). "Reconceptualising the Determinants of Risk Behaviour." Academy of Management Review **17** (1): 9–38.

Sitkin, S. B. and L. R. Weingart (1995). "Determinants of Risky Decisionmaking Behavior." Academy of Management Journal **38** (6): 1573–1592.

Slovic, P. (1972). "Psychological Study of Human Judgment: Implications for Investment Decision Making." The Journal of Finance **27** (4): 779–799.

Slovic, P. and R. Gregory (1999). "Risk Analysis, Decision Analysis, and the Social Context for Risk Decision Making" in J. Shanteau, B. A. Mellers and D. A. Schum (ed) Decision Science and Technology: Reflections on the Contributions of Ward Edwards. Boston, Kluwer Academic: 353–365.

Smith, A. (1759, republished 2002). The Theory of Moral Sentiments. Cambridge, Cambridge University Press.

Smith, A. (1776, reprinted 1937). The Wealth of Nations. New York, The Modern Library.

Smith, G. (2012). Why I Left Goldman Sachs: A Wall Street Story. New York, Grand Central Publishing.

Smith, K. V. and M. B. Goudzwaard (1970). "Survey of Investment Management: Teaching Versus Practice." The Journal of Finance **25** (2): 329–347.

Solon, O. (2015). "Human Performance Analytics Are Coming to an Office Near You". The Sydney Morning Herald. Sydney. 16 August 2015.

Soros, G. (1994). "The Theory of Reflexivity." Speech to the MIT Department of Economics World Economy Laboratory Conference, Washington DC Retrieved 12 November 2003, www.soros.org/textfiles/speeches/042694_Theory_of_ Reflexivity.txt.

Standard & Poor's (2015) "2014 Annual Global Corporate Default Study." www. standardandpoors.com/.

Statman, M. (1999). "Behaviorial Finance: Past Battles and Future Engagements." Financial Analysts Journal **55** (6): 18–27.

Statman, M. (2010). "What Is Behavioral Finance?" in A. S. Wood (ed) Behavioral Finance and Investment Management. Charlottesville VA, Research Foundation of CFA Institute.

Steil, B. (2004). "Get Tough on Soft Commissions". Financial Times. London. 21 December 2004

Stein, J. C. (2008). "Conversations Among Competitors." American Economic Review **98**: 2150–2162.

Steiner, E. (1988). Methodology of Theory Building. Sydney, Educology Research Associates.

Stracca, L. (2006). "Delegated Portfolio Management: A Survey of the Theoretical Literature." Journal of Economic Surveys **20** (5): 823–848.

Straus, S. E., J. Tetroe and I. Graham (2009). "Defining Knowledge Translation." Canadian Medical Association Journal **181** (3–4): 165–168.

Stuart, A. and K. Ord (2009). Kendall's Advanced Theory of Statistics. London, Edward Arnold.

Subrahmanyam, A. (2007). "Behavioural Finance: A Review and Synthesis." European Financial Management **14** (1): 12–29.

Sundaramurthy, C., D. L. Rhoades and P. L. Rechner (2005). "A Meta-Analysis of the Effects of Executive and Institutional Ownership on Firm Performance." Journal of Managerial Issues: 494–510.

Tang, C. F. and H. H. Lean (2009). "New Evidence from the Misery Index in the Crime Function." Economics Letters **102** (2): 112–115.

Tetlock, P. E. (2005). Expert Political Judgment: How Good Is It? How Can We Know? Princeton NJ, Princeton University Press.

Thaler, R. (1987). "Anomalies: The January Effect." Journal of Economic Perspectives **1** (1): 197–201.

Thaler, R. (1999). "Mental Accounting Matters." Journal of Behavioral Decision Making **12**: 183–206.

Thaler, R. H. (1988). "Anomalies: The Winner's Curse." The Journal of Economic Perspectives **2**: 191–202.

Thaler, R. H. (1989). "Anomalies: Interindustry Wage Differentials." The Journal of Economic Perspectives: 181–193.

Thaler, R. H. and E. V. Johnson (1990). "Gambling with the House Money and Trying to Break Even: The Effects of Prior Outcomes on Risky Choice." Management Science **36**: 643–660.

Tirole, J. (2006). The Theory of Corporate Finance. Princeton NJ, Princeton University Press.

Tosi, H. L., A. L. Brownlee, P. Silva and J. P. Katz (2003). "An Empirical Exploration of Decision-Making Under Agency Controls and Stewardship Structure." Journal of Management Studies **40** (8): 2053–2071.

Tourangeau, R., M. P. Couper and F. Conrad (2007). "Color, Labels, and Interpretive Heuristics for Response Scales." Public Opinion Quarterly **71** (1): 91–112.

Treynor, J. L. and F. Black (1973). "How to Use Security Analysis to Improve Portfolio Selection." The Journal of Business **46** (1): 66–86.

Trimpop, R. M. (1994). The Psychology of Risk Taking Behavior. Amsterdam, Elsevier Science.

Tuckett, D. and R. J. Taffler (2012). Fund Management: An Emotional Finance Perspective. Charlottesville VA, CFA Institute.

Tufano, P. (1996). "Who Manages Risks? An Empirical Examination of Risk Management Practices in the Gold Mining Industry." The Journal of Finance **51** (4): 1097–1137.

Turner, A., A. Haldane, P. Woolley, S. Wadhwani and C. Goodhart (2010). The Future of Finance: the LSE Report. London, London School of Economics and Political Science.

US Census Bureau (2014). Statistical Abstract of the United States. Washington DC, United States Department of Commerce.

US SIF (2015) "US Sustainable, Responsible and Impact Investing Trends." http://www.ussif.org/Files/Publications/SIF_Trends_14.F.ES.pdf.

Van Beurden, P. and T. Gössling (2008). "The Worth of Values-a Literature Review on the Relation Between Corporate Social and Financial Performance." Journal of Business Ethics **82** (2): 407–424.

van Hoorn, A. (2014). "The Global Financial Crisis and the Values of Professionals in Finance: An Empirical Analysis." Journal of Business Ethics **130** (2): 253–269.

Viscusi, W. K. (1993). "The Value of Risks to Life and Health." Journal of Economic Literature **31** (4): 1912–1946.

Wallace, W. L. (1983). Principles of Scientific Sociology. Hawthorne NY, Aldine.

Walls, M. R. and J. S. Dyer (1996). "Risk Propensity and Firm Performance: A Study of the Petroleum Exploration Industry." Management Science **42** (7): 1004–1021.

Walras, L. (1877, reprinted 1954). Elements of Pure Economics. Homewood IL, Irwin.

Wang, X. T. (2004). "Self-Framing of Risky Choice." Journal of Behavioral Decision Making **17** (1): 1.

Warther, V. A. (1995). "Aggregate Mutual Fund Flows and Security Returns." Journal of Financial Economics **39** (2–3): 209–235.

Weiss, D. (2010). "Cost Behavior and Analysts' Earnings Forecasts." The Accounting Review **85** (4): 1441–1471.

Wen, F. and X. Yang (2009). "Skewness of Return Distribution and Coefficient of Risk Premium." Journal of Systems Science and Complexity **22** (3): 360–371.

Wermers, R. (2000). "Mutual Fund Performance: An Empirical Decomposition into Stock-Picking Talent, Style, Transactions Costs, and Expenses." The Journal of Finance **55** (4): 1655–1695.

Westphal, J. D. and M. K. Bednar (2008). "The Pacification of Institutional Investors." Administrative Science Quarterly **53**: 29–72.

White, H. C. (2002). Markets from Networks: Socioeconomic Models of Production. Princeton NJ, Princeton University Press.

Whitelaw, R. F. (2000). "Stock Market Risk and Return: An Equilibrium Approach". The Review of Financial Studies **13** (3): 521–548.

Williams, J. B. (1938). The Theory of Investment Value. Flint Hill VA, Fraser Publishing.

Williams, S. and S. Narendran (1999). "Determinants of Managerial Risk: Exploring Personality and Cultural Influences." The Journal of Social Psychology **139** (1): 102–125.

Wolfers, J. (2006). "Point Shaving: Corruption in NCAA Basketball." AEA Papers and Proceedings **96** (2): 279–283.

Wu, G., C. Heath and M. Knez (2003). "A Timidity Error in Evaluations." Organisational Behavior and Human Decision Processes **90** (1): 50–62.

Yan, X. S. and Z. Zhang (2009). "Institutional Investors and Equity Returns: Are Short-Term Institutions Better Informed?" Review of Financial Studies **22** (2): 893–924.

Yates, J. F. (1990). Judgement and Decision Making. New Jersey, Prentice Hall.

Yuan, K., L. Zheng and Q. Zhu (2006). "Are Investors Moonstruck? Lunar Phases and Stock Returns." Journal of Empirical Finance **13** (1): 1–23.

Zackay, D. (1984). "The Influence of Perceived Event's Controllability on Its Subjective Occurrence Probability." Psychological Record **34**: 233–240.

Zhang, G. (2000). "Accounting Information, Capital Investment Decisions, and Equity Valuation: Theory and Empirical Implications." Journal of Accounting Research **29** (1): 271–295.

Index

A

Adverse selection, 64

Agency theory, vii–xv, 2, 76, 81, 165, 168–9, 207

Allen, Franklin, 162

Anderson, Evan W, 58, 143, 166, 172, 186

Applied Investment Theory
core tenets, 166–8
investment application, 209–11
precis, vii–ix, xi–xvi, 179–93
research agenda, 204–8
structural model, 194
teaching, 208–9

Arbitrage pricing theory, 16, 22–3

Australia, 99, 115, 123, 124, 214

Austrian School of economics, 27, 28, 146

B

Behavioural finance, ix, xv, 2, 10, 11, 27, 29–31, 47, 49, 52, 80, 206, 214

Black-Scholes option pricing model, 16, 18, 55, 76

Bounding, 8, 30, 31, 38–40, 48, 134

C

Capital asset pricing model (CAPM), 15, 16, 20–225

Counterparty risk, 17, 53, 117, 200

D

Disposition effect, 35, 40, 49, 50, 139

E

Efficient markets hypothesis, vii, 2, 7, 8, 28, 101, 118, 199–200, 207

Equator Principles, 55

Equities, vii–xiv, 71
determinants of returns, xiii, 7–8, 71, 77, 80, 87, 95, 99–101, 103–12, 118, 134, 146, 155–7, 181, 186–7, 205

© The Author(s) 2016
L. Coleman, *Applied Investment Theory*,
DOI 10.1007/978-3-319-43976-1

244 Index

Equities (*cont.*)
market evolution, 146
prediction of returns, xiii–xiv, 33,
35, 104–12, 133, 135, 155,
172, 178, 210, 238
price, 83–120, 138–9, 169–71
price fall, 2, 8, 9, 62, 172
risk premium, 59–62, 84, 98
sawtooth price pattern, vii, viii, 83,
90–2, 117, 165, 167–8, 170,
181, 207
turnover, 5, 87
valuation, viii–ix, 2, 5–7, 17–19,
21, 24–7, 32–8, 54, 57,
77–8, 104–6, 118, 161,
165–8, 174–9, 183, 188,
195, 198, 209
Ethics, 68–70, 160
Experts and expertise, xiii, 3, 10,
33, 41, 43, 45, 67, 78, 117,
119, 125, 134, 143, 148,
149, 154–6, 161, 203,
209–10, 214

F

Factor models, 18, 22–4, 49, 153
Factor X, 115–6, 209
Federal Reserve, 63, 122, 159
Ferreira, Miguel, x, 4, 69, 112
Fibonacci, 139
Financial system facts, 84
Financial system reliability,
8–9, 129, 154
Framing, 34, 40–1, 46, 48–50
Fund managers, vii–xv
compensation, 7, 78, 128, 156,
161–2, 180, 207
conduct, ix, xii–xv, 117, 145, 147,
192, 196
herding, xv, 41, 144–5, 192
impression management, 143–4,
186, 197

socialisation, viii, xii, 7, 131,
140–3, 148–9, 162, 184–6,
193, 195, 197
valuation of equities, ix–xv

G

Global financial crises (2007-2011),
x, xvi, 8, 85, 125, 213
Global Reporting Initiative, 55, 212
Governance, ix, xii, xiv, xvi, 1, 7, 9, 27,
54, 68–70, 102, 122, 125,
128–9, 135–7, 140–1, 157,
185, 188–9, 195–6, 212
Greenspan Put, 63, 122

H

Herding, 7, 30, 33–4, 41–2, 49,
145, 183
Hindsight bias, xiv, 34, 42, 50, 115,
167, 176, 189, 190, 198

I

Information, xi–xii, 30–5, 69, 122,
131, 133–4, 136–8, 141–3,
145, 149, 166, 168–9
human control, vii, viii, 27, 31, 83,
97–8, 120, 146, 165, 166,
168–73, 178, 181–2
as input to equity valuations, ix, viii,
xii, xiv, 7, 16, 18, 27, 38–41,
48, 83–8, 96–8, 104–5,
112–15, 117–20, 173, 178,
181–8, 193, 195–202, 209
Information asymmetry, viii, xi, xiii,
48, 53, 54, 69, 96, 105, 117,
121, 125, 128, 141, 152, 160,
161, 169, 179, 183, 190, 195,
199–202, 212
Insurance, 20, 34, 35, 38, 55,
65, 66, 71

Investment, vii–xvi, 1–4, 9–11, 15–20,
22, 24, 26–8, 131–49,
166–71, 173–6, 178, 180,
182, 185–90, 192, 193,
197–9, 202
building blocks, 17–19, 27, 80
puzzles, ix, xv, 2, 4, 29, 76, 78, 81,
91, 170, 196–9, 204
using Applied Investment Theory,
209–11
Investors, viii–xvi, 1–3, 8, 15–22, 24,
26–8, 53–72, 172–3
decisions, 7, 29–52
in equities, 3, 10, 77, 90, 92, 96,
100, 101, 112, 115, 117,
122–5, 127–8, 132, 133, 136,
138, 140, 157, 160–2,
169–72, 175–9, 181–3, 185,
186, 188–92, 195, 198–200
institutional, x, 2–4, 10, 47, 64, 89,
92, 97, 105, 113, 124, 147,
153, 170, 178, 182, 196
utility functions, 57, 138–40, 167,
171, 189, 201, 206

K
Keynes, Lord John Maynard,
10, 77, 146, 149, 207
Knowledge risk, 55
Kuhn, Thomas, 16, 84, 213

L
Law of One Price, 19, 30, 84,
102–3, 201
Lunacy of Modern Finance Theory
& Regulation, xvi, 213

M
Mental accounting, xiv, 35, 44, 48–9,
51, 64, 167, 189, 198
Merton, Robert, xi, 16

Modern portfolio theory (MPT), x, xi,
1, 2, 15–17, 30, 143,
199–201, 208
practical application, x, 10, 185
shortcomings, x, xvi, 1, 2, 7, 10
Moral hazard, ix, vii, xii, 18, 54, 65,
69, 122–3, 128, 131, 152,
157, 160–1, 165, 167–9,
192–3, 195, 207
Mutual fund managers
Fund Managers
Mutual funds, vii–ix, xv–xvi, 3, 4, 8
and 9, 70, 81, 85, 87, 92, 99,
102, 124, 126–9
business model, viii, xii, xv, 9, 121,
125, 127–8, 161, 179–80,
193, 214
conduct, 126–9
lack of ethics, xv, 157–60
performance, x, 151–62, 168–9
size, ix, 4, 99, 123–4
Mutual funds industry, 147,
157, 161
influences, 122–3
regulation, xvi
structure, xii, 3, 121–9

N
Norway, 124, 214

O
Overconfidence, 30–1, 35–6, 44–5,
48–9, 51, 189

P
Padley, Marcus, 157
Prospect Theory, 35, 45–6, 66, 120

Q
Queen Elizabeth, 8

246 **Index**

R

Real options, 59
  as features of equities, vii–ix, xii, xiv, 53, 72, 166–8, 174–7, 189–91, 198–9, 207
Reflexivity, 27, 145–7
Regret aversion, 35, 46–7, 51
Regulation, xii, xvi, 38, 64–5, 122, 137, 141, 169, 185
  of mutual fund industry, 122, 203, 206, 212–14
Risk, vii, viii, xv, 8–10, 15–28, 34–8, 45–9, 81, 105, 115, 119, 122, 125, 127–8, 142, 154, 166–9, 172–6, 186–91, 201, 207
Uncertainty
  risk-return trade-off, 18, 21, 37, 57–66, 70–2, 90, 106, 143, 186, 199

S

Seasonality in markets, 88
Securities and Exchange Commission, 88, 103, 122–3
Shakespeare, William, 19
Smart beta, 104–5
Soros, George, 27, 116, 146
Stewardship Theory, 206

T

Technical analysis of equity prices, xiv, 7, 26, 27, 35, 84, 92, 117, 135, 138–9, 149, 167, 170, 171, 183–4, 195, 198
Theory, 1–2, 10–11, 16–17, 26–7, 75–81, 148, 213
Three component model of equity prices, viii, xiv, 168, 173–8, 190–1

U

Uncertainty, vii–ix, xiii–xiv, 7–8, 20, 26–7, 45–6, 53–72, 96, 102, 115–19, 134–7, 140–2, 167–8, 172–7, 186, 190, 195, 199, 201–2, 206–9, 214
Risk
Utility theory, 20

Structure-conduct-performance (SCP)
  paradigm, ix, xii, 75–81, 92, 129, 135, 151, 152, 160–2, 165, 168–9, 192–3, 196, 205, 207
Sustainability, xiv, 32, 68–9, 97, 128, 137